Knowing Yourself Inside Out
For Self-Direction

Knowing Yourself
Inside Out
For Self-Direction

SEVEN THEORIES OF PSYCHOLOGY

Jerry Cross
Diablo Valley College
and
Pauline Bondonno Cross

Crystal Publications
Berkeley

Library of Congress Number 83-070449

ISBN 0-9610820-8-9

If names of persons or companies in this book bear any similarity
to those of actual persons or companies, the similarity is purely
fortuitous.

Website	www.crystalpublications.net
eMail	CrystalPub@aol.com

To Lois, John, Fern, Paul,
John Paul, Jason and Julia

Overview

Table of Contents

CHAPTER SEVEN

Cultural Psychology:
Awareness and Self-Direction   277

CONCLUSION   319

Preface

*T*he world has changed so much since the last edition of
Knowing Yourself was published. In response the authors
have updated this third edition with new research and expanded it with a new chapter on cultural psychology and
a new section applying the basic core concepts of seven
theories of psychology, illustrating how to use the multiple
perspectives approach to cope with today's pressing issues.

Knowing Yourself has been written with a keen awareness of the importance of bridging academic and personally
relevant concerns. The goal is to make the ideas of psychology accessible to the general reader in a meaningful
and useful form and to aid in developing a better understanding of oneself and one's personal resources to more
fully direct one's life.

The focus is on liberating the self as a positive force
for clearer, more flexible thinking; to step out of everyday
attitudes, emotions and conditioned responses that can limit
transformation and growth. The book is designed to eliminate thinking of oneself in a context of a particular concept,
model or point of view and to open one's thinking for
greater self-direction.

This book provides an opportunity for the reader to
combine the insights of seven different theories into a single multiple perspectives approach to psychology for maxi-

mizing its usefulness in understanding one's own unique life situation. Complete theories are concisely presented, using realistic examples, to make the ideas and concepts more understandable and useful.

The book's structure facilitates developing oneself rather than simply presenting a single viewpoint. Through developmental psychology, we gain insight into how we change with different life stages and how self-direction is a life-long skill that we refine as our motivations change. Psychoanalytic psychology offers an understanding of unconscious motives; why we may become victims of our emotions, responding to issues in immature ways that may limit our ability for adult fulfillment. Through humanistic psychology we explore how one becomes self-actualized and develops his or her highest potentials. Behaviorism helps us to discern which attitudes have been conditioned and how old habits can be changed. Through social psychology, we study how a sense of security, in which to develop our own individuality, can be gained and how to avoid being swept away and dominated by social forces. With Carl Jung's theory, we can get in touch with a deeper wisdom, with our "inner guide," that can be overwhelmed by social forces. In cultural psychology we develop an awareness of how culture is an invisible determiner of our fundamental views of ourselves and influences how we think, feel and act.

In this new edition we have included an additional chapter, an addendum, to the seven theories of psychology, to illustrate how to apply the multiple perspective approach for self-direction to two of the ongoing crisis of our time, identity and terrorism.

This multiple perspective view of psychology can provide new insights into old problems and create an understanding for applying psychology theories to everyday life for developing our capacity to be self-directive.

As you read this text, the authors hope that you will find the concepts not only understandable and illuminating, but also emotionally meaningful and a catalyst for personal change.

We would like to thank Harrington Young, Inc., text graphics, cover, and typesetting; John Diestler, cover and graphic design consultant; Carol Hicks, text graphics; Charlotte Ayers, cover model; Karen Keyes and Sharon Patton, proofreaders; Jacqueline Payne, for listening; and Snell Putney and James Steele, former teachers.

We would like to express our special gratitude for suggestions and comments from colleagues: Paul Jeffery, University of Missouri; Larry Foster, Cleveland State University; Bruce Lerro, Dominican College; Mary Lou Corbin Sicoli, Cabrini College; James Daley and Lee Rode, Diablo Valley College; and Anna Napoli, University of the Redlands.

Our appreciation to my colleagues for sharing their enthusiasm, thoughts and suggestions which helped refine this new edition and to the many students for their enthusiasm and comments on the original text. We would like to thank our children, John Paul, Jason and Julia, for their patience. A special thanks to those who allowed us to use their copyrighted materials.

—J.C. and P.B.C.

The Scientific Approach
Self-Direction:
Inside Out? Outside In?

The Scientific Approach
Self-Direction: Inside out? Outside In?

A. The Method of Scientific Inquiry
B. The Importance of Perception
C. The Value of Scientific Theories
D. Alternating Perspectives in Psychology

The Scientific Approach
Self-Direction:
Inside Out? Outside In?

Why do we have difficulty overcoming loneliness and maintaining intimate relationships? How do we lose our objectivity and detachment and get swept away by emotions? Why do men and women get into arguments over trivia, saying things which may permanently damage their relationship? Why do male-female relationships sometimes "seesaw" back and forth, alternately hot and cold so that the pair just miss each other? Why do we often have so much difficulty understanding our mate? Why do we participate in social institutions that may influence us against our self-interest? How can we take more *self-direction* in these kinds of situations rather than be taken over by feelings?

Some people are stunned when things go wrong. To them such events seem to occur randomly without apparent causes or connections. Blame shifts to husbands, wives, children, parents. Yet, we may have a freer hand in determining the situation than we think once we see the relationship between our behavior and the occurrences in our lives. We'll examine many cause-and-effect models that simultaneously give a greater sense of control, responsibility, and self-determination to the individual. Some will focus on *inside systems* such as thought and emotion, while others will emphasize *outside systems* such as social roles and models.

To be human is to be in continual transformation. Living effectively and fully is not something we do just once: rather, over and over again, continually rediscovering and developing ourselves. The theories we examine are designed to speed up the learning process, to reintegrate ourselves more effectively in each life stage, as what motivates and makes us happy changes. Today, we see that the individual's personality and level of functioning are not fixed at a certain age, but can change with the discovery and development of one's potential.

We are in the midst of major conceptual changes about the world and ourselves, moving toward an expanded view of human potentialities where the focus is on inner resources and the capacity for growth. This emphasis on the individual is in contrast to the once dominant approach of a "psychology of social adjustment," an approach that was supposed to "fit" the person into society. Today, the field of psychology recognizes that defining oneself by the limited role society assigns as man, woman, parent, child or employee, means giving up some of what is unique to the person.

The Method of Scientific Inquiry

Our capacity for self-direction is based on how completely we understand ourselves. How do we control and shape our behavior for our own betterment? How do we tap our inner resources more completely? How do we distinguish the "inner" from the "outer" forces to more effectively direct the self? The individuation process is so distinct for each of us that institutions or even psychology cannot provide all the answers for directing our lives in the most fulfilling way. Although ultimately we must do this ourselves, we can use the unique idea of a *multiple perspective* approach to psychology as a rich source of understanding and insight.

Such insights and understanding derive from a "tentative approach" such as that taken early by the Greek philosopher, Socrates, formulated over time in the "scientific method" and, in psychology today, exemplified by Piaget's concept of *alternating multiple perspectives.*

Socrates, in about 400 B.C., searched his native Athens, bent on discovering a wise person. In the course of interviewing well-known figures, Socrates asked questions that demonstrated the wise person's limited understanding. Socrates concluded that neither he, nor the individual reputed to be wise, had any knowledge to boast of. Socrates thought that while the wise man believed he himself possessed knowledge, Socrates knew himself to be ignorant. Thus Socrates concluded that he was wise insofar as he could perceive that he didn't know.

Socrates' conclusion is still relevant today. A recent study lends scientific support to his observation over 2000 years ago that some people tend to overestimate how much they know; people who think they know a great deal may actually know less than they think. In 1999 Kruger and Dunning at Cornell University found that those students who were most incompetent in logical reasoning and English grammar tests were oblivious to this fact and even overestimated their abilities: they were more self-assured and overconfident than the most competent students. In other words, people who knew the least on the two tests were the most likely to overestimate their knowledge. This study shows the importance of questioning our assumptions.[1]

This position of continuous tentativeness, an openness
to other views, to constantly questioning and reevaluating
answers, looking for alternative explanations, is built into
the structure of scientific inquiry. Science can bring us
closer to more clearly perceiving reality by freeing us from
our past, from the assumptions of the group we live in, the
biases of our friends and cultural limitations. Our perceptions are not always accurate. We must continually check
our assumptions. In some cases we find that what appeared
to be reality was an illusion without substance, or perhaps
an idea promoted by the strongest, the most powerful or
even by a good friend who wanted to help us. Rather than
rely on personal impressions, convictions, opinion or
hearsay, scientific studies require discipline to overcome
our preconceptions about ourselves and others. We are a dynamic and very complex subject matter in which, by the
very nature of the subject, we are personally involved. The
kind of being we are makes it very difficult to develop the
objectivity central to the scientific method. The scientific
method demands an openness to new views and new ways
of looking at the world that allows the person to formulate
alternative conclusions separate from what has been assumed to be reality. It liberates the individual from a single
viewpoint for greater self-direction.

This "openness" is incorporated by the Swiss psychologist, Jean Piaget, into his theory of *alternating multiple
perspectives;* that is, an individual's capacity to make a
hypothesis and, at the same time, to consider alternatives
transcending the presumed reality; to imagine and conceive
of other approaches to life's situations. Piaget terms this
capacity the highest level of intellectual functioning.

According to Piaget, the individual ultimately must
solve problems through personal struggle and growth.

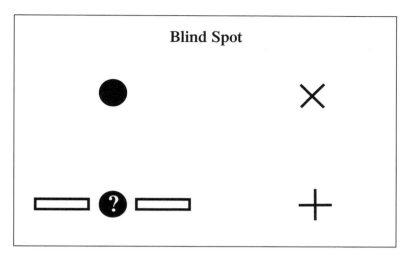

Giving a person an answer may prevent self-discovery and internalizing the knowledge to become more independent and self-directive, as well as ignoring one's individuality.

Alternating perspectives liberates one's thinking from traditional ways of looking at the world and puts the individual in a position to make freer choices, to direct one's life, to look more objectively at one's feelings.

The Importance of Perception

What is reality? What is truth? Can we ever know it? The study of perception can help us appreciate the importance of the tentative approach, continually questioning our perception of reality. Consider what William James, the founder of American psychology, said: "Genius, in truth, means little more than the faculty of perceiving in an unhabitual way."

A simple *blind spot* experiment illustrates how we perceive only part of reality. Hold the book about 20 inches in front of your face and line up the X in the above diagram with your nose. To the left of the X is a dot. Place your hand over your right eye. Without moving your eye off the X you can see the spot in your side vision. Now very slowly move the book toward your nose, keeping your eye focused on the X. Vary the distance as needed until you notice the dot has disappeared, about 6–8 inches from your face. Then stop. If the spot disappears briefly and then reappears move the page more slowly and be sure your eye is staying fixed on the X. At first only part of the dot may disappear so you may have to move the page slightly up, down or sideways to make the dot totally disappear. The spot will reappear as you move the book in closer. Now cover your right eye again and focus on the cross as you slowly move the book towards your nose. Keeping your eye fixed on the cross, you can see a dot with a question mark between two bars in your side vision. Notice when the question mark disappears that the brain fills in the gap by connecting the lines of the bar. Everyone who can see has a *blind spot* in each eye where there are no receptor cells. Where the optic nerve, which transmits the nerve impulse to the brain, leaves the eye there are no receptors for light, therefore the blind spot. Many people are not aware of the blind spot because with two eyes one eye can see what the other misses and because the brain can "fill in" whatever stimulus is missing.

Perception is a process of interpreting the meaning of sensations or stimuli, it determines how we "see" the world, therefore how we behave. Perception involves both sensing and interpreting. Our perception is an interpretation of a stimulus. The world seems so objective and real, many go through life thinking there is no difference between the real world and the world as we perceive it. It is the philosopher who questions "Can we ever know reality?" Our perceptions are not exact copies of the outside world or even the stimulus sensations from energy triggering our nerves, but are processed and transformed by the brain. Often even the most unusual behavior is understandable if we can see it from the other person's viewpoint.

Consider these two opposing views of reality. Mother goes outside and finds her child in the dirt with a worm. She says in surprise, "You've cut the worm in half. That's horrible." The child says "No, now he has a friend to play with."

As an experiment, Jane Elliot, a teacher in an all white, rural Iowa farm community, told her third grade students that brown-eyed students were more intelligent that blue-eyed students. Blue-eyed students' self-esteem and academic performance plummeted. They described themselves as "bad" or "stupid." The next day she told her class she had been wrong; actually blue-eyed children were superior and deserved special treatment; at which time their performance went up and the brown-eyed students' performance went down.[2] They were no longer confident about themselves. What influence did the teacher's statement have on the students? When the teacher expected them to be superior, they perceived themselves in such a way. Our expectations influence our perceptions or how we see things. Our assumptions can put our thinking in an invisible straightjacket. They can limit our thoughts, imagination and therefore our behavior. If a person cannot think about something, how can he or she imagine doing it? Unquestioned assumptions or expectations of others can have absolute influence over us, limiting, misleading, even leaving us open to being manipulated. This is why the systematic questioning and tentativeness of science is important.

With only one way of seeing the world there is no questioning. For example, students accepted the teacher's initial tenet, that brown-eyed students were superior. Let's add another model or perspective. For example, what if I

An Illusion

Studying illusions can make us more conscious of our perceptions. What do you see in this picture? It depends on how you
look at it. What you think, expect (assume), want to see or are
looking for, can each affect what you do see. Our expectations
influence what we see and how we interpret the drawing. As
you alternate your perspective, you will find that there is more
than one way of looking at the figure. If you can switch your
perception back and forth you will see not only a vase but the
profiles of two faces. *Archives of the History of American
Psychology, University of Akron.*

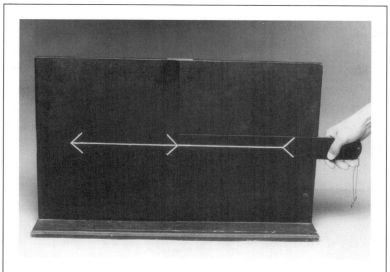

Muller-Lyer Illusion

Which side of the line is longer? Actually, both sides are equal, even though the right side appears longer. You can verify this by measuring with a ruler. When the line has arrow-feathers, it appears longer than when it has arrowheads, causing the viewer to misinterpret the length, leading to the mistaken view that one side is longer, further illustrating the importance of becoming aware of our assumptions and questioning our perceptions. *Courtesy of the Archives of the History of American Psychology, University of Akron.*

maintain that blue-eyed people are superior. Now we have two ways of looking at reality. With two models there is conflict, "either or thinking," a lot of time is spent on arguments between "I'm right and you're wrong" or vice-versa. In contrast, with three or more models we can step out of the system, become model-free and experience flexible thinking and ultimately freedom of thought. The person is no longer attached to any single idea or belief. The issue is no longer my way of seeing things; a particular idea or belief I am attached to. William James encouraged using multiple models, thinking of more than one theory at a time, finding that different models were useful for understanding different data and situations. Some models of thinking may be useful, even if not necessarily true, for they may have a *heuristic value*, which means they encourage further independent investigation and questioning. The structure of this text, alternating multiple perspectives, is designed to encourage this questioning, loosen up our assumptions, our childhood conclusions, becoming more flexible, innovative and creative.

The Value of Scientific Theories

In everyday life, do you ever notice or observe things and question, "How does this work?" One question leads to another as you try to figure it out, until you piece together the most likely explanation. You might make a guess, for instance, "What makes me sneeze?" and then test your hypothesis. This is how a theory begins. Scientific theories are basically a refinement of what you already do when you search for understanding. Scientists do this, but in a formal, systematic manner, open to public questioning and evaluation. A *scientific theory* is an explanation based on observations which are testable and repeatable. Yet theories go beyond our personal observations, experience and present knowledge. They organize what we know into a more meaningful and complete understanding, revealing the relationships between ideas from which new questions and insights may be generated. This is the process of discovery which stimulates further scientific inquiry.

What is the value of theories? They connect ideas and provide a model to predict alternative outcomes and understanding of behavior. This gives additional meaning to what otherwise might be just a collection or encyclopedic list of unrelated facts and ideas. Meaningful, organized material is more useful, as well as easier to understand and remember. Similarly, from the context of a theory and its implications, we can formulate new understandings and alternate responses for our unique life situations.

Let's take these rules and find out how the Russian scientist Ivan Pavlov came up with a theory. Pavlov, a physiologist, was busy studying how much dogs would salivate at the taste of certain foods, when his experiment was disrupted. What surprised Pavlov was that the dogs' mouths started watering even before the food got there, in fact when the animals heard the laboratory assistants' footsteps coming down the hall. Pavlov wondered, "Could they be taught to salivate at something other than food?" Based on his observations, he took a guess that, indeed, they could be made to salivate at something totally unrelated to food; he would try a bell. He decided to test his guess, called a *hypothesis*. He rang the bell before feeding the animals, so they began to associate the bell with the food. Eventually the dogs would salivate upon hearing the bell without any food (as students' mouths start watering with the noontime lunch bell), supporting his hypothesis. Were his results testable and repeatable, following the rules of science? He and other scientists repeated his experiment and had the same results. Here was real scientific evidence and a procedure others could follow to study learning and build upon his theory.

Theories vary in their strengths and focus. While some theories have a broad, comprehensive focus, organizing a lot of information to explain many aspects of behavior, other theories emphasize more limited objectives which are more easily tested. Many psychologists therefore use several different theories, called an *eclectic approach,* often finding that theories complement each other, resulting in a more complete and meaningful understanding.

Alternating Perspectives in Psychology

This book goes beyond any single point of view of psychology and consists of the concise and realistic presentation of seven major theories that, collectively, provide a base from which one can develop the capacity for alternating psychological perspectives to more completely understand himself or herself.

Developmental psychology explores the continual transformations and growth that occur at each life stage, from girl to woman, from youth to midlife, from middle age on, and how self-direction is a life-long skill that we refine over and over again, continually rediscovering, developing and reintegrating ourselves more effectively in each life stage as the focus of what motivates us changes.

Through psychoanalytic psychology, one can develop a thorough understanding of how the unconscious affects daily life; of emotional stumbling blocks left over from childhood that are irrational and counterproductive; and how to free up more personal resources for attaining self-direction and long-lasting intimate relationships.

Humanistic psychology is concerned with the uniqueness and wholeness of the individual, with becoming a fully functioning person by sorting out the potentials and experiences of a self-actualized person and how to become self-actualized. An understanding of how these higher potentials relate to more basic needs can help in achieving more self-direction.

Through behaviorism, we learn how we can perform more efficiently and how conditioning can accelerate or reduce optimal performance. We look at the dynamics of stress, its relationship to health and well-being, and how to operate more effectively for more fulfilled lives; distinguishing responses based on one's best interest from those based on habit or cultural conditioning.

Social psychology provides an understanding of how social forces can contribute to or detract from self-direction, and how to distinguish inner forces from the outer forces of society that can overwhelm self-identity and sweep the person along into conformity or cultism at the cost of being oneself.

Through Jung's work, one becomes aware of the unconscious as a guide for self-direction toward the ultimate unfolding of our individuality. How to transcend everyday life to get in touch with our deepest potentials through understanding dreams, art and mythology is the subject of this study.

Cultural psychology can deepen our appreciation of the influence of culture as an invisible determiner of how we think, feel and act and our fundamental views of ourselves. We will look at psychology outside the assumptions of Western culture. The aim is to develop our cultural competencies to relate successfully to people in other cultures for our own personal enrichment and successful participation in the global economy.

The multiple perspective approach is illustrated in the addendum chapter in which the seven theories are applied to pressing issues of our time: identity, terrorism and globalization.

The goal of this book is to liberate the self from "inside systems," such as emotion and thought, as well as from "outside systems," such as social roles and models. Using these theories as a collective tool, the reader can be freed "inside out" to, as the Greek sages admonished, "know thyself" for transformation and growth.

CHAPTER ONE

Developmental Psychology

**The Changing Self: Developmental Stages
Erik Erikson's and Jean Piaget's Theory**

A. The Shaping of Personality
B. Different People at Different Stages
C. Piaget: Growth Through Struggle
   1. Intellectual Development
   2. Accommodation and Assimilation
   3. Integration of Opposites
D. Erikson's Theory of Life Stages
   1. Self-Discovery
   2. Life Tasks
      a. Trust versus Mistrust
      b. Autonomy versus Doubt
      c. Initiative versus Guilt
      d. Industry versus Inferiority
      e. Identity versus Role Confusion
      f. Intimacy versus Isolation
      g. Generation versus Stagnation or Self-Absorption
      h. Ego Integrity versus Despair
E. Conclusion

The Changing Self:
Developmental Stages

*I*magine for a moment that your existence began in old age. As you progressed through life, accordingly, you became youthful, and finally returned to and disappeared in your mother's womb. At your "birth" you'd know exactly how long you had to live and might be much less likely to let a day or even an hour slide by, living each moment to its fullest. Initially, while your physical movement was restricted by the limitations of old age, you'd be attending school.

The way things are now there are in fact times when life seems backwards. When you're still so young and full of energy, yearning to be with friends, to go to the beach, to hike in nature, to be under a blue sky, you're confined to classrooms. Wouldn't it be so much better to study during old age when it is difficult to get around anyway? When you turned sixty your parents would come to life and you'd never have to worry about burying loved ones. When you were ill, you'd always recover.

By age thirty-five you could have your schooling completed, your house paid off and retire in your youth to enjoy life. You'd be healthy, full of energy, ambitious, with all your time to call your own. You could travel, do whatever you wanted. There would, of course, be one drawback: eventually as you became a teenager, you'd begin to lose privileges—you'd have to be home at a certain time and even have to ask for the car keys.

The Shaping of Personality

Although this seems at best a playful notion, it suggests that if you lived your life backwards your personality would be different. We face different challenges at each life stage. How we cope with them determines how we continue "to grow up" in adulthood. The problems we face at each period of life, says eminent psychologist Erik Erikson, are a main force in shaping our personalities. How effectively we meet the crises of each life stage gives us a foundation for future fulfillment and determines how self-directing we will be. For example, childhood feelings of mistrust for parents, which linger into adulthood, may reduce the individual's capacity to trust others and thereby future fulfillment.

Erikson says that personality development is continuous throughout life. It doesn't end with adulthood at the magic age of twenty-one. Rather, each stage of development presents new challenges which affect whether our personalities disintegrate or grow. If we stop striving at one stage, unwilling to let go of a particular way of being, it will eventually reduce our fulfillment. The thirty-five-year-old former high school homecoming queen who believes she achieved the high point in her growth at age eighteen, may be a sad figure at the high school reunion, her past triumphs now inadequate to fulfill her. Happiness requires continued growth because each life stage presents new problems.

Different People at Different Stages

We change radically as we grow up. An eight-year-old has very different perceptions, motivations, problems and interests than an eighteen- or sixty-five-year-old. In a sense we are different people at different stages in our lives. An eight-year-old boy may do everything he can to avoid touching a little girl's hand. This is the stage where boys and girls see themselves as very separate groups. Still not really confident about the male role, the young boy overreacts by rejecting girls. But, by the time he reaches twelve or thirteen, he'll have become very interested in the opposite sex. In fact, he may want to hold the hands of many girls.

As we grow, our self-fulfillment is based on how effectively we meet life's demands. We may feel as though we had it made at one stage of life. Thinking back, we may recall that at a particular period, say age nine, we really had a terrific time, felt great, had a sense of wholeness. Or, for others, a favorite time may have been at sixteen, in high school. Our actions seemed purposeful, there was a coherence in our experiences, we weren't confused, we didn't work against ourselves. There was a sense of equilibrium that lasted until we were faced with a new life stage and task, such as choosing a career or mate.

When I was a child we asked each other, "What are you going to be when you grow up?" We fantasized about our perfect lives. Somewhere around the age of eighteen to twenty-one everything would be our way: we could stay up as late as we wanted, we could buy anything, we wouldn't be required to study, no one could tell us what to do, we wouldn't have any problems. We perceived adults as having their way; we would too, someday.

Developmental psychology, however, challenges this notion, as do our lives. As soon as I turned twenty-two, I realized that I had just as many problems as ever—I was just another year older. Developmental psychology is based on the idea that we grow, struggle and change throughout our entire lives. To be human is not easy; it's an achievement. Even if we live to grow old, it doesn't mean all our potentials will be fulfilled. The qualities of character we respect—wisdom, love, courage, appreciation, self-awareness—do not occur automatically, are not simply inside of us, waiting to emerge on a certain birthday. They must be cultivated, and they require environmental opportunities. Many characteristics such as intelligence and destructiveness, once thought of as inherent in the individual, are now seen to a larger degree as being determined by the environment.

Piaget: Growth Through Struggle

Let's turn to Jean Piaget's studies that have revolutionized the concept of intellectual development. Piaget, along with Erikson, postulates that our growth occurs in periods of crisis, struggle and questioning.

A central idea is that for us to grow from our struggles, we must deal with our problems on our own. Piaget believes that when we teach a child something, we deprive the youngster of discovering it and making the knowledge his or her own. Clearly, says Piaget, telling a child the correct answer is not as important as the child's struggle to reduce the inconsistencies he sees in the world around him.

Likewise, Maria Montessori, whose Montessori method of education was originally designed to bring order to poor children's lives and to help them escape the ghettos

Maria Montessori studied at the University of Rome and graduated in medicine in 1894, and became the first woman physician in Italy. After educating children with learning disabilities, she concluded that similar methods could be applied to normal children. She began teaching her methods in Rome. Some advocates of orthodox education regarded her system as destructive of discipline. But many reformers supported her and in 1922 she was appointed government inspector of schools in Italy. Today her ideas are practiced throughout the United States in Montessori schools. *Courtesy of Ernest Ulmer, Artist; and Creative Process, Inc.*

of Rome through self-reliance, followed this premise. She said that if a little girl has difficulty buttoning her coat, and is showing interest in mastering the skill, give the child the opportunity to do it on her own, to develop her competency at coat buttoning. The most important thing is not to have the coat buttoned correctly, but to allow the child to concentrate on the act of buttoning. Here lies the opportunity for individual growth; for the child to learn independently.

Yet aspects of American educational philosophy are rooted in the concept of molding the child into some preconceived form, like "cookie-cutter people," who have been taught the answers. Such an approach assumes that virtues are outside the child and must be hammered in through instruction. It raises a very basic question about human nature. Are concentration, self-reliance and kindness, for example, potentials largely within the individual for adults to cultivate, or does the child have innate negative traits such as destructiveness and laziness that first must be overcome?

Piaget would say that children don't learn to think intelligently as the result of being taught logic. Instead, their thoughts are reflections of living in a lawful universe. Organizing the environment intelligently can help the child discover and interact with the laws of nature.

Intellectual Development

The young child's perception of reality is based upon how things look. In early stages, very simple assumptions lie behind how the child discriminates and reasons. As the youngster grows older and perceives that the world is more complex than immediate impressions, the child realizes that truth is not easy to come by.

Jean Piaget's focus was not on whether the child had the right answer, but rather on discovering the underlying structure or organization of children's thoughts by studying their incorrect answers.[1] Piaget noticed that their incorrect answers were not random, but made sense, when he discussed with the children their understanding of what they were doing. *Courtesy of the Archives of the History of American Psychology, University of Akron.*

Through a simple experiment Piaget gives us a striking example of how intellectual ability develops. Imagine two glasses filled with lemonade, both the same height and width. The experimenter asks a five-year-old, a seven-year-old and an eleven-year-old if one glass contains more than the other. Each youngster says they are the same. The experimenter pours the lemonade from one glass into a taller, more slender glass and proceeds to ask the five-year-old if the amount in this glass is the same as in the other glass. The youngest child says that the tall, slender glass does indeed have more lemonade; the seven-year-old agrees, while the eleven-year-old dissents, saying they are still equivalent. Then the experimenter takes the tall glass of lemonade and pours it back into the original container. The five-year-old says the glass still contains more lemonade even though they look equal. The youngest child's perception is dominated by the image of the tall glass of lemonade that looked like more. (This kind of thinking is the basis for the young child's acceptance of magic.) The eleven-year-old maintains the two glasses are still equal and begins to find the experiment boring. Not the seven-year-old. The child looks confused upon seeing a tall, narrow glass of lemonade poured back into a short, wide glass and realizes there has been a mistake; the problem was more complex than realized. Up to this point the seven-year-old operated on the principle of height as an explanation of size. Up to now, this concept seemed to have worked: big brother who was taller was also "more than" the younger child; a tall ice cream cone contained "more" ice cream. But now there is a new variable—the child's thinking must become more complex to include width and, still later, depth. The amount is no longer determined solely by height but rather, by height interacting with width.

The relevance of Piaget's study extends beyond the children's perceptions. The study, says Piaget, is an example of a *conservation* problem: the quantity remains the same despite changes in appearance, which can be manipulated. If we don't understand the conservation of matter despite changing forms, we are vulnerable to deception. Just like the two-year-old who thinks there is more ice cream when it's stacked high, an adult in a hurry may buy a tall, thin box of food that seems larger than it is. Those deceived by packaging can learn to appreciate another variable: the weight stated on the label. At each stage the world seems consistent for a short time until the person perceives more complexity. As new problem-solving situations arise, a child will naturally consider new variables unless inquiry is blocked by being punished for not having the right answer immediately or by being pampered and given the answer. Ideally, parents or teachers can provide opportunities for the child to develop more complex reasoning.

Accommodation and Assimilation

Piaget explains growth as an exciting process that involves *assimilating* (similar to absorbing or taking in) and *accommodating* (adapting or adjusting to) the world around us. For example, if someone speaks to us we may hear what we already know, what we want to hear. In other words, we *assimilate* information and make it fit our understanding of the world. In contrast, with *accommodation,* we adapt to fit reality. We listen very carefully to understand the uniqueness of what the other person says, his or her perception of the world, and how they differ from our current understanding.

Who is the "accommodator" in Piaget's experiment? Is it the five-year-old who interprets the experiment as being

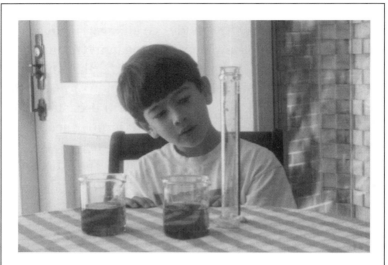

The seven-year-old says the two glasses are the same.

The experimenter pours the lemonade into the taller more slender glass.

The seven-year-old says the slender glass contains more.

The seven-year-old, upon seeing a tall, narrow glass poured back into a short, wide glass, realizes there has been a mistake.

magic or the eleven-year-old who is bored with it all? Whose perception of quantity, or reality, changed? It was, you recall, the seven-year-old who realized the mistake, that the concept of quantity was more complex than was previously thought. In a moment of confusion, the child accommodates the experiment, listens carefully, bends to understand the mistake. Piaget demonstrates that a person must reach a certain stage of development to appreciate the problem. The five-year-old had not yet reached this stage; the youngster assimilates the experiment and explains it on the basis of what is already known. It goes right over the child's head, who is not even aware that a question was missed. The eleven-year-old, already familiar with volume, assimilates the experience correctly.

We're continually exposed to new situations. In some cases assimilation is more appropriate; in others, accommodation. Different life stages require new responses. For example, although it may have been appropriate to assimilate a situation in the past, this may no longer work because the individual has grown older, one's perceptions of the world have changed, and society will no longer tolerate the same behavior. If the person doesn't accommodate a changing reality, one's fulfillment in life may decrease. On the other hand, by modifying impressions of reality, the individual grows.

Integration of Opposites

This may be better understood if we see it in terms of the larger concept of incorporating an awareness of opposites. The individual's perception of reality develops through life experiences. Within the ideal family environment, the infant's main impression is one of love. However, this changes beyond the boundaries of the family as the child learns that love cannot be expected from everyone and that in fact, some people actively work against the youngster's welfare. From such a contrast, the child develops an *appreciation* of love. Similarly, an understanding of heat develops when the child comes into a warm house, shivering from the cold, or of justice when he or she is wronged.

The experience of opposites can contribute to our growth and understanding. George Hegel, a German philosopher, says truth is the unification of contrary elements through a process that he calls the dialectic. As we become aware of opposing dimensions, we experience tension that forces us to reevaluate our view and incorporate new information, becoming aware of new ideas. We can no longer consider size solely in terms of height. In order to come closer to reality, which in our example is volume, we must add the dimension of width. The integration of these opposing elements results in a more complex and complete view of life.

Erikson's theory is based on the tension of opposing forces at each life stage: trust versus mistrust, identity versus role confusion, intimacy versus isolation. What keeps the individual striving for intimacy is loneliness. The capacity for intimacy emerges from the tension of feeling separate from other human beings. When the individual is able to integrate these contrary feelings—seeing oneself as separate from other human beings, yet still desiring companionship—the person achieves what Piaget calls *equilibrium,* a balance between opposing forces.

Within a relationship, there is a continual struggle for equilibrium between intimacy and isolation. If one partner is overprotective, the other will pull back, increasing the tension, which eventually forces acknowledgment of their separateness. In the very moment of estrangement lies the opportunity for the relationship to grow as the couple appreciates one another's separateness and individuality.

As we grow and understand the different aspects of reality, we become more complex and differentiated (*different*-iated); our uniqueness becomes more apparent. In this process of self-actualization, we transcend the limitations of how we saw ourselves and related to the world in earlier stages of life.

Erikson's Theory of Life Stages

Have you ever wondered why some people read the obituaries? Comedian Bill Cosby talks about his grandfather reading the obituaries every day and saying, "Well, a lot of people died yesterday, I guess I won't be around much longer." The grandfather's concern may seem extreme to a young person caught up in growth and life. Yet taking the problems of other age groups seriously can enrich our lives. For example, how much more rewarding youth would be if we mastered an art of the old, to live each day to its fullest as though it were the last.

Life struggles begin in our earliest years. A baby tries to walk, falls, and experiences frustration. But, even so, the toddler tries again until walking is mastered. In time, as more complex awareness develops and new inconsistencies become apparent, the child raises new questions about the world which require growth. Later, as an adult, there will be the challenge to achieve intimacy, compassion, courage, appreciation and wisdom, ideal human traits that don't come easily except through a recognition of opposites. Around us are people who live through the hardest of times and yet somehow emerge as examples of life at its richest.

Self-Discovery

While growing up, many accept certain traditional roles: the thrill of cooking with pots and pans, of playing house, of dressing up in uniforms and becoming a Scout. Later, as the person masters these roles, their inconsistencies become more apparent. Consider this person's experience:

> In the beginning, I was one person, knowing nothing but my own experience.
>
> Then I was told things, and I became two people: the little girl who said how terrible it was that the boys had a fire going in the lot next door where they were roasting apples (which was what the women said)— and the little girl, who, when the boys were called by their mothers to go to the store, ran out and tended the fire and the apples because she loved doing it.
>
> So there were two of I.
>
> One I always doing something that the other I disapproved of. Or other I said what I disapproved of. All this argument in me so much.
>
> In the beginning was I, and I was good.
>
> Then came in other I. Outside authority. This was confusing. And then other I became very confused because there were so many different outside authorities.
>
> Sit nicely. Leave the room to blow your nose. Don't do that, that's silly. Why, the poor child doesn't even know how to pick a bone! Flush the toilet at night because if you don't it makes it harder to clean. DON'T FLUSH THE TOILET AT NIGHT—you wake people up! Always be nice to people. Even if you don't like them, you mustn't hurt their feelings. Be frank and honest. If you don't tell people what you think of them, that's cowardly. . . .
>
> The most important thing is to have a career. The most important thing is to get married. The hell with everyone. Be nice to everyone. The most important

thing is to have everyone like you. The most important thing is to dress well. The most important thing is to be sophisticated and say what you don't mean and don't let anyone know what you feel. The most important thing is to be ahead of everyone else. The most important thing is a black seal coat and china and silver. The most important thing is to be clean. The most important thing is to always pay your debts. The most important thing is to love your parents. The most important thing is to speak correct English. The most important thing is to be dutiful to your husband. The most important thing is to see that your children read the right books. The most important thing is to do what others say. And others say all these things.

All the time, *I* is saying, live with life. That is what is important.

But when I lives with life, other I says no, that's bad. All the different other I's say this. It's dangerous. It isn't practical. You'll come to a bad end. Of course . . . everyone felt that way once, the way you do, but *you'll learn!*

Out of all the other I's some are chosen as a pattern that is me. But there are all the other possibilities of patterns within what all the others say which come into me and become other I which is not myself, and sometimes these take over. Then who am I?

I does not bother about whom am I. I *is,* and is happy being. But when I is happy being, other I says get to work, do something, do something worthwhile. I is happy doing dishes. "You're weird!" I is happy being with people saying nothing. Other I says talk. Talk, talk, talk, I gets lost . . . .

I is human. If someone needs, I gives. "You can't do that! You'll never have anything for yourself! We'll have to support you!"

I loves. I loves in a way that other I does not know. I loves. "That's too warm for friends!" "That's too cool for lovers!" "Don't feel so bad, he's just a friend.

It's not as though you loved him." "How can you let him go? I thought you loved him?" So cool the warm for friends and hot up the love for lovers, and I gets lost.

So both I's have a house and a husband and children and all that and friends and respectability and all that, and security and all that but both I's are confused because other I says, "You see? You're lucky," while I goes on crying. "What are you crying about? Why are you so ungrateful?" I doesn't know gratitude or ingratitude and cannot argue. I goes on crying. Other I pushes it out, says "I am happy! I am lucky to have such a fine family and a nice house and good neighbors and lots of friends who want me to do this, do that." I is not reason-able, either. I goes on crying.

Other I gets tired, and goes on smiling, because this is the thing to do. Smile, and you will be rewarded. Like the seal who gets tossed a piece of fish. Be nice to everyone and you will be rewarded. People will be nice to you, and you can be happy with that. You know they like you. Like a dog who gets patted on the head for good behavior. Tell funny stories. Be gay. Smile, smile, smile . . . I is crying . . . "Don't be sorry for yourself! Go out and do things for people!" "Go out and be with people!" I is still crying, but now, that is not heard and felt so much.

Suddenly: "What am I doing?" "Am I to go through life playing the clown?" "What am I doing, going to parties that I do not enjoy?" "What am I doing, being with people who bore me?" "Why am I so hollow and the hollowness filled with emptiness?" A shell. How has this shell grown around me? Why am I proud of my children and unhappy about their lives which are not good enough? Why am I disappointed? Why do I feel so much waste?

I comes through, a little. In moments. And gets pushed back by other I.

I refuses to play the clown any more. Which I is

that? "She used to be fun, but now she thinks too much about herself." I lets friends drop away. Which I is that? "She's being too much by herself. That's bad. She's losing her mind." Which mind?

Barry Stevens *Person to Person*[2]

This woman is experiencing role confusion. For most of us it begins in adolescence when an individual realizes that he or she acts differently with friends than with parents or at work. The teen experiences a discrepancy in roles, a disequilibrium, a tension, raising a question about identity. Tom may find that he treats his girlfriend differently if she intrudes on him and his pals. He may even slight her because he has not integrated his role with his steady girlfriend and his role as a member of a male group. At this stage, young people don't always want different parts of their lives to come together because it emphasizes inconsistencies in themselves that they may not have worked out.

As time passes, Tom learns to think of himself as an individual, separate from his role expectations. He is no longer merely the child of his parents, a member of the boys' club, an employee. He is a unique person more than the sum of these roles. Each must go on an individual search to define the self, through conflict, hurt and loss.

This understanding of who "I" is increases our ability to be intimate, to achieve a long and lasting relationship which takes the individual into even greater depths of the self.

Life Tasks

In focusing on personal and social development, Erikson discovered that our development and the tasks we face in life take place in a certain sequence. Achievements in life don't necessarily occur at a particular age, but instead at a specific life stage. Erikson elaborated on Freud's four childhood stages of psychological development, saying that personal and social development occurs throughout one's lifetime. He identified eight stages of development, from infancy to old age. In each stage there are unique problems or tasks. When we successfully deal with these tasks, we grow. If we don't, they act as barriers to further growth. Although many of these conflicts may not be completely resolved, they must be worked out to a large degree in order to move into the next developmental stage and successfully cope with new challenges.

Trust versus Mistrust. We all recognize the helplessness and dependency of a baby. In fact, the infant's very survival depends on the care others provide. The child is seeking security, love and care through feeding and comforting from an affectionate parent.

Erikson says the relationship that develops between parent and child during this early period is the child's basis for trust throughout life. Yet the infant also experiences the opposite, mistrust, when he or she cries and Mother doesn't appear immediately. A central issue for the child to deal with is, "How can I trust you if you don't always show up?" The baby must learn to trust Mother to return if the infant is to move on into the next stage of development. When the toddler tries to walk, a sense of mistrust is reactivated upon falling. Although afraid to get up and try again, if the child resolves the ambivalent feelings to trust, he or she will learn to walk, recognizing the dangers of the world, yet maintaining an openness to it.

Autonomy versus Doubt. During the "terrible twos," parents seem to spend most of their waking hours telling their child, "No." The child's newfound independence is at odds with parental control. One sensitive, exasperated mother felt so bad about continually telling her toddler "No" that she wished she could walk her youngster through the house for a day and say nothing but "Yes," pointing out everything the child could do.

This stage includes the second and third year of life. Up to this age the youngster has been very dependent. Mother controlled when and how much the infant would eat. Even if the baby wasn't hungry, the mother might put the baby to her breast. Now the child is seen as asserting him- or herself, experiencing will and individuality. This person differs biologically, perceptually, intellectually and socially from the infant in the crib; in short, an independent and autonomous being (auto means self; autonomous means self-directing or self-starting). If Mother puts the child down for a nap, she can't be sure the youngster won't climb out of the crib and come find her in another room.

As exciting as independence is, unchecked it puts the toddler in opposition to social and physical forces. For example, the child who climbs up the stairs too quickly may fall and scrape a knee. The physical properties of the stairs limit the toddler's independence. The mobile youngster is capable of doing things that bring great pleasure, but also great harm. The limitations are not only physical, they are also social. The child reaches for an object on the coffee table, Mother says "No." In the middle of this expression of free will, the child suddenly experiences self doubt. Thrown out of equilibrium, the youngster now must incorporate control from an outside source.

Too much authority, as well as no authority, can result in the child becoming an over- or underlearner. If the parent exerts too much control instead of allowing assertiveness, the toddler may remain a dependent personality, even throughout life. The two-year-old who is continually told "No" may begin to have self-doubt, to lose self-esteem. The loss of autonomy may undermine the person's determination and creativeness, crucial elements to solving the complex and subtle problems of self-direction one is confronted with later in life. Erikson calls this person the *overlearner,* the individual who becomes very anxious to do the right thing and tries too hard to please authority figures at the cost of being oneself. This child may grow up to win great achievements, but at a great personal cost because the person never does what he or she really wants.

If the child experiences too much or too little external control, the youngster may also rebel, failing to integrate submission with willfulness. The person may become destructive and stubborn, spending the remainder of life fighting authority. Erikson calls this personality the *underlearner.* Rather than learning to accept authority as a child, the adult may be uncontrollable, spurred by the impulsive desire to get one's own way, even at the cost of hurting oneself. If the child feels the parent tried to break the developing self-esteem or autonomy, the offspring may have a subtle hostility toward authority throughout life, unable to accommodate even if things are in his or her favor.

The child must balance self-assertiveness with accommodation to avoid being caught in a struggle to either please others or to rebel against authority. This requires developing the ability to affirm oneself while, at the same time, being able to yield in order to move into the next life stage.

Initiative versus Guilt. I remember when I was four, playing Indians, cops-and-robbers or house almost every day. The preschool child's days are filled with dramatic play; the child makes a game of almost everything. The sense of autonomy from the previous life stage is the basis for emerging initiative. The young child is imitating the adult world, initiating activities with direction and purpose, specific games with roles. They are important activities. Acting out sex roles influences sexual identity and sexual attitudes later in life. The child plays cooperatively with others, spontaneous and open to the world, confident of love and a place in the family. This stage usually occurs about four to five.

Play, the spirit of games, as distinguished from competitive sports in school, stimulates and sharpens the senses, according to Erikson. He says that modern life allows too little time for the pleasures of the senses. The child starts to lose touch with the senses in school when play is called "a waste of time" or "laziness."

Preschoolers believe in magic. The boundary between the child's fantasies and "reality" is undeveloped. A youngster may think events can be influenced through one's will. If something goes wrong after the child has wished someone harm, a great sense of guilt may follow. At this age the little person may begin to have general fears of monsters or other frightening creatures.

As the child's awareness of body parts increases, there is a consciousness of physical vulnerability and a growing concern that the body remain intact. A young lad may see having his tonsils removed as losing part of himself.

Industry versus Inferiority.   From ages six to ten, the child's physical and social environment expands rapidly beyond one's own backyard. The youngster is an explorer, looking through junkyards and construction sites, climbing fences, hanging from trees and from monkey bars. These are the elementary school years: The child's world expands to include a classroom of 30 students. The youngster becomes independent of parents; life becomes dominated by peers.

Children focus on the world unfolding before them, with countless things to do. They have a great sense of industry as they begin to learn the skills of the adult world: to read, to write, to work. They are busy playing ball, riding bikes and horses, jumping rope, ice-skating, mastering computer games and making friends. If they are encouraged and praised, they will learn to produce, to be a worker; to build tree houses, model airplanes, to sew, to bake and to paint. They can play team sports as they learn to follow rules and to take turns.

The child who fails to produce, either because of lack of encouragement, being made to feel stupid, or being ill, may develop a sense of *inferiority*. Erikson says the child's development is based not only on encouragement from parents but also from social institutions. A warm, supportive teacher can do a great deal to encourage a child's creative processes, even if the youngster is discouraged at home.

We must all deal with a sense of inferiority, which stems from coming into the world undeveloped. We are a developmental achievement. Each of us knows how it feels to be inferior as a child as we try to learn new skills, says psychologist Alfred Adler. There is no way to learn how to pour milk without spilling it. The struggle to overcome a sense of inferiority can motivate the adult to contribute to society. For example, the youngster deeply touched by death may choose a profession where he or she can help others to heal. Adler says a key to evaluating one's behavior is whether or not it is socially useful.

There are, of course, he points out, some children who may be overwhelmed by a profound sense of inferiority and lack faith that, through struggle, they will master the necessary skills.

"I can't do it, I can't do it," they may say. On the other hand, a person can overcompensate for an overwhelming sense of inferiority by adopting an attitude of superiority, that he or she is better than others, a posture that separates the individual from intimate relationships and prevents growth.

Identity versus Role Confusion. Between the ages of nine to twenty, one begins to break with parents and family, becoming a person in his or her own right. At first the child may be shaken and feel alone in an empty universe. These feelings accompany the breaking of ties with parents as one learns more about the self and as their individuality slowly emerges. During this period the person also matures sexually. At this time, young people seek emotional support from peers; they begin to develop a life of their own outside the home, to live in their own society with their own social rules, and to eventually become independent emotionally.

This stage includes the struggle to define oneself, to begin living as a separate entity. Doubts are not only raised about one's sexual role but, for the first time, the individual sees life as a finite entity from birth to death and asks the question, "What's it all about?" Up to this point the young person has taken in information about the world, but now there are questions concerning underlying assumptions. In college, beliefs are challenged as students become aware of themselves in a new way. As one person said, "I was born intellectually at eighteen."

There are many contradictions in adolescence that can be quite unsettling. There are pressures to be oneself, to act like an adult, yet at the same time one is economically dependent. There are demands to select a job, to break emotional ties with the family and to find a mate for life. Some choose to escape through drugs, destructiveness or even dropping out because the developmental task—discerning one's identity—seems overwhelming. Others may remain dependent on the family at the cost of expressing their individuality. For many, however, the struggle results in success at being themselves.

Intimacy versus Isolation. The greatest challenge of young adulthood (ages twenty to thirty-five) is to achieve intimacy, a task that involves integrating many different roles and thinking of others. To a large extent, one's capacity for commitment is based on no longer being identified with one's roles. The male who spends his time being "macho," the individual wrapped up in business, or the woman who sees her role as being submissive to men, may all have difficulty achieving intimacy. They can only relate to another human being in a limited fashion.

We are faced with the difficult issue of trying to maintain "I" in the midst of "we"; of trying to overcome our aloneness and achieve intimacy. We may fail, but the sense of isolation and desolation forces us to try again, to work through our hurt and learn to live closely with others.

The focus of happiness shifts from being responsible for oneself to include the welfare of others. For example, Sam found that when he regularly came home late, his wife Hazel's affection seemed to cool. She was limiting her emotional involvement because it hurt too much to be so intensely concerned. As Sam got a clearer self-perception, he became more aware of Hazel's concern and stopped staying out so late. She could be more open and intimate now because Sam was demonstrating his concern for her needs.

Those who have difficulty achieving intimacy may respond by becoming bitter, by conforming, or by giving up their aspirations. Some people see the world as a jungle, put up walls to retreat from it, or decide they will hurt others before they are hurt. It is during adulthood that cynicism may develop, that a person may say, "I'm going to make it no matter what; I'm going to market this product even if it does cause cancer."

This period is one of experimentation; through dating many different people and trying different jobs, the individual deals with two developmental tasks: to work and to love.

Important choices are made—most people choose a mate and a career in which they strive to establish themselves during their twenties and thirties. This is a time of building foundations, of establishing a family, of making a home. Traditionally during this life stage, the individual gets in touch with the potential for deep interpersonal relationships—with a husband or wife, with children, with friends and one's parents.

Generation versus Stagnation or Self-Absorption. In *A Christmas Carol,* Scrooge portrays the classical example of self-absorption and stagnation—wrapped up in business, out of touch with other human beings, concerned only with possessions and physical well-being. The ghosts of Christmas past will remind him of the task of adult development he missed, and encourage him to break out of his

Erik Erikson developed the theory that one progresses through eight distinct life stages. *Courtesy of Jon Erikson.*

isolation and cultivate younger generations. This period normally occurs between the ages of thirty-five and fifty.

Erikson says we grow at this stage through *generativity* —feeling a voluntary obligation to care for others. Generativity is primarily the concern for establishing and guiding the next generation, taking care to pass on what you have to contribute to life. It includes caring for others, having empathy and concern.[3]

Erikson said that generativity is lacking in modern life—making the world better for our children through the way we live, and promoting positive values in the lives of the next generation. Generativity may involve not only contributing to one's children, but helping others in the community at large, for example, by working for the control of harmful substances that may affect generations to come. Generativity includes being more productive and creative— those who miss it stagnate, wrapped up in themselves.

In a comedy routine about basketball, Bill Cosby reminisces about how his body went downhill as he approached thirty. Up to that time he would go out on the court, think "Jump!" and he was off the ground, dunking the ball in the basket. Then he turned twenty-eight, went out on the court and thought "Jump!" But his feet never left the ground. Again, "Jump," but still nothing happened. His body had gone bad on him! By age thirty-five many people begin to feel their energies start to decline. Their world is not expanding as rapidly as it did when they were younger, so they try to consolidate the gains they've already made.

Around age forty many people face a midlife crisis. The individual has "crossed the bridge" halfway through life. There is the knowledge that youthfulness has peaked and life is limited. The magic of achieving a particular career, status or lifestyle, which could make life complete, has diminished. It is time to take stock of what's behind and what's ahead. The question, which first appeared during adolescence, reappears with new intensity: "What's it all about?" The issue was probably submerged during young adulthood because the person was too busy holding down a job, raising a family and fixing the roof. Now there is a pause to reevaluate the life direction one worked so hard to establish during the twenties and the thirties. For many there is serious questioning of all aspects of their life direction; they may no longer like what they've been doing for the last 15 years; perhaps the job has become unfulfilling or they feel distant from family. Radical changes can take place at this stage, disrupting marriages, switching careers or lifestyles. Tom, for example, still sees himself as idealistic and nonmaterialistic. Suddenly, he's aware of the discrepancy between that image and his present lifestyle. Life turns upside down. He sells his home, opting for a low-keyed lifestyle in a small beach town with fewer materialistic goals. Sue, a mother and housewife, now has time to look back on the dreams of a career she discarded at twenty-five to support her husband's vocation and to raise children. She may reevaluate these old aspirations and decide to pursue them, once again incorporating the image of a competent professional self in her identity. Career women, as well as men, may wonder if they made the right decision; some who had both a career and children may wonder if they succeeded at either; while others find themselves out of a marriage—or as a single parent—and forced to have a career or different lifestyle. Such experiences may sharpen one's awareness, appreciation, understanding and judgment in deciding how to spend the rest of one's life.

Ego Integrity versus Despair. Somewhere between age fifty or sixty and death, a period of evaluation and decline sets in. The older adult's life tasks include caring for aging parents, losing them and dealing with questions about the meaning of life and death.

The developmental task now is to affirm one's life, to resolve the ambivalence between what the person has been able to achieve and what hasn't been accomplished. But, no matter how many goals the individual has achieved, certain ambitions may remain illusive or only partially fulfilled. All of us have to deal with the feeling that life is too short; that even if we lived to be one-hundred-and-ten years old, we couldn't accomplish all of our dreams; that we have not succeeded in all of our objectives. Yet there is an alternative to depression and despair when our overall life experience leaves us with a sense of fulfillment, our integrity and dignity intact.

In old age, we face a challenge to see ourselves as part of the continuity of all life, as the passing generation, to let go of physical faculties and, eventually, our lives. This is a time when one can continue to experience productivity by sharing one's wisdom and cultivating the young.

The fruits of the earlier seven stages of life—having in some way taken care of people and things, having adapted oneself to the triumphs and disappointments which come with life, accepting one's life and circumstances as they were, given the historical moment one lived in—may ripen into ego integrity.[4]

Youth belongs not only to the young. It lives on everywhere minds are kept vital, where ideas and creativity are free-flowing. Youthfulness is a child's excitement at that first step or a seventy-year-old applying the last touches to a painting of the seashore; the parents' first sight of their newborn or an eighty-year-old playing the piano or teaching a young person how to study the signs of rain in the sky. Youth is the child and the grandmother, both breathless at the sight of the sunset, as though it were the first one ever seen.

Generativity includes cultivating the younger generation. Youth is a child and grandmother sharing a secret.

Conclusion

Human beings are a developmental achievement—their intellectual ability and capacity for intimacy and for self-fulfillment is dependent on the struggle to resolve problems at each life stage. Each of Erikson's stages of development presents new challenges that affect whether the person grows. There is an inherent tension at each developmental stage as the individual attempts to assimilate and accommodate the world. Out of crisis comes the opportunity for growth. In order to move solidly into the next developmental stage he or she must, in turn, integrate trust and mistrust, autonomy and doubt, initiative and guilt, identity and role confusion, intimacy and isolation, generativity and self-absorption, and finally, ego integrity and despair. If the individual is able to balance these contrary elements he or she lives more richly and fulfilled, with a new understanding of the self and the world.

CHAPTER TWO

Psychoanalytic Psychology

Discovering the Unconscious World: Sigmund Freud's Theory

Discovering the
Unconscious World

*W*hile visiting relatives in Italy, I met a young man who told me that he prided himself on his reputation, as all of his young Italian male friends did, as one of the world's greatest lovers. In fact, he considered wining and dining and courting a woman a profession. He cultivated his image as a man with a passionate nature and a disarming ability to make the woman of his choice feel as though she were a queen, as though she were fulfilling his wildest dreams and passion—in short, the ideal romance. Then, to my surprise, he fell deeply in love and married. With a marriage certificate in hand and a gold ring to prove his undying devotion, the relationship changed. Something was drastically wrong. The passion was gone. All of a sudden he was no longer Don Juan, bringing his wife roses, whispering sweet nothings in her ear, telling her how strong his love was. He began to treat her like, of all people, his mother, with great respect and an accompanying respectful distance. For some unusual reason, she was no longer the object of his sexual fantasies. Instead, he turned to someone else. So the two became a trio: the husband; his devoted wife, whom he admires; and his mistress, who shares his passion.

I realized this was not an isolated incident in Italian society but occurs with people of many cultures. It illustrates a common dilemma in marriage, which I had first read about in Sigmund Freud's theory: The couple had difficulty integrating passion and respect. Once the relationship has been legitimized, passion flies out the nearest window. Why does this occur?

Freud, the founder of psychoanalysis, sheds light on why a man may only be able to relate to a woman in narrowly defined roles, either as a sex object or as his mother. For Freud, the past holds the key to overcoming prejudices toward the opposite sex, freeing the individual to achieve deep and lasting intimacy. Intimacy is central to adult fulfillment; being capable of loving someone and being ourselves while we are close to that person. Why do we sometimes behave irrationally with the people we love most? Freud says we may act as we did in childhood, regressing to a conflict we never quite resolved. Freud's basic premise, which forms the basis for much of modern psychology, is that the earliest impressions in life, particularly during the first five years, determine much of our adult personalities. They shape our emotions, our receptiveness to pleasure and dependency on others later in life.

In dealing with patients who suffered physical disabilities because of emotional conflicts, Freud asked what could be so painful that it literally immobilized these people? (One patient's legs were paralyzed; another had no sensitivity in her hand.) He found when he asked, "Who are these people? What are they really about?" that the answer was far more complex than the smooth veneer of the personality.

Sigmund Freud, the founder of psychoanalytic psychology, established a new direction for psychology. *Courtesy of the Archives of the History of American Psychology, University of Akron.*

The Unconscious and the Id

Freud pointed out there is far more to the human personality than what we see on the surface. Freud was the first to systematically explore the *unconscious,* that part of the psyche not directly accessible to the conscious, which includes repressed desires and conflicts, and to explain how it directs much of our activity. Through Freud's work, people have glimpsed greater dimensions of the human personality. He called the primitive part the *id,* which includes the psychic experiences that we inherit from our species. It is very powerful, for the id is the major source of all our basic drives and pleasure impulses. The id is not constrained by considerations of reality; it does not include the rational or the critical restrictions of logic. The id operates by what Freud called the primary processes and is expressed in wish-fulfillment images, fantasies or dreams. Such images are free of the restraints of logic, time and space and can be experienced in a daydream, while sleeping or in the delirium of a fever.

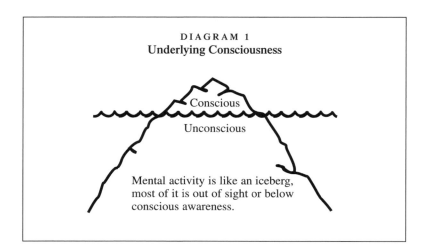

DIAGRAM 1
Underlying Consciousness

Conscious

Unconscious

Mental activity is like an iceberg,
most of it is out of sight or below
conscious awareness.

What makes a husband treat his wife as though she were his mother? Certainly he loses out as well, no longer deriving pleasure from the intimacy he once knew with her. Or have you ever wondered why it's so hard to stay involved with someone to whom you are really attracted? Or to feel passionate for someone with whom you were initially friends and then only later considered dating? According to Freud, behavior in such cases is directed by the unconscious.

Freud finds cause for the apparent inexplicable—things that seem to occur by chance or accident. He postulates the unconscious to make sense of nonsense: irrational dreams, accidents, certain physical disabilities and slips of the tongue can all be explained. In fact, according to Freud, many of the choices we make in life (spouse, profession, attitudes and even vices) may be determined by something far more subtle than a conscious decision.

You may find some of Freud's ideas startling, for he explains parts of the psyche or mind obscured by Western culture, going against social, scientific and religious taboos. His work has created great controversy, for he maintains that both forces beyond conscious control and sexuality determine much of personality development. Although some people feel this reduces our free will, by becoming aware of these forces, which were previously unconscious, we can increase our ability to be self-directive.

As you read this chapter you may catch yourself daydreaming, losing track of an idea. Freud calls this *resistance,* referring to the individual's reluctance to take a deep look at his or her personality, at unresolved feelings that have been buried below the surface for years. For some, bringing these feelings to the surface can be painful. Yet Freud found dealing with these conflicts gratifying—

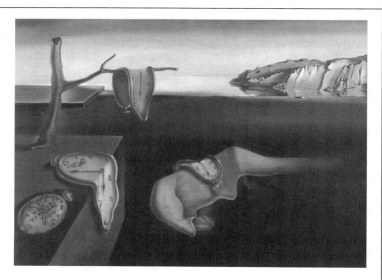

Freud's influence is widespread in the modern world. Consider
Freud's description of the psyche as an iceberg. What part of the
psyche may have stimulated the artist who created this picture?
The unconscious. In Salvador Dali's painting *The Persistence of
Memory* (1931) the image of time is not subject to the critical
restrictions of logic. Dali taps into the primary processes and
makes the unconscious conscious. It is an expression of the id.
In his painting Dali stretched time to resemble the shape of soft
camembert cheese, unrestricted by the shape of a watch. This is
an artistic manifestation of the subjectivity of time, how time
can slow down, or in other instances go more quickly, restricting
one's activity. Using a dreamlike state, Dali creates a painting in
which things happen outside the limitations of time and space.
Dali studied psychoanalysis and the works of Freud before joining the surrealistic painters. Dali's surrealistic method has been
used in poetry, fashion, film and other arts. *Courtesy of the
Museum of Modern Art, New York. Oil on canvas, 9 $\frac{1}{2}$ x 13.*

psychoanalysis freed patients from paralysis and other ailments.

While the nature of Freud's ideas shocked the people of Vienna where he lived and worked, today his concepts permeate society and many psychologists have built on Freud's most basic premises.

Eros and the Death Instinct

Can you remember the last time you experienced joy? What were you doing? Running on the beach, hugging a loved one? At that point you may have been aware of a strong current of life energy running through you. Freud calls this energy *libido,* which is shaped and expressed in pleasure-seeking activities.

Freud maintains that human beings are born with two basic urges or drives. The first he calls *Eros,* named after the Greek god of life and love. It is the instinct of life and love—love of self, love for others and the desire to preserve the self and the species. Eros represents all life forces within us, such as hunger and thirst. From Eros flows the energy of the libido. The libido is the basis for anything that makes one feel good, from the satisfaction an infant experiences in nursing to adult sexuality.

Just as there is a wish for life, there is a desire for death, an urge to escape the stress of living by becoming inanimate. There is a basic antagonism submerged in the unconscious between the death instinct and the wish for life. This self-destructive impulse can be turned outward as well. For example, a man obsessed with fantasies about his own death may, at the last minute, turn his aggression on someone else and commit murder.

The Id, the Ego and the Superego

At birth, we're totally directed by the id. It's only as we develop and accumulate experience that the ego emerges. The *id* is based solely on strong biological drives to achieve pleasure without taking into account physical threats or social mores. The id says, "I want this and I want it now," as though there are no consequences. Most striking and unabashed is the id of a one-year-old. Confident of the world, the child is ready to try anything until the youngster gets hurt seriously enough to modify a particular activity.

Through contact with harsh reality the *ego* develops. The ego's main task is self-preservation, so it adopts rational principles such as concern for safety. It operates on the reality principle: "what is" versus "what I wish" or "what should be."

If the ego is based on the child's experiences (the discovery of the hot stove occurs upon touching it) the *superego* is based on "hearsay," on what others tell the young person. The superego develops at about age four or five when the child internalizes the values of parents and society. The superego embodies the morals of society, how our family and subculture tell us to behave. It includes feelings of guilt that the individual experiences when the dictates of the conscience aren't followed. People unconditionally striving for fame may be driven by the superego, a desire to receive praise from society that originated in trying to please their parents. When successful at living up to society's ideal, an individual may feel "high," on an ego trip. Or, more appropriately, on a "superego trip."

It is important here to note that, in the healthy adult, the ego subordinates the superego and the id so the person is not dominated by pleasure drives, aggressive feelings, guilt or an ego ideal.

Let's see what happens when the personality is controlled by the id. The one-year-old has few learned experiences and therefore an undeveloped ego. The superego doesn't exist, for society's expectations have not been incorporated. The baby is pure, undifferentiated id, a state that gets the child into a lot of trouble. The toddler has no rational checks (the ego) to stop him or her from touching a hot stove or from trying to jump out of Mother's arms or out the window after something that takes the child's fancy. Mother must act as the youngster's ego, grabbing her offspring by the seat of the pants and pulling the child back, until safety principles are more thoroughly learned through experience. Meanwhile, external reality threatens complete annihilation! The toddler begins to realize just how vulnerable he or she is. Burn yourself on the stove, fall off the chair, scrape your knees, bump your head; there are so many dangers. As a result, the personality is forced to give up some of its pleasure-oriented energy to remember to watch out for hot stoves or to be careful not to lean too far over on a chair. Memory and reasoning ability are the basis for the child's developing ego, which acts as an intermediary between powerful internal drives, the superego, and the external world.

The youngster's undeveloped ego can be overpowered by the strong pleasure drives of the id. That's what happened to four-year-old Julie when her mother decided to leave her daughter alone in the house for a few minutes.

It all started when Mother said, "While I'm gone don't eat any cookies. Do you understand, Julie?"

Anxious to please her mother, Julie responds, "Yes, Mom."

Her mother walks out the door. Julie thinks about being a good girl and not eating any cookies. The word 'cookies' passes through her mind again. She looks at the cookie jar.

"Cookies," she thinks. "Cookies," she mumbles softly. Soon her whole awareness is taken over by her desire for cookies. (The Sesame Street Cookie Monster represents the dimensions of this urge once it possesses a child.)

Julie walks over to the counter, opens the jar, looks inside. Those sweet, round cookies are irresistible. She picks up one and stuffs it in her mouth, chews and swallows, then again and again. No sooner has she swallowed the last bite than she feels bad, anticipating her mother's return.

Sure enough, her mother comes in, sees cookie crumbs all over Julie's face and asks, "Did you eat a cookie?"

Julie's trapped. The child's ego, having succumbed to the overwhelming desire for cookies, doesn't want Mother to be angry, so Julie answers, "No."

"Julie, don't lie to me. Did you eat two cookies?"

"No."

"Did you eat three?"

"Yes."

Julie's superego or sense of guilt doesn't prevent her from eating cookies. Up to age five, right versus wrong is based on verbal or physical threats. The child's id is seeking pleasure and avoiding pain or discomfort. If Julie does something wrong, she knows she will get scolded.

In a scene with her peers, Julie might have answered, "Well, Billy ate a cookie, John ate a cookie, everybody ate a cookie. I had to eat one."

In this case, Julie is using what Freud calls a *defense mechanism* to camouflage a weak spot in her personality. Defense mechanisms are unconscious ways of handling situations that overwhelm the ego and result in anxiety or threaten self-esteem. Julie uses a defense mechanism called a rationalization (a thinking process separate from reality) to justify her position. So reality becomes second to maintaining integrity.

The defenses we develop as children emerge much the same in the adult personality. Listen to Joe explain why he's late for work:

"I'm not late. The buses aren't running. The subway is on strike. The car wouldn't start."

Although ego defenses serve to ward off anxiety, they also slow down further personality growth because the individual fails to confront important issues, such as an overpowering desire for cookies or a tendency to be late.

Fixations

As the young child, full of life energy or libido, grows, there are obstacles that interrupt the youngster's pleasure-seeking activity. For example, the infant's earliest pleasure, sucking, is soon taken away. Freud believed that how the fledgling ego deals with the ensuing frustration is central to the development of the adult personality. If the child feels deprived or overwhelmed, this can result in a *fixation,* an interruption in the emotional growth of the youngster. The ego may become fixated, according to Freud, at a childhood stage of life. That childhood frustration may follow into adulthood, motivating the person to act as a two-year-old might when stress hits the fixated part of the personality.

This helps explain why one person can handle intense stress while another doubles over under the same pressure. For example, you admire how well a friend generally performs on the job, thinking how competent and strong he is. Yet, there are certain issues with which he just can't seem to cope; he becomes distraught, anxious, unnerved. It's as though somebody pushed his button. He flies off the handle.

You wonder why he can't seem to deal with certain situations. A key is that only highly developed parts of the personality can handle intense stress. Other areas are vulnerable; they have been stunted; fixed in the provisional incomplete organization of a child's ego that is so easily overwhelmed.

Certain areas of the personality may remain vulnerable. A particular comment can elicit completely unexpected behavior from a friend.

You think, "I can't believe the words coming out of your mouth. You're not like that. Why are you so angry?"

According to Freud, the individual at this point *regresses,* backing up in time, so to speak, to handle the anxiety as a child would.

Yet, if the childish nature of the personality becomes obvious, it will endanger adult relationships the person has worked hard to maintain—with a mate, with an employer, or with friends. For example, say you're in the office with a business associate and an important deal falls through. This fellow quietly crawls under the desk clutching his coat and begins to suck his thumb. People are hesitant to catch his eye; they may talk about him in the cafeteria. The secretary tells clients that he's out to lunch, so to speak. The boss calls him in and puts him on probation and his wife is humiliated to be with him at office parties. He probably won't keep his job very long.

Generally, the personality disguises the infantile nature of its motives through adult expressions such as smoking. In our society, smoking signifies adulthood. First, the smoker must be an "adult," age 18, to purchase cigarettes. Second, billboards and advertisements point out how one can achieve a sexual identity by smoking: be "macho," or become a liberated woman.

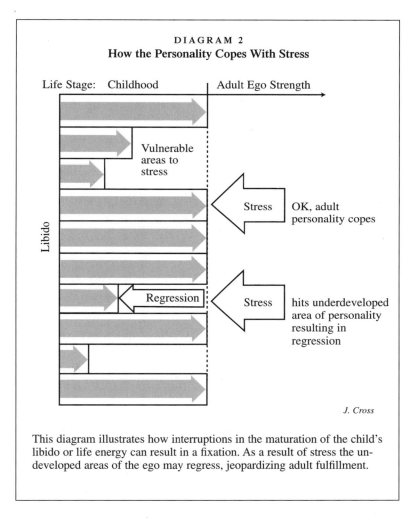

DIAGRAM 2
How the Personality Copes With Stress

Life Stage: Childhood | Adult Ego Strength

Vulnerable areas to stress

Stress | OK, adult personality copes

Regression | Stress | hits underdeveloped area of personality resulting in regression

Libido

J. Cross

This diagram illustrates how interruptions in the maturation of the child's libido or life energy can result in a fixation. As a result of stress the undeveloped areas of the ego may regress, jeopardizing adult fulfillment.

The difficulty is that such oral habits are not rational choices—they have never been subordinated or evaluated objectively. Rather, they are based on childlike impulses. The danger is that such substitute satisfactions can become excessive in the personality, so that the individual doesn't choose to take a drink or light a cigarette based on rational considerations.

Such ways of dealing with stress create only more stress in the long run. Listen to this conversation a friend has with an alcoholic:

"You know, this is the third job you've had in two years. If you keep drinking and don't show up for work, you'll lose your job."

"Yeah," he answers. "It sure is upsetting. I think I'll have a drink."

In desperation the friend says, "Your wife is going to leave you and your children are so mixed up they're going to the school psychologist. You know, your whole life is a mess."

"Yeah, I know it."

"If you keep drinking, I'm going to leave you too."

"Well, that's really horrible. I'm going to have two drinks."

Even in milder cases, these fixations may result in deviousness, deceptiveness, or duplicity, unconscious motives in the person's behavior that have not surfaced into conscious awareness.

Such an individual may wonder, "I don't understand myself. Why do these things keep happening to me?"

Or, "It's difficult for me to be close to other people because I'm not in control of how I relate to them. I have these uncontrollable impulses that detract from our relationship." Lacking an understanding of oneself, the person's behavior is not in his or her best interest.

If it's true that human beings can be irrational, even wrecking their lives because of these fixations wrought in childhood, what are we going to do about it? At this point Freud presents us with a great challenge. He says that people can be freed, releasing the libido that has been fixated. With the newfound life energy, the individual can go forward, ready to resolve issues and live a richer life. Let's look at fixations more carefully to see how this works.

The Psychosexual Stages of Development

Freud divides the first seven years of life into developmental stages based on the child's sexual development or pleasure-seeking activities. These *psychosexual stages* are associated with erogenous zones of the body (sensitive parts of the skin and mucous membranes). They include the *oral stage* (at birth the infant is capable of sucking); the *anal stage* (which occurs at about a year-and-a-half when the child gains control of the anal sphincter muscles), and the *phallic stage* (at about age three when the youngster becomes aware of the genitals).

The Oral Stage.   The newborn is most content blissfully sucking at Mother's breast, the whole body relaxing as a deep satisfaction overtakes the baby. The first and dominant source of pleasure is through the mouth, first through sucking and then later through biting and chewing. The infant experiences the world through the mouth. Whatever is found on the floor—bits of paper, pins, toys—is put in the mouth. If it's too big to put into the mouth, the child will put his or her mouth on it, sucking a chair leg, for example.

If the infant experiences a great deal of frustration through difficulty in nursing or lacks a supportive environment, this may be reflected in the personality as an adult. Perhaps the mother finds nursing distasteful or feels overwhelmed by the infant's complete dependency on her. The child's experience with sucking forms the emotional attitude towards pleasure throughout life, including adult sexuality. Does one have to compete for pleasure or does it flow naturally? If the child isn't fulfilled, he or she may be destined to always struggle to meet an insatiable need for security. The individual may also generalize the need for oral gratification from mother to a dependency on others, behaving passively in social relationships, looking to others for guidance and direction. In his or her mind, fulfillment is something you take in from the environment. Such people expect others to make them happy. They may also become angry in counseling when the therapist refuses to tell them what to do with their lives.

The orally fixated person is highly sensitive to any act of kindness or deprivation. Suppose one day you can't oblige a friend and give him a ride because you're studying for finals. He answers, "It's okay, don't worry about it. I knew we weren't friends anyway. You don't really care."

You've touched an area in which he's oversensitive, a part of his personality stunted in infancy, and so he may respond like a child, in an embarrassing, immature manner.

On the other hand, if you do turn around and do him a favor he may overwhelm you with his appreciation, ready to turn his life over to "his friend," to move in, let you do his laundry, and take care of him.

A fixation can result in a neurotic response, too strong or too weak a response to the situation, based on emotional rather than rational considerations. A neurotic response could be expressed through excessive eating, drinking, or smoking. For the alcoholic, drinking may provide a temporary feeling of well-being—a substitute for nurturing maternal feelings that were unfulfilled as a child.

In mild cases, fixations result in character traits that interfere with adult fulfillment because the person has never successfully subordinated or integrated oral needs. Many of us have some form of oral habits we use to soothe ourselves.

Perhaps if a friend is depressed you suggest, "Let's go buy an ice cream. It'll make you feel better." Or maybe a milkshake. Slushing it around, sipping from a straw, one begins to feel better.

A voracious appetite, the ability to almost inhale a meal, may indicate feelings of being emotionally deprived. For instance, let's say you have a big date who calls at the last minute Friday afternoon and cancels.

You sound very adult over the phone, "We'll do it another time. I'll see you again, soon."

No sooner do you plunk down the receiver than you head for the refrigerator.

"Let's see, chicken, salami, bread, cookies."

You sit down in front of the television and literally gorge yourself all night. However, overeating won't help the dating situation; in fact, it may make for more frustration in the future if you have a weight problem.

Our consumer-oriented society offers substitute satisfaction for oral needs through the consumption of large amounts of goods, appliances and gadgets. Happiness becomes something you can buy.

"Oralness" can even affect one's professional interests. Nurses may be motivated to care for someone else to experience vicariously the nurturing they wanted as children. The chef who delights in feeding clientele also feels nurtured through the guests' satisfaction. Both salespeople and teachers make a living based upon their oral activities. Business executives may become consumed by symbolically incorporating the world by swallowing up other businesses through corporate takeovers. Not all people in these professions, of course, are fixated. The key is whether they choose the profession based on rational considerations or to fulfill unresolved emotional conflicts. The individual acting out a fixation needs to keep the client dependent, as does the nurse who only helps the patient recover up to a point because of the need to nurture someone.

In support of the notion of oral character traits are such scientific studies as the one by Blum and Miller. They watched a group of eight-year-old boys and girls through a one-way mirror and counted their nonpurposeful mouth movements such as lip licking and thumb sucking. Then, after telling the youngsters they could eat as many one-ounce cups of ice cream as they wanted, they watched to see who ate the most. Most of the children ate about eight ounces, a few 10 ounces, one child 16 ounces. The researchers found the children consuming the most ice cream were, as Freud would have predicted, the ones exhibiting the most nonpurposeful mouth movements. Such experiments help verify the idea of underlying character traits in understanding the oral personality. Such youngsters could be dominated by consumption, seeking security orally.

The Anal Stage. Why does one person spend an hour on the toilet each morning while another is in and out of the bathroom in two minutes? Freud says there are reasons for this kind of behavior that go back to our early childhood experiences and that our toilet habits may reflect our feelings about control as an adult.

All societies require some form of toilet training for children. The period from age one-and-a-half to three is known as the anal stage, what Freud calls "the battle of the chamber pot."

It is during this period that children become increasingly independent, walking and navigating for themselves. Moreover, by about a year-and-a-half they exert their own will more forcibly. A parent puts the child to bed, the toddler climbs out. Mother makes a request, the child says "No." At this age, children express their needs and desires; for the first time they are in charge, they have something to negotiate with: whether or not they will go to the toilet. They are learning to control their anal sphincter muscles and, according to Freud, they find great pleasure first, through the expulsion of feces and, later, through retaining them.

Let's explore the youngster's viewpoint for a moment. Children feel their feces are a product of themselves and have value; they often wave good-bye to them in the toilet. The child may have already had the first pleasure, nursing, taken away. Now, the adult world says, "We're going to take away your new pleasure, or at least bring it under our control."

So, follows the struggle of wills. The will of a two-year-old is strong and cannot easily be intimidated. The youngster will take on an adult many times bigger without compromise.

We can get a clear perception of the child's feelings in the following dialogue between a grandmother and her three grandchildren who've just finished eating dinner.

She tells the oldest to go study, the second to help her clear off the table and orders the youngest, a girl, "Go to the bathroom. You've been wiggling a lot. You have to go."

Everyone gets up from the table except the little girl.

"I thought I told you to go." The tension is building.

"I don't have to go."

"I told you to go. You get in there."

"I don't have to go and I'm not going."

"Oh, really?" Grandma walks over, sweeps up the child. Arms and legs fly, the youngster screams as her grandmother carries her down the hall and places her on the toilet.

"Now you sit there until you go," she commands.

The child's heart is beating fast, her blood pressure is up, there's no way she can have a bowel movement. In order to go to the bathroom the child needs to relax.

These same anxieties may follow her into adulthood. She'll find herself taking a stack of books or magazines to the toilet where she settles in for an hour, trying to relax. Think of it, an hour a day, seven days a week, 52 weeks a year. If you were choosing how to spend your life, you certainly wouldn't sign up to spend five percent of it on the toilet.

If toilet training is imposed on the child, then the issue of control may dominate as an adult. This can occur if the training is premature (before a year-and-a-half) or if the parent approaches the child as if to break the youngster's will, as in the scenario above.

For the rest of the lives of such children, situations involving control and power may elicit the overwhelming feelings they had when Grandma forced them on the toilet. As adults, they may have difficulty responding rationally to authority, thus limiting their relationships with supervisors or others in power. Or they may have difficulty enforcing authority.

Unnecessary pressure to conform in toilet training may result in a fixation leading to under- or overconformity as an adult. In the latter case, the individual may be exceptionally clean and orderly to avoid activating the old emotional conflict with authority. Or, one may defy authority, be disorganized and messy, refusing to conform, to avoid the overwhelming stress experienced as a child in dealing with control. The person may rebel against social institutions or even try to destroy them in order not to feel reduced to the powerlessness of a child. To overcome these feelings, the individual must go beyond the unpleasantness of certain childhood experiences. Otherwise the person may act irrationally when authority is exerted.

For instance, when Jim walks in late for tennis class, the instructor says, "Just stand over there."

Jim overreacts, "I thought so. I know your type, trying to push me around already. Just forget it!"

He gets up abruptly and leaves, depriving himself of the opportunity to learn to play tennis.

Mike, a compulsive personality who overidentifies with authority, shows up half an hour early for the same class, asking the teacher, "Where do you want me to sit? Am I holding the racket correctly?"

Anxious to please authority, he can't really relax and enjoy the class, so he makes the learning experience more difficult than it has to be. Both students are using ego tactics to protect themselves from the overwhelming childhood emotions. One handles the anxiety by trying to anticipate everything the authority might want while the other pupil reflexively rebels to avoid the deep-seated emotional conflict that would surface in an authority relationship.

In a sense, we may inherit social patterns that lead to fixations just as we inherit physical characteristics. As a child, Grandmother was probably put firmly on the toilet and told to go. She grew up with the notion that control was a central issue and so she raises her offspring in a similar fashion instead of providing toilet training in a noncombative atmosphere, as a joint effort between parent and child.

The child who grows up under the iron grip of authority may choose a profession such as politics in order to exert power. This individual may be so dominated by the drive to maintain control through a job that the person sacrifices intimacy with loved ones and time to cultivate oneself to get ahead professionally.

The Phallic Stage: Oedipal and Electra Complexes.
Freud says the young child, from three to five years of age, is especially attracted to the parent of the opposite sex. Girls form a strong attachment to their fathers, boys to their mothers. Freud argues that this period is critical, that, in fact, these feelings can determine the child's attitude toward the opposite sex throughout life. The child's sexual interest in a parent corresponds with the discovery of pleasurable feelings associated with genitals. Freud termed this period of development the *phallic stage,* since the presence or absence of a penis becomes a defining factor. For the first time, a little boy becomes aware that he has a penis, while a little girl discovers that she doesn't have one, that they are, indeed, different.

The young boy's strong sensual feelings for his mother blossom into an unconscious desire for incest that brings him into competition with his father. Freud calls this the *Oedipal complex,* named after the Greek tragedy in which Oedipus, separated from his family as a child, acts out a prophecy, killing his father and later unknowingly marrying his mother.

If such a cultural taboo strikes you as unbelievable, remember that Freud says these feelings are unconscious. While the little boy knows there's a great mystery behind the closed bedroom door, it's unlikely he has any idea about the mechanics of sex. He simply wants the exclusive relationship with Mother that Dad has; to hold his mother's hand; to sleep with her. Through the course of the day it's almost as though he's his mother's lover. Her attention is relatively undivided; she plays with him, talks to him. In short, he's the prince until six o'clock when Dad comes home and Mother's interest shifts to her husband.

How does the four-year-old feel? Freud says the boy is jealous of Dad or any male who wants to compete for a special position with his mother. One little fellow I know acted on his feelings—when he saw his mother's boyfriend holding her hand he moved in, separated their hands, put them back on their respective laps and placed his hand firmly on her hand. If Dad has a business trip, his young son may help him pack, anxious to see his parent leave. In his desire to get rid of his competition, the lad may even go so far as to wish his dad were dead, not fully realizing that being dead is permanent.

What can the boy do to defend his position? Dad is so much stronger, he can pick his son up with one hand or throw a chair across the room. The youngster finds himself drawn into an overwhelming conflict: his desire for his mother versus his fear of his father. He is sure that his father can read his mind (after all, his mother can tell if he eats cookies while she's out) and will punish him, probably by taking something away from him. Freud says the boy unconsciously fears his father will retaliate by injuring his genitals. Why not? The breast, unfettered toilet pleasures, have all been taken away. Why not this too? Freud calls this the castration complex. Although this may sound extreme, remember that some youngsters are still told today, "If you don't stop playing with that thing, I'll cut it off."

This crisis is significant for children. In fact, unless they resolve this conflict, as adults the attachment to the opposite sex parent may remain the most intense relationship they will ever know.

The boy's fear of his father drives him into repressing his sexual feelings. *Repression,* the most basic of the defense mechanisms, involves keeping thoughts and desires that make the person uncomfortable from entering the conscious. For the rest of his life, he will sublimate his feelings and only be aware of tender affection for his mother. *Sublimation* is another defense mechanism through which socially acceptable forms of behavior are substituted for unacceptable instinctual drives.

What occurs next is central to the adult's feelings for the opposite sex. Since his culture forbids him from feeling sexual desires for his mother, a deep split in the personality occurs between passion and respect. If they are not integrated, he will grow up unable to simultaneously feel passion and respect for the same woman, as in the example at the beginning of this chapter.

As the youngster abandons his passion for his mother and anger for his father, he replaces the latter with a strong drive to follow in his father's footsteps, socially inheriting the attitudes of the male subculture. Freud calls the son's new-found orientation *identification with the aggressor.* Identifying with the aggressor is an ego defense mechanism the child employs for survival since he cannot physically overcome his parent. The lad tries to dress and behave like his father, following him around, saying, "It's you and me, Dad. We'll take care of the women." Now, instead of feeling bitter jealousy, he delights in seeing his father hold his mother's hand.

The child's hostility toward the parent is turned inward, channeled into the superego, where it's expressed as self-criticism. So the boy's former intense anger for his father, who represents authority, now becomes a source of depression and guilt if he goes against the morals of society.

The female counterpart of the Oedipal complex, called the *Electra complex,* is based on the little girl's attraction to her father. Freud says the child feels penis envy, which has

been modified by many modern psychologists to be interpreted as her desire for the privileges men have in a male-
dominated culture. According to Freud, the little girl blames
her mother for allowing her to be deprived of a penis and
begins to identify with her father, becoming Daddy's little
girl. After all, she'd rather be having fun, climbing a tree
like her brother. Yet, in order to fit into society she, too,
eventually submits, repressing her feelings for her father
and identifying with her mother.

Freud says competition between men and women
is the result of penis envy. Women, feeling deprived and
inferior because they lack a penis, may enjoy teasing, per-
plexing and hurting men to prove that males aren't superior.

One might also, however, make an argument for
"womb envy." Men can never experience the ultimate
involvement in creation that a woman knows through having a child grow in her body. Instead, men may be driven to
participate in the (re)productive process by creating great
structures—building towering skyscrapers and spaceships
to go to the moon.

Rejection, neglect, inconsistent treatment or spoiling
can overwhelm the child's developing ego, resulting in
a fixation. The youngster's growth can be stunted by demanding too much or by doing everything for the youngster.
During this period, the child may feel unable to live up to
the demands of the parent. For instance, if Dad pressures his
son to perform like a "pro" baseball player in Little League
or if Dad is very successful and the child is expected to
match him, the boy may be overcome by the difference
between what he perceives to be his ability and his father's
expectations. Or, suppose that Father is always away on
business or relates to his child as if he were handling a
high-powered business deal, the youngster may well be

estranged. If, on the other hand, the parent doesn't encourage the child's potential for independence, lavishing the child with affection and spoiling the youngster, a desire to grow and to master one's environment can be undermined.

Adults can minimize the potential crisis for the child at each of these developmental stages by encouraging the child's efforts without overwhelming the young person. For instance, a father can minimize the effects of the Oedipal complex by spending time with his son in a non-competitive situation so the boy discovers himself through his father. Or a mother and father might let their young son sit between them before going to bed so he doesn't feel rejected.

"I want a girl just like the girl that married dear old Dad."

Freud says the Oedipal stage is crucial: it set the limits and determines the style of adult interpersonal emotional involvements. Unresolved feelings for the opposite sex can result in neurosis later in life. For those suffering from the Oedipal complex, every potential mate is measured against the expectation they had of the opposite-sex parent at age three, personified in the song above. There's one problem— a three-year-old's image of mother doesn't include her faults—so this leads to a perfectionistic attitude. How can anyone ever live up to Mother? Shortly after marriage, a man fixated in the Oedipal stage begins comparing his wife to his mother.

"You make lousy meatloaf," he says, "nothing like Mother's. You never keep the house clean."

She may respond, "What about you? You're no prize. You read the newspaper at breakfast, leave your dirty clothes laying around, and when you come home from work you put your feet on the couch, drink beer and watch television. My dad always had time to talk to me. You never do."

Karen Horney's pioneering efforts in psychoanalytic theory contributed significantly to putting the psychology of women and
men on an equal footing. Karen Horney disagreed with Freud's
view that having or not having a penis, called the phallus, was
the primary focus for both sexes, leaving women permanently in
a state of discontent or "lacking." Rather, Dr. Horney thought
women's behavior was more determined by the culture they
were brought up in. If a woman felt cheated or limited, that was
the result of living in a culture which favored males. She found
that her male patients also expressed envy of women's ability to
give birth, to suckle new life, as well as not having to compete.
Horney had the unusual ability to step out of culturally limiting
assumptions. Her own breakthroughs and cross-cultural sensitivities were stimulated as a young child traveling on long voyages
with her sea captain father. *Courtesy of the Association for the
Advancement of Psychoanalysis of the Karen Horney
Psychoanalytic Institute and Center.*

As we saw earlier, the Oedipal complex can result in a split in the psyche between passion and respect for the opposite sex. The male suffering from an Oedipal fixation may treat a woman either as a sex object or as his mother— the difficulty lies in treating her as a whole person. It is the male's emotional involvement with the female that triggers his unconscious response, echoing his conflicting feelings from the Oedipal years.

For instance, Stan finds he has difficulty being physically attracted to a woman he respects. He has a "good girlfriend" who he takes home for Thanksgiving dinner and a "fun girlfriend" to indulge in his sexual fantasies. His good girlfriend may be someone else's fun girlfriend, but not for Stan, because she knows he can't handle both feelings for the same person. This may be true for her as well.

The individual may simply be in love with the unattainable, as in childhood, with the opposite sex parent. So, for example, Martha is madly in love with Larry, who's only mildly interested in her. But one day Larry's passion mounts and he professes his great love. Now that she has him in her pocket her interest diminishes. So a relationship may see-saw for years, the two never in love at the same time, a replay of the one-sided love affair the child knew. When Larry's "cool," Martha doesn't have to get to know him too well so she avoids conflicting feelings of respect and passion. Meanwhile, Larry fits her unrealistic childhood image of the perfect mate.

This also explains how the Oedipal complex can lead to infidelity in marriage—the search outside the bonds of wedlock for the unattainable or the perfect mate. Part of the enticement may be that these affairs are often self-limiting. A couple who meet for a torrid afternoon affair probably won't see all the faults they would note living with one another. Thus it becomes easier to maintain the aura of perfection.

One might further suppose that the split in the psyche between passion and respect may make it difficult for a woman to get involved with "nice" guys. When Kathleen meets men at work or school, she's not particularly interested in getting involved with them. Carl, a friend with whom she studies, asks her for a date.

"I couldn't," she says. "I think of you as a brother. Why wreck a good thing?"

She'd prefer to date someone she meets at a dance. She finds it difficult to get emotionally involved with someone she respects and understands. Relationships that are initially intense may cool off later and run out of steam as the pair get to know and respect each other.

Is it surprising, then, that the Oedipal complex can result in a great deal of hostility and disrespect for the opposite sex? At the extreme, women may refer impersonally to a man as a "hunk," while men may objectify a woman as "a piece."

Latency Period.   When the child represses intense emotional involvement for the opposite-sex parent to avoid negative consequences, he or she also represses the conscious desire for all members of the opposite sex. As a boy enters the latency period, at about age six, he feels that little girls are to be avoided like the plague. Still, he'll spend time conniving how to scare them or how to shock them by putting a frog on their chairs, for example. Little girls as well spend a lot of energy ignoring boys. They may go to any ends to avoid touching a boy, giggling about them, how they jumped one of the girls and tied her to a tree. Freud explains such antics as an expression of interest in the opposite sex which has become unconscious through massive repression. This repression also estranges children from their earliest memories, accounting for *infantile amnesia.*

Genital Stage (Adulthood).   This stage is the culmination of healthy psychological development. It has five main characteristics:

Strong Awareness of Self-Interest.   The adult has a clear perception of self-interest and is careful not to undermine his or her own identity and integrity, choosing activities that contribute to self-fulfillment. The person is capable of great care and empathy, yet doesn't get entangled in others' problems at the cost of his or her own identity.

More Energy Available.   Because the adult is not acting out unconscious conflicts, the person has more energy to be productive in life. Unpreoccupied with infantile striving, the individual avoids depleting energy in relationships based on dependency or control or by driving oneself with guilt or the desire to become famous at the cost of one's integrity.

Autonomy.   The person is capable of autonomy or independence of thought and action, taking responsibility for personal happiness.

Ego Control.   The mature personality is dominated by ego strength, choosing the person's best interests based on rational considerations. The ego subordinates the superego perfectionism to reason. Similarly, the individual is not driven by the instinctual passions of anger and sexual or pleasure-seeking desires, but uses these energies for enlightened self-interest.

Maturity.   This individual has an immense capacity to work and to love, achieving strong, sustained, reciprocal intimacy with others because he or she is neither struggling for power nor forcing others to fit into unrealistic childhood ideals.

In summary, the psychologically healthy adult knows and likes himself or herself and makes choices for directing life based on his or her best interests.

Marital Relationships

The fixations can play such an important role in the adult personality that they may form the basis for marriage, according to psychologist James Steele. Let's look at three marriages to see how these childhood feelings are transferred.

The Oral-Passive Marriage.   John, who works as a salesman, is married to Sarah, a motherly, nurturing woman who waits on her husband hand and foot. Although she works all day as a nurse, when she comes home John expects her to prepare dinner. Meals are an important time in this household. They're eagerly anticipated. But even if the dinner is late, John won't get up from his easy chair to help. He had a difficult time when their first child was born because Sarah was busy with their newborn and didn't have the energy to nurture him. John finds his son's greediness at the table disturbing, particularly the other night when Nathan took the last biscuit from the dish and John thought, "Here I am again, always being deprived, running short of what I really need."

John prefers that his wife initiate sexual relations but this makes her angry—she wishes he'd take the initiative. Yet, she reminds herself, she had the opportunity once to marry an assertive, independent male, but she was afraid he might desert her. At least with John she always knows where he is, sitting in front of the television waiting to be fed.

In this marriage, the relationship is based on dependency. In fact, dependency comes before intimacy. The wife satisfies her own orally dependent needs by marrying an orally dependent male, gaining indirect fulfillment by nurturing him.

Anal Fixation. Mike, a statistician, and Jane, an accountant, both have jobs that demand a great deal of detailed work. Their incomes are in the median range, they live in a suburban home and own two cars. They're preoccupied with control and the acquisition of property. Even their children are seen as possessions: they have one of each sex to play in front of their neat, freshly painted house. Things must be orderly—the pair are particularly concerned about scheduling and budgeting so that money doesn't slip through their fingers. Even sex may be scheduled in, most likely on Saturday nights because Thursday is already taken with bowling and Friday with bridge. Both Mike and Jane shower before and after sex and usually stay home on Sunday to repent for all the fun they had by cutting the lawn and fixing up the house.

Basically, they are not very comfortable with themselves. The relationship lacks spontaneity and intimacy. Their repressed hostility for the control their parents exerted on each of them as children may be directed at others. They may be prejudiced or complain about their unrestrained neighbors. What they're really bothered by are their own feelings: as long as "everything's under control," they won't be overwhelmed by their stifled emotions from childhood.

Their anger can also turn inward, leading to stress-related illnesses such as ulcers or hemorrhoids.

Oedipal-Electra Marriage. Tom, a successful thirty-three-old lawyer, doesn't know what to do about his marriage. It's only been a short time since he and Sue, his twenty-year-old secretary, were wed. He can't understand why her interest cooled so soon. After all, he was the one who was reserved, perhaps even a little reluctant about developing the relationship. It was strange, the more he hesitated, the more she became attracted and pursued him. So they finally got married. The first few weeks were great. But, by about the fourth month, Sue was no longer sexually interested in Tom. In fact, she seemed to be impulsively attracted to other men: the other day she had the nerve to bring home a man she picked up at the laundromat.

Sue was initially attracted to Tom because he seemed to be unattainable, just as her father had been. She finds herself always wanting what she doesn't have, and once it's hers, her interest diminishes. Now that they're married, she feels guilty and sexually uninterested.

How successful will these marriages be? These fixations sidetrack the couples from the satisfaction they're capable of achieving. In the last case, the chances are slim. Oedipal marriages are very short, often less than a year. The oral marriage may stay together by default since both partners may be too dependent to get out of it. The anal marriage may last because the relationship has a lot of social support and approval. After all, the pair has invested a lot of money in their home and possessions. They're in control of their social responsibilities: they pay their bills and show up to work, able to maintain successful jobs.

Conclusion

Freud acquaints us with the child within us by making the unconscious conscious. His theory demonstrates how unresolved childhood feelings can determine our responses to situations as adults. The individual fixated in the oral stage, the anal stage or the phallic stage may respond immaturely as an adult when an action triggers the overwhelming childhood conflict. These fixations may diminish the adult's life by leading to dependency, rebellion, an insatiable search for power, or to difficulty achieving sexual intimacy.

People may unconsciously relate to one another symbolically, not seeing each other for what he or she objectively is, but rather in terms of infantile needs and conflicts. Through understanding these childish motivations we can reduce them and relate to other human beings in a more rational fashion.

This chapter can help us to develop skills in self analysis to determine what motivates our emotional responses. When the veil of the unconscious is lifted and childhood conflicts are resolved, the individual is no longer compelled to manipulate others to fulfill unconscious needs for dependency or control. Overcoming these feelings requires reviewing unpleasant childhood experiences. The adult can handle many feelings that overpower the child. The goal is not to regress but to deal with anxiety in constructive ways that we'll explore in other chapters of this book.

Freud's Life (1856–1939)

Amid the grandeur of 19th-century Vienna, Sigmund Freud, a physician, struggled to establish himself and his work, the field of psychoanalysis. As a culture, Vienna was at its pinnacle, known for the magnificence and wealth of the Hapsburg empire. Its palaces, theaters, operas, balls and nobility epitomized Western culture. Great musicians such as Johann Strauss were inspired by its style. In the midst of this cultural prosperity, however, were the starvation-level poor and one of the highest suicide rates in Europe.

This was the age of rationalism; reason was thought capable of explaining almost anything. Control and order were reflected in the palaces and gardens of the formal Viennese society. Criticism was intense for those who did not conform to society's expectations, so much so that the architect of Vienna's lovely opera house committed suicide after public disapproval of his creation.

For all its cultural achievement, Vienna, Freud thought, was a sick society. Imagine living in a world dominated by Victorian morality that suppressed sexuality. Women were not expected to look at themselves nude nor were they to enjoy sex. Frigidity was the norm in marriage. As a result, women had almost no sex with their husbands, who deferred their sexual desires to prostitutes. The society was, in short, too "civilized." Freud said that because these people were cut off from their physical selves, repressing their sexual needs, other parts of their personalities had been repressed in the process. In extreme cases this resulted in neuroses manifested in physical ailments. These were the desperate people who came to Freud for treatment after being treated with harshness and contempt by the medical establishment that said there was no apparent cause for their illnesses. From his work with patients suffering hysterical paralysis based on emotional conflicts, Freud developed psychoanalysis, lifting the veil of the unconscious which, since childhood, had been pulled over their awareness.

Freud proposed ideas that shocked Western culture. When he talked about infantile sexuality at a scientific meeting in Hamburg, Germany in 1910, one of his colleagues got up from his seat and began banging the podium shouting, "This is a matter for the police." Not only did Freud analyze the traumas inflicted on the innocent infant, he pointed a finger at the child's parents, taking on motherhood, the most sacred of institutions, noting that the mother-child relationship would influence the child's behavior as an adult. In the midst of a frigid society he said that socially taboo fantasies such as the unconscious desire for incest were taking place in normal parent-child relationships.

Freud drastically changed people's view of themselves. In 19th-century Vienna people did not consider that childhood experiences could have a profound effect on adult behavior. Dreams were considered nonsense until Freud began to analyze their hidden meaning to understand his patients. Slips of the tongue or pen and accidents were considered unintentional, rather than the result of hidden urges or desires.

It's no surprise that Freud's ideas, which revealed serious flaws in the fabric of society, met with great resistance and hostility from the closed society of Vienna. In fact, Freud received little formal acknowledgment from the world until 1909, when G. Stanley Hall invited Freud and his followers to lecture at Clark University in Worcester, Massachusetts. It was in the United States that Freud received great acclaim for his work and the world finally recognized his genius.

The Debate on Freud Today

Controversy still rages around Freud's ideas today. On the one hand, about 10–15 million Americans are involved in

Francis Sumner, first African-American Ph.d. psychologist. Born
in Arkansas, 1895–1954. The ripples of influence from Freud's
visit to Clark University were still being felt when Francis
Sumner completed his doctoral thesis, "A Psychoanalysis of
Freud and Adler" in 1920. At 25 years old, the World War I
veteran became the first African-American psychologist to earn
a Ph.D., in spite of social and economic barriers. At the time,
nearly one-fourth of African-Americans were illiterate and
there were 239 recorded lynchings. Sumner went on to establish
his own psychology department at Howard University in
Washington, D.C. *Courtesy of Clark University Department
of Psychology.*

some kind of talking cure largely based on Freud's ideas, although not always acknowledged. In fact, Freud's influence may have actually increased in the past 40 years.[1] Psychoanalysis has been a dominant model for thinking and talking about human behavior in the 20th century. How will it do in the 21st century?

Freud's ideas have spread well beyond professional psychoanalysts into popular culture. Even people who have never read his work are familiar with ideas that come from Freud: ego, id, superego, repressed memories.[2]

However, Freud and his ideas still continue to attract sharp attack. From the 1950's onward, as brain research increased and drug treatment became more popular, biological explanations began to gain favor over Freud's views. By the 1980's it became increasingly popular to treat emotional problems as chemical imbalances in the brain rather than as the result of an interruption in the maturation process during infancy.

Alan Stone, professor of psychiatry at Harvard, while acknowledging Freud's genius, says Freud's theory has no scientific method and cannot be verified.[3] Mistakes, such as those regarding female sexuality, have been taken as scientific truths which misled and limited the fulfillment of some women. While some say his theory cannot be built on, others point out how many theories have been spawned or influenced using Freud's ideas as a stimulus.

In 1997 Stone thought that Freud's influence would decline with further scientific advancements such as more research on genetics, drugs and the reliability of childhood memories. However, he expected it would continue to survive in the humanities, literature and popular culture to help people to understand or make sense of their personal life

Freud at Clark University: seated in front, Sigmund Freud, G. Stanley Hall, Carl Jung; standing, A. Brill, E. Jones and S. Ferenczi. *Clark University Archives.*

histories. Stone said, "I know of no other work in psychology so powerful, so lucid and so immediately convincing."

Freud expected people to criticize his ideas because his approach would bring up repressed material that by definition the person did not want to think about. They found this uncomfortable, resulting in what he called resistance which, in turn, was then interpreted as further support for the theory. Some critics say the theory is a closed system, scientifically unquestionable.

Freud's supporters disagree and argue that it can be studied objectively through scientific research, pointing to studies which support many of Freud's ideas.

Current Research and Freud's Ideas.   It's important to remember that Freud was a highly regarded neuroscientist in his day. He wanted to invent a science of the mind, but it was difficult to test his theories because of the limited scientific tools of the Victorian era. Today a number of studies, using modern scientific technology, support some of Freud's ideas such as unconscious motivation, repression and the effects of early trauma on adult responses to stress. Recent neurological mappings of the brain generally correspond to Freud's conceptions of the id, ego and super-ego. For example, the core brain stem and limbic system— responsible for instincts and drives—roughly correspond to Freud's id.[4]

Let's look at two recent studies. The first study is related to repression. One of Freud's key claims was that people repress unpleasant memories. He believed that they could emerge disguised in slips of the tongue or dreams. Skeptics long doubted whether repression actually occurred in the brain, finding it difficult to imagine how such a process could occur and concluded it was not scientifically verifiable.

Yet in 2003 Stanford University researchers found that the brain's primary function is not only to remember, but also to forget, in order to keep the circuits from being overloaded. There is so much information in the course of a day the brain must repress some of it.

Researchers used brain scans, called magnetic resonance imaging (MRI), to create pictures to demonstrate which areas of the brain are involved in repressing memory. In the experiment 24 volunteers between the ages of 19 to 31 memorized two sets of word pairs like "steam-train" and "jaw-gum." Lying inside the MRI scanner they observed the words flashing above them. They were shown the first word of a pair and asked either to recall and think about the associated response or to prevent the associated word from entering consciousness at all. Later they were tested on recall of all word pairs. The result showed that subjects had a harder time recalling words they previously tried to forget. The MRI scanner demonstrated that certain brain regions (prefrontal cortex) thought to be involved in repressing memory were more active (as measured by increased blood flow and oxygen consumption) while the subjects were trying to forget words. The part of the brain connected with memory, the hippocampus, had less activity during these periods of forgetting.5

What are the implications?

Dr. Charles P. Fisher of the San Francisco Psychoanalytic Institute says the work at Stanford "upholds one crucial piece of Freudian psychoanalysis—the existence of motivated forgetting."

Anderson, one of the nation's leading memory researchers, says of his study, "It's no longer possible to say that human beings can't actively forget. Our research demystifies the idea of memory suppression."

While Matthew Erdelyi, a researcher at Brooklyn College in New York, says Freud was first a neuroscientist, one who understood that the brain's subsystems could work against each other. Anderson says his findings show how modern technology can take century-old science a step further. They show how the human brain blocks an unwanted memory.

The second study looks at Freud's premise that adult personalities are influenced by early emotional experiences. Traumatic experiences in childhood may manifest effects in the adult's personality. For example, if a person is overwhelmed as a child by a stress, resulting in an interruption of emotional growth or a fixation, the capacity to deal with stress may be weakened. Results of a recent study on abuse, stress and brain chemistry are consistent with Freud's theory. He thought that early trauma could interrupt the maturation of the child's ego, leaving the child's underdeveloped ego vulnerable and more easily overwhelmed and overreacting even to mild levels of stress.

At Stanford University (2003) researchers found that women who were physically or sexually abused in childhood did indeed have exaggerated physiological responses when exposed to mild stress. These responses were particularly pronounced in women who suffered from depression. They experienced a higher heart rate under stress and secreted a higher level of hormones (ACTH and cortisol) associated with stress, as much as six times as high, as those women without such histories.[6]

"Clearly, here is an environmental event that causes changes in the brain," says Dr. Charles B. Nemeroff, of Emory University and co-author of the study.[7]

Such experimental results support Freud's observation that adults who are traumatized as children may respond to stress at exaggerated levels as adults.

These studies demonstrate how Freud's theory can suggest directions for contemporary investigations. The weaker points in his theories are being supplemented and revised with more research. Increasing numbers of neuroscientists are joining with psychiatrists discovering the usefulness of Freud's model as an intellectual framework for seeing the big picture and coherently arranging emerging details from modern research. It provides a conceptual framework to organize the findings of these studies and a basis to interpret their significance, according to Professor Mark Solms, chair in neuropsychology at the University of Cape Town in South Africa.[8]

And So the Debate Goes on. However not everyone is enthusiastic about the reappearance of Freudian concepts in the mainstream.[9] There are critics that say that psychoanalysis is in big trouble and no amount of neurobiological tinkering can fix it. Professor J. Hobson of Harvard Medical School says psychoanalysis needs such a radical overhaul that many neuroscientists would prefer to start over.[10]

As a therapy, supporters caution that even if it does not work as a cure for everyone, psychoanalysis can still be valuable as a method to reveal unconscious material for understanding.[11]

French psychoanalyst Serge Leclaire says that the French do not have the same conflicts, nor do they attack Freud as do American psychoanalysts, because they use the theory with greater flexibility, changing with the times, rather than trying to freeze the theory into a rigid doctrine.[12]

Ultimately, on a personal level, the value of Freud's ideas may come down to whether a Freudian perspective is useful in understanding one's life.

Finally, Freud considered himself an explorer, bent on bringing to light unconscious conflicts to liberate the personality. He wrote his epitaph:

> I am not really a man of science . . . I am nothing
> but by temperament a conquistador—an adventurer . . .
> with the curiosity, the boldness and the tenacity which
> belong to that kind of being.[13]

As a result of Freud's emphasis on child development and unconscious motivation, the modern world has never been the same.

Self-Actualization/
Humanistic Psychology

Self-Direction Through Self-Actualization:
Humanistic Psychology
Carl Rogers' and Abraham Maslow's Theories

A. Phenomenological Reality
B. Positive Regard and Conditions of Worth
C. The Development of Incongruence Between the
   Self and the Experience
D. The Experience of Threat and the Defense Process
E. Organization of the Personality
   1. Socialization Process
   2. Personality Integration
   3. The Authentic Self
F. Socialization and Sense of Self
G. The Self-Actualization Process

Abraham Maslow's Theory
A. The Hierarchy of Needs
   1. Physiological Needs
   2. Safety Needs
   3. Belonging and Love Needs
   4. Esteem Needs
   5. Deficiency Motivation
B. Self-Actualization
   1. Characteristics of Self-Actualizers
   2. The Jonah Complex
C. Conclusion

Self-Direction
Through Self-Actualization

I shed the mental structure and feelings of civilization like an overcoat as my awareness broke through to the excitement and vividness of watching the eternal rhythm of the ocean waves; walking on the sand, smelling the fresh salt air, feeling the force of the wind blow in my hair, the warmth of the sun, watching sea gulls gliding unpredictably on wind currents overhead, listening to their wild calls. The eternal forces of nature and life were being revealed to me. The concerns of everyday life paled as trivia in comparison.

• • •

We would sit and talk with Aunt Hazel for hours at a time. Her eyes had a girlish twinkle which dissolved generation gaps. When she spoke there was a sense of timelessness as we traveled with her to her childhood as she rode bareback with Indians through deep pine forests. Listening was effortless, we had no consciousness of ourselves, we seemed to transcend time, for the stories she told were eternally true. She was a rich self-actualized person who made

us feel in touch with ourselves, and that life was always new
and fresh.

· · ·

One warm spring day I was swinging in a hammock, watching the leaves shimmer and the branches sway below the
bluest of skies. As I was gently being rocked by the wind, I
felt the boundaries of my body disappear; the air and the
warm sunshine were within me and without me. It was as
though I had become a ring on God's finger, I felt the energy
flowing through me and all around me, encircling me.

· · ·

Deep in the redwood forest I felt a sense of peace and one-
ness overtake me, as though I was part of the woods and the
warm sunshine beating down on my back. The silence of
the forest was part of the deep solitude within me. My
senses were uncluttered by the sounds of cars, the pressures
of urban life; my mind was freed of structure. I had no consciousness that I ought to act a certain way, project a particular image to these trees. Life seemed so clear; fear and
suspicion dropped away. I was free.

· · ·

As I watched my two-year-old running toward me with an
expression of wild uncontained happiness, it was as though
time stopped—a long moment was pulled back and en-
graved in my memory. He ran, his hair blowing freely in the
wind, his bright face animated, his eyes shining. All of his
energy and love were focused on me. Bystanders stopped,
watched, smiled, absorbed in the moment which stood out
in a world which deals so much in appearances. It was a
universal timeless experience which everyone could relate
to; older people remembered their own youngsters, since

grown up, while young adults were touched by images deep within them of children not yet born.

• • •

Moments to hang on to, to savour, to remember forever. What do all these experiences have in common? They are universal, timeless, vivid, they simply can't be improved upon. They validate the self; one seems more fully alive and experiences life firsthand with all one's senses. Abraham Maslow calls such events *peak experiences* or *magic moments.* Such intense occurrences can take place in the context of virtually any activity. Maslow says that anything with real excellence, real perfection, absolute justice or values tends to result in a peak experience. A beautiful work of art, a strong interpersonal relationship, a beautiful moment in nature such as a moving sunset, can all produce peak experiences. In these moments, events and objects are perceived as they truly are, not distorted to meet our needs or desires. These happenings are comparable to deep religious experiences in which the person senses eternal forces. During a peak experience one feels whole; conflicts and ambivalences are resolved.

How many such experiences do we miss because we are not in touch with ourselves, functioning at our best in a particular moment? Maslow says that everyone has peak experiences, but that some people aren't aware of or forget them. How can we increase the number of such intense moments in life? What situations encourage peak experiences? They are more likely to take place in a non-threatening environment in which there is a sense of positive regard and empathy from others, in other words situations in which we feel understood, in which we can be ourselves, in which others are being themselves and not putting on any facades.

The number of peak experiences depends not only on outside forces but on our own inner world, how we perceive ourselves and our relationship to others; our openness and lack of defensiveness. According to Maslow, it is the *self-actualization* process—creative growth in the direction of self-realization—which will increase the number of peak experiences. Maslow goes on to explain more precisely self-actualization: it is becoming the best one is able to be, becoming fully human. The theories of Maslow and Carl Rogers are both concerned with helping people to function at their highest level, with producing greater happiness and fulfillment in life.

They maintain that the struggle for self-actualization is inherent, a lifelong challenge which begins in infancy as the young child tries to master the world. In spite of painful falls, a baby keeps struggling to walk, immediately pulling him or herself up to try again. It is Carl Rogers who draws our attention to the young child, noting that the desire for mastery and growth is a tremendous force in children. Consider how they ask questions about every aspect of the world around them, trying to fully understand how it works and their relationship to the universe.

Rogers asserts that it is this inclination which engages the adult as well as the child in struggle. Imagine the adult intent to mountain climb, poised on a dangerous precipice, legs aching, adrenaline pumping following a near mishap as rock crumbled beneath groping boots. From such exertion arises a sense of achievement, of mastering the mountain. Even the plant growing along the rocky cliff exemplifies this great effort. It sprouts in an arid, infertile terrain, even in an inhospitable environment. Similarly the child is born with the urge to master the world in spite of difficulty, to join the quest to self-actualize, says Rogers.

Phenomenological Reality

One's perception of reality determines how this struggle for growth takes place. What we call objective "reality" is actually very subjective. It is not so much based solely on people and events as they are, but on likes and dislikes, on hopes and dreams and fears, what we read into the world around us. Rogers calls this private world of experience, which makes a unique personal frame of reference, the *phenomenological* viewpoint. He says a person reacts to reality as it is perceived from one's own point of view. He presents us with the example of two men who listen to a radio speech by an unknown political candidate:

> One perceives the candidate as a trickster, a false prophet, and reacts accordingly. The other perceives him as a leader of the people, a person of high aims and purpose. Each is reacting to the reality as he has perceived it. In the same way two young parents each perceive differently the behavior of their offspring.[1]

Such a subjective view colors our self-concept and may even prevent us from seeing our assets. For example, a world weight-lifting champion focuses not on his strength, but on the one set of triceps which are not fully developed. While his fans hail his fantastic form he is still overcome by a sense of inadequacy.

Rogers' basic premise for therapy is that to change an individual's behavior one must first alter the person's self-concept. The individual's manner makes sense according to how he or she views the world. For example, students who have a self-concept of being inferior, in need of help, yet being ignored, may tend to perpetuate their self-view by not seriously trying, even when real opportunities for help are available.

Similarly, such a phenomenological viewpoint influences the success of marriage. Carol, an insecure person, feels that her husband doesn't love her enough. She gets very angry at him for what she perceives to be his waning affection. She begins to drink heavily to numb herself to her feelings. Her husband drifts and her marriage fails even more. Her reaction is a self-fulfilling prophecy which fits her perception of reality, for she sees herself as unlovable and her life as a dead end.

It is only when the individual's perception changes that one reacts differently to reality. Rogers illustrates how a new enlightening perception about a parent can soften old feelings:

> As long as a parent is perceived as a domineering individual, that is the reality to which the individual reacts. When he is perceived as a rather pathetic individual trying to maintain his status, then the reaction to this new reality is quite different.[2]

The individual's self-concept is formed in childhood as the child's sense of self-regard grows. Rogers says, "He perceives himself as lovable, worthy of love and his relationship to his parents is one of affection."[3] This gives the child a great sense of satisfaction and forms the core of the self. The phenomenological viewpoint is enhanced as the child's perception of the self develops. In infancy, co-author of *Normal Neurosis,* Snell Putney, reminds us of the pain of self-discovery when the baby bites his or her own thumb instead of the pacifier. Here a clear-cut differentiation between the self and the rest of reality takes place. As time passes the child learns to respond to a name which again differentiates the youngster from others.

The self continues to be distinguished from others as the child is evaluated by parents who say, "Johnny is a good boy" or "a bad boy." The youngster, feeling self-regard threatened, may answer back, "No, you are bad," trying to maintain a positive sense of self.

Positive Regard and Conditions of Worth

Rogers calls our inner circle, made up of parents and others who make a profound impression on us, *significant others*. What these people think of us matters a great deal, for their evaluations form the basis of our positive regard. As awareness of self emerges, the individual develops the powerful need for positive regard. The child learns that some behavior is more worthy of positive regard than other types of behavior.

Significant others are indeed selective and will only give positive feedback for certain conduct. For example, when parents become angry with their toddler for throwing a spoon in the restaurant, the child senses a loss of positive regard.

Here Rogers notes that *conditions of worth* are attached to positive regard. That is, the child must fulfill certain requirements to receive positive regard from others. The child learns how to realize these conditions of worth, so that eventually they may be incorporated into the child's self-concept.

"If I always share my toys, if I don't tear books, if I smile at relatives, my parents will be pleased and tell me how good I am," the youngster might think.

Eventually the person may seek experiences solely for positive regard rather than because they are genuinely desirable for development and expressions of the true self. For example, a male may associate with a woman because she is popular or powerful rather than because he really likes her. He believes their relationship will enhance the positive regard he receives from others.

These conditions of worth are a result of experiencing *conditional positive regard* from others. In other words, "I will like you if you do what I say." In contrast, if the individual had experienced only *unconditional positive regard,* no conditions of worth would have developed. If Mother or Father had said, "I love you no matter what you do," the child wouldn't be forced to hide or distort certain feelings from the self-concept, to deny certain experiences. For example, if we discern that our parents refuse us their love when we exhibit anger, we may deny feelings of indignation in order to maintain parental affection. We may have been led to believe that we will not be worthy of love if we disagree.

How do people lose touch with their feelings, with living authentically? The individual's base of operation shifts from an internal reference of self-esteem, to what the world says it approves of. When the individual becomes dependent on others to feel good about him- or herself, the person allows others to direct his or her life. The individual gives people the power to determine his or her behavior and feelings about the self, putting that person in a vulnerable position indeed. At times such a person may even appear to be working against oneself in the distorted or misdirected attempt to get positive regard from others without fully considering one's uniqueness.

Positive regard includes acceptance, liking, warmth, empathy and respect from others. Each individual needs positive regard from people who are significant to him or her. It helps the person to accept and to be oneself, reducing the need to be defensive and to conceal true feelings. In accepting and expressing oneself, the person tends to develop feelings of positive regard for others which facilitates communication and the development of a healthy and satisfying relationship.

In contrast, if there is a lack of positive regard both members of the relationship become more defensive and rigid in their perceptions, merely acting in social roles. Their communication becomes superficial. The relationship is unsatisfying and tends to deteriorate into a destructive relationship which no longer promotes growth or fulfillment.

In summary we need positive regard. But our experience with significant others—parents, relatives, teachers—tells us that only certain behaviors are worthy of this. In this quest people can lose consciousness of their own sensory and emotional experiences, and may ignore feelings of anxiety or displeasure, not even registering them at a conscious level. Even though they may feel strongly against certain behavior or uncomfortable with a particular person, they may still take part to meet conditions of worth for positive regard. In such instances the desire for positive regard contradicts the person's sensory experience or "gut" reaction.

The Development of Incongruence Between the Self and the Experience

Becoming "hooked" by conditions of worth has significant ramifications. First of all, the individual perceives experiences selectively in terms of what is in accordance with conditions of worth. Experiences that run contrary to one's conditions of worth may be denied or distorted.

For example, Carol's marriage continued to sour. She had married a man twice her age against the advice of her family and had moved hundreds of miles away from loved ones. The idea of having a successful marriage was tied to Carol's concept of conditions of worth. So, when she visited her sister she said her marriage was good, although the couple quarreled daily. Carol denied to herself that the marriage was failing because such an admission would reduce positive regard from others and she might feel even worse.

In such cases we can see that the person loses touch with aspects of the real self. Rogers says that certain experiences are not permitted into consciousness, except in a distorted form. Sensory reaction, what one experiences in the here and now, is ignored.

"A concept of self based in part upon a distorted symbolization has taken their place," says Rogers.[4]

The individual has an image of the self to protect. So if an experience doesn't fit this self-concept, the person may not accept it. Consequently some experiences now occur which are not recognized, perceived or organized into the self-structure.

Ideally the self-structure should be constantly changing and growing as new perceptions are integrated. However, the opposite can take place if the need for positive regard overshadows authentic growth. The self-structure becomes stagnant and distorted because of the need for positive regard. The individual may have so many conditions of worth that are not being fulfilled that the self grows out of touch with reality.

For example, Carol had a sense of inferiority, that she really didn't deserve positive regard. She read magazines which described torrid love affairs, elaborate wardrobes and Caribbean vacations as part of the fulfilled woman's life. She began to incorporate these fantasies into her concept of marriage. When her first husband fell short of them she divorced him, stating simply that she couldn't stand the way he buttered his toast. In describing her plans to marry again, she talked about her fiancé's money. Carol had so many conditions of worth she needed to satisfy to be worthy of positive regard from others. To feel good about herself required a particular amount of money, a certain house with the right furniture, a singular vacation. In order to accept positive regard from her husband and her family, these conditions of worth had to be fulfilled.

Yet somehow many other things weren't right. There were more arguments until finally he asked her to leave. She was no longer fulfilling conditions of worth of a successful wife.

In contrast, if Carol had no conditions of worth attached to her self-concept, there would be no tension between her sensory experience and the need for positive regard. Without conditions of worth the individual is open to all experience, clearly perceives all feelings, including affection, tenderness, hostility, aggression and sexuality. Instead Carol felt more and more anxiety because of the growing discrepancy between her experience and what she accepted as reality.

Simply because a person doesn't admit an experience doesn't mean it didn't occur. Our perceptions are an interpretation of a stimulus. For example, one of the authors, traveling home from the Southwest, repeatedly felt inside his suitcase and thought he had found a thistle. He wondered what a thistle was doing there, yet when he pulled out his hand it was bloody. He looked inside to find that what he perceived as a prickly thistle had been a sharp razor.

We all have an actualizing tendency; however, when experiences are not admitted into consciousness they cannot help shape the personality. In other words, the self-concept cannot be modified to fit these new events. When they are not incorporated conscious control becomes more difficult. As a result the self-concept becomes increasingly incongruent with experience, with what one really feels and senses and, therefore, out of contact with reality.

The Experience of Threat
and the Defense Process

These inconsistent experiences loom as a threat to the self-concept. The more contrary events the individual undergoes, the more defenses are developed. John may get angry at others for not helping him when he really needs assistance. His feelings are a threat to him because he's been taught not to get angry, particularly not to say critical things to loved ones. So the unresolved tensions may be expressed as disguised rage towards loved ones or towards himself as depression.

A number of experiences are not incorporated into the self-concept. The self with its conditions of worth cannot accept these events or the individual's self-concept would no longer be consistent, the person would no longer feel whole or good about the self. The self-concept would be challenged.

For example, following an argument with his wife, a husband may have a hard time feeling good about himself. He wants to make up with his wife, for her to tell him how much she loves him. Rogers might interpret the male's move to resolve the quarrel as his desire for his wife's esteem to once again fulfill his conditions of worth.

During the argument his wife may have become defensive to protect her feelings of worth. Her husband said she wasn't taking care of the house or giving the children enough time. This did not fit her self-concept, so she became defensive to prevent these comments from entering consciousness, from lowering her self-esteem.

Instead, she hears things selectively, distorting some things, denying others in order to keep her perception consistent with the self-structure and conditions of worth. The results are a rigid and inaccurate perception of reality and breakdown in communication. How many times have we missed hearing something a friend or spouse told us which didn't fit our self-concept? As we have seen, three things may occur in this process—one denies reality, distorts it, or only selectively perceives it.

A curious thing happens as the individual becomes more rigid and defensive: one doesn't seem to be conscious of certain events and only partially perceives others because they are inconsistent with the narrowly defined conditions of worth and a threat to the self-concept. The person is simply out of touch with reality, so the individual's level of functioning begins to disintegrate, says Rogers.

However, this can be reversed through a moving event such as a peak experience, the death of a loved one, an emergency, a religious experience, or a supportive environment of unconditional positive regard which doesn't threaten the person's defenses. For a moment the individual's perceptual constructs, the phenomenological perception, is set aside. It's as though the curtain opens: reality becomes clear, the self and life are seen as they really are, separate from all the social strivings and conditions of worth. This glimpse of truth occurs because the conditions of worth are dwarfed by the intensity of the event, whether it's the loss of a loved one or a peak experience. One becomes detached, freed from conditions of worth, from socialization and from roles.

If, on the other hand, the personality continues to disintegrate there is the risk that experiences eventually will directly conflict with one's self perception. If the self and the experience become very discrepant, then the person's defense mechanism may not function effectively, resulting in anxiety. The Gestalt, the sense of being a unified whole, is broken by this experience. The result—the person may behave in one of two very different ways. Initially there is confusion, disorganization. From this a shift may occur, the old self may emerge, without all the conditions of worth attached. Or, unable to handle the present reality, the person may regress back to childish feelings and reasoning.

Carol was overwhelmed by the magnitude of the problems in her marriage; she didn't know how to cope with them. Again her husband asked her to leave. He largely treated her with disregard, ignoring her conditions of worth. So while Carol was dependent on conditions of worth, she lacked a supportive environment; as a result her sense of self-esteem was failing.

At times Carol seemed to be very much in touch with her feelings, she talked angrily about her mate. Yet, in the next instant, she spoke of how their marriage was successful and they were happy. One night they had a particularly severe fight. She went to visit friends and talked to them of things that were important to her as a girl. She regressed to a childish way of thinking, saying that people should anonymously leave baskets of food for the needy on their doorsteps. Then her thoughts became more disorganized. She said she must return home to her children. On the way she had a head-on collision and died.

The more overwhelmed the person is by unrealistic conditions of worth, the more defenses are used to protect the self-concept. To maintain the self-concept then requires ignoring or distorting experiences inconsistent with the self, selectively perceiving reality, which may jeopardize the person.

Organization of the Personality

According to Rogers, there are two regulatory systems which govern individual behavior: the *organism,* which includes

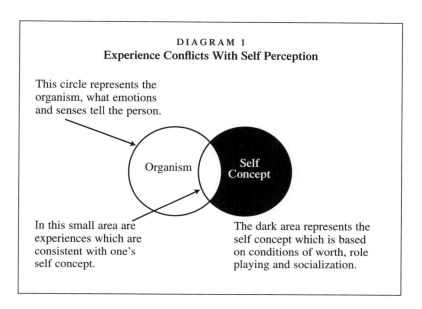

DIAGRAM 1
Experience Conflicts With Self Perception

This circle represents the
organism, what emotions
and senses tell the person.

Organism

Self
Concept

In this small area are
experiences which are
consistent with one's
self concept.

The dark area represents the
self concept which is based
on conditions of worth, role
playing and socialization.

inborn senses and emotions, and the *self-concept,* the individual's perception of who he or she is. The organism represents the here and now; it disregards the self-concept. For Rogers an important step towards the self-actualization process is to get in touch with the organism. (See diagram 1.)

To do so Rogers asks, "What do you really feel?"

He is after the real "me," the experience that people have when they let go of their roles and socialization. Rogers' approach to therapy, called client-centered, encourages people to find out for themselves what they really want to do and be, to trust their own feelings, thoughts and perceptions, accepting and valuing themselves.

In contrast, if the individual has been told what to think and taken on many roles, the self-concept may be very different from the organism. If there is a severe discrepancy, then psychological maladjustment results because only a small part of one's experience agrees with the self-concept.

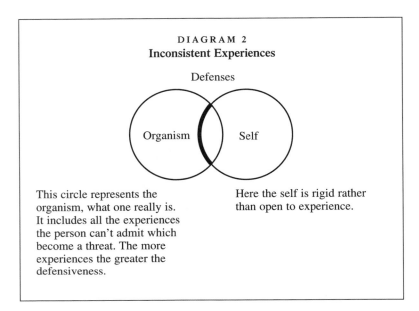

DIAGRAM 2
Inconsistent Experiences

Defenses

Organism   Self

This circle represents the
organism, what one really is.
It includes all the experiences
the person can't admit which
become a threat. The more
experiences the greater the
defensiveness.

Here the self is rigid rather
than open to experience.

Inconsistent experiences which don't fit one's self-concept are seen as a threat to the self-structure. The more inconsistencies in the individual's life, the more defensive and rigid the person becomes to prevent this contradictory information from entering consciousness. The adult lives around the truth, not acknowledging certain aspects of reality. The self becomes closed and perhaps even boring, losing touch with the vitality of life. (See diagram 2.)

Socialization Process. The socialization process can lead a person to deny very real feelings and other aspects of the self such as anger, spontaneity, assertiveness, intelligence, talent, competency, sexuality or childlikeness, because these qualities may not fit the conditions of worth set by one's significant others. These characteristics are still part of the organism, yet they are not admitted into the self-concept. (See diagram 3.)

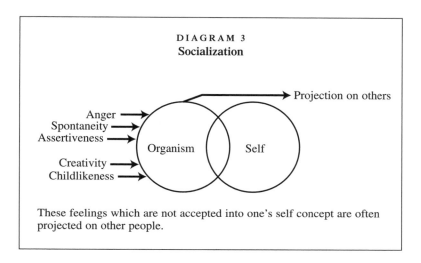

DIAGRAM 3
Socialization

Anger
Spontaneity
Assertiveness

Organism   Self

Creativity
Childlikeness

Projection on others

These feelings which are not accepted into one's self concept are often projected on other people.

As a result, these alienated feelings are projected on other people. A man learns to repress his feminine characteristics, such as tenderness and nurturing, projecting them on the women in his life. Another person has learned to hide childlike feelings. So instead of admitting them, he projects them on his friend, saying, "You're so childish."

Personality Integration. In contrast, for the individual functioning well psychologically, there is a close rapport between experience and awareness. By and large, experiences agree with the self-concept. Through therapy and life, the person can regain a sense of completeness. (See diagram 4.)

The Authentic Self. In this case the person is more authentic because the organism and the self are nearly the same. (See diagram 5.)

Rogers describes the characteristics of the individual whose experience agrees with the self-concept. Such a person is open to experience. The self is flexible, spontaneous,

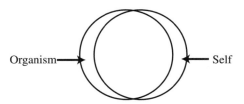

Personality Integration

Organism → ⭘ ← Self

Here the circles overlap very closely because there is a close rapport
between what the person sees and feels, between the organism and the
self concept.

ready to change and benefit through experience. The center
of evaluation is within the person—decisions are made
according to what is felt and sensed. Because the person
doesn't look to others to feel good about the self, there are
no conditions of worth and the individual experiences
unconditional self-regard.

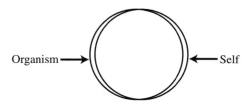

DIAGRAM 5
The Authentic Self

Organism → ⭘ ← Self

Here the organism and the self are nearly the same. One's experience
agrees with the self concept.

The person finds the self a trustworthy guide and values living up to his or her potentials. The self is respected because experiences are not distorted or denied. All experiences, whether positive or negative, provide a basis for growth. Life has personal meaning; the individual approaches it creatively to deal with the uniqueness of each experience.

How can one raise children so that self-worth will be determined within the person? After all, parents are forced to let a child know that certain behavior displeases them and doesn't fit socially. The major difference, according to Rogers, is that even when children are rebuked, they know they are loved.

"In this relationship the child experiences no threat to his concept of himself as a loved person," says Rogers.[5]

The parent does not withhold love until the child behaves in a satisfactory way. Rogers uses the example of the youngster who feels aggressive toward a baby brother, who he enjoys hitting. The parent accepts both positive and negative feelings experienced by the child. Through the parents' example the child is allowed to perceive these sentiments rather than deny or distort them. Yet, the child knows that such behavior is disagreeable.

How does this work in practice? For example, you find your little boy twisting his baby sister's foot to hear her cry at a particular octave. You would prevent his endeavor without telling him that such behavior makes him unlovable or separates him from humanity.

Rogers concludes:

> Because the budding structure of the self is not threatened by loss of love, because feelings are accepted by his parent, the child . . . does not need to deny to awareness the satisfaction which he is experiencing.

The youngster can freely admit to awareness of both positive and negative feelings.[6]

Categorizing the child's behavior also attaches conditions of worth to it.

For example, if the parent tells the child, "You are acting childish," or, "You are silly," the youngster learns that it's not acceptable to express childlikeness or to be silly. These all become experiences which may be denied later in life until a particularly supportive non-evaluative environment or a jolting occurrence may bring the individual in touch with true feelings again. If some event makes the discrepancy clear, the person may see a better alternative to the unrealistic aspect of the self-concept.

Socialization and Sense of Self

As we have seen in this chapter, our self-concept is influenced by others. Let's look at how an adult's response to a child modifies the youngster's sense of self. (See diagram 6.)

Circle number one represents the young child in a state of wholeness—in other words the youngster's feelings and thoughts are one and exist without concern of fitting into society. The white area represents the child's total experience.

Circle number two suggests three main aspects of the child's experience: positive, warm and caring feelings (+); negative, fearful and hurt feelings (-); and the experience of wonder and questioning. How might social experiences shape and reduce the child's contact with these aspects of life?

Let's take a simple example.

Johnny's mother says, "Give me a big love."

Johnny responds spontaneously with a big, uninhibited hug and a wet kiss. Yet very quickly his mother retreats,

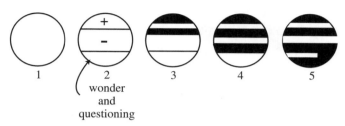

DIAGRAM 6
The Effects of Socialization on the Sense of Self

Circle number one (1) represents the young child in a state of wholeness. Circle number two (2) includes positive feelings, negative feelings and the experience of wonder and questioning. The shaded area in circle number three (3) represents the feelings of love the child learns to block out. In circle number four (4) the expression of negative feelings is restricted to what is socially acceptable. In circle number five (5) his sense of wonder and questioning are frustrated so that the individual is aware of only the unshaded area, a small part of one's experience and potential.

unable to deal with her own unresolved hurts which restrict her ability to express affection. Johnny experiences the discrepancy between her verbal request and her withdrawal from him. The child learns that he should express only so much love. The shaded area in circle number three represents how Johnny blocks out some of his feelings of love. The child learns what society means by love.

Certain experiences are unthinkable and certainly unspeakable. Like the day Johnny started talking about rats to his grandmother who was visiting. Suddenly his mother became very upset, told him not to talk that way, threw up her arms, unable to accept him talking about such "filthy creatures." Socially he learns that one only talks about certain negative thoughts such as horror movies and ghosts— but only at Halloween. So Johnny learns to deny other feelings and experiences. Perhaps if a parent dies, he is expected to accept that the parent is "better off" and things are really "just fine" this way, rather than dealing more personally with his feelings. In circle four the expression of negative emotion is denied.

In circle number five Johnny's sense of wonder and questioning is frustrated. Johnny is fascinated by an apple falling to the ground, commenting to his father how its path is straight down.

His father, pleased, begins a discourse about gravity, concluding with a beaming smile and a pat on Johnny's shoulder, "Anytime you have a question son, don't hesitate to ask."

Johnny perks up. "I did want to ask one more thing— what did you mean when you said gravity was a 'force'? What exactly does 'force' mean?"

"Well, I'll tell you, it's—well—ummm—hmm. Will you stop asking so many questions!"

There is a blunting of the child's experience. The youngster's concepts and awareness are narrowed in favor of social communication and adult acceptance. The child's idea of love, his concerns, curiosity, excitement and desire for understanding is much deeper than society encourages.

In circle number five the individual is aware of only the unshaded area which represents a small part of experience and one's potentials. This area symbolizes his socialized consciousness, how he has been conditioned to talk and think about things. One can understand why such people may be anxious or bored with life because they are alienated from a large part of the self.

In this process, many conditions of worth are being put upon the child.

"I am going to give you more positive regard only if you love me in a way which is acceptable to me"; or "I am going to give you more positive regard if you ask me appropriate questions" (this may mean questions which I can answer to meet my own conditions of worth).

The Self-Actualization Process

Rogers says the direction taken by those who truly want to be themselves is not an easy one. Still, he notes:

> I have yet to find the individual who, when he examines his situation deeply, and feels that he perceives it clearly, deliberately chooses dependence, deliberately chooses to have the integrated direction of himself taken by another. When all the elements are clearly perceived, the balance seems invariably in the direction of the painful, but ultimately rewarding path of self-actualization and growth.[7]

The self-actualization process can only take place for those who are given more than the usual freedom of choice. Individuals must be in environments in which experiences are clearly perceived in order to make the best choices for personal growth. They must be willing to let down their guard and accept all experiences, whether positive or negative. If experiences are denied or distorted, the individual becomes less self-actualizing.

Rogers describes how the self-actualizing person is unwilling to distort the self for approval from others and rather moves "away from facades, away from oughts" (away from the image that he or she must be good in the eyes of parents), "away from meeting expectations" (as an employer, as a friend, as a host), "away from pleasing others. . . . Clients define their goal by discovering some of the

Carl Rogers liked to see what contributed to growth, both in people and gardens. Throughout his life he enjoyed being in his garden every day. This thread can be traced back to his early childhood when his family moved to a farm in Illinois and he became interested in scientific agriculture. His later studies at the Union Theological Seminary in New York and then psychology at Columbia University may have contributed to his extraordinary respect and appreciation of others as separate persons. He had the ability to put himself aside, take the other person's perspective and be at their service in sorting out their own direction of personal growth. Rogers credited his insights to over 40 years of trying to understand and be of therapeutic help to people and the curiosity and questioning of his students at Ohio State University who stimulated him to clarify what he was doing. Eventually his ideas on trust and communication spread beyond psychology into the worlds of business, health care and international relations. *Courtesy of Carl Rogers Memorial Library.*

directions that they do not wish to move . . . . They do not wish to mold themselves and their behavior into a form which would be merely pleasing to others."[8] They do not wish to be anything artificial, anything which is defined by others. They do not value these goals even though they may have lived by them.

The aim is to be that person who one truly is: fully functioning, both intellectually and emotionally. Part of the self-actualizing process is to be open and honest in the face of new experiences. The person listens to the self, getting in touch with ambivalences, rather than shutting them out from consciousness. The individual trusts his or her own intellect, experience and feelings, taking into account all information before acting. In this way a sense of security and strength is derived from personal competence rather than from dependency or submissiveness to institutions or a code of behavior established by others.

In the self-actualizing process the individual has a sense of moving forward, of changing. One is not the same year after year; feelings towards a particular person or event may alter with the passage of time because the person is constantly in the process of becoming. This "becoming" does not take place over a short period of time, but is a continuing process towards self-direction, towards more responsibly choosing meaningful behavior.

In this process one is more accepting of others for what they are, there are no demands that people behave differently from their natures.

Abraham Maslow's Theory

From Freud we learned that the past exists now in the person. Now we must learn, from growth theory and self-actualization theory, that the future also now

exists in the person in the form of ideals, hopes, . . .
goals, unrealized potentialities.[9]

Abraham Maslow

Abraham Maslow believes that there is a tendency for
positive growth or self-actualization in individuals which
directs behavior. He presents a positive image of human
nature, stating that, if left to their own resources, people will
display a kind of biological efficiency.

The Hierarchy of Needs.   According to Maslow, people
have inborn needs which are arranged in a hierarchy of
decreasing importance for survival. The individual must
satisfy the most basic needs at the bottom of the hierarchy
before the self-actualization process can take place. The
lower needs, which are shared with other life forms, are the
most basic and powerful. (See diagram 7.)

Maslow says that the higher needs of human beings are
instinctoid, which means inborn like an instinct but weaker,
so that the needs whisper, rather than shout, at us. We can
ignore or even act against the higher needs and not fully be
our true self, acknowledging creative, spontaneous expression of authentic feelings or our unique personal awareness.
The higher needs can be overridden by society, for instance
by seductive advertisements, demanding people or the pressures of modern life. We can lose sight of the requirements
of our nature and probably survive, but we may not escape
the consequences of anxiety, boredom, destruction, depression, alienation or life without meaning.

Physiological Needs.   The most powerful and basic
needs are for food, water, air, sleep and sex. If one doesn't
have air to breathe, death results. If a person is starving, other
needs are blocked out. If one goes for days without sleep,
everything else loses importance. In developing countries

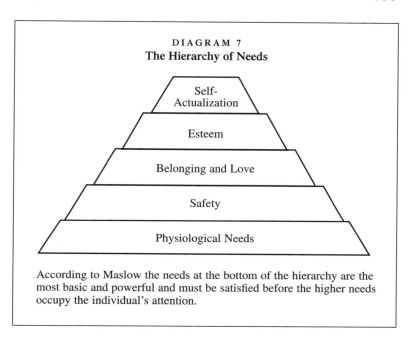

DIAGRAM 7
The Hierarchy of Needs

Self-Actualization

Esteem

Belonging and Love

Safety

Physiological Needs

According to Maslow the needs at the bottom of the hierarchy are the most basic and powerful and must be satisfied before the higher needs occupy the individual's attention.

many people must concentrate on these very basic needs. Sheer survival may far outweigh the self-actualizing process. In the modern world our most basic needs are largely met, so we can concentrate on higher requirements. The primary needs are the most urgent. Once they are satisfied, the next most powerful group becomes conscious.

Safety Needs.   All of us need to be safe from foe and from natural disaster in order to feel secure enough to think about higher aims. A child's need for safety is manifested through the desire for an orderly world and protection. For an adult, structure, order, organization and routine all provide an element of safety.

Belonging and Love Needs.   The need for belonging and for love are strong forces which can be satisfied through intimate relationships with other people or with a group or society at large. If a person does not satisfy the need to love, he or she will not be adjusted, according to Maslow. The child who is deprived of love in early years may be unhappy, sick or even neurotic as an adult. The failure to satisfy this need is one of the fundamental deficiencies of our culture, says Maslow.

The more mobile the society becomes, the less the need to belong is satisfied. When people move frequently, as some modern jobs require, they don't have the opportunity to know their friends and neighbors as well or to achieve a sense of roots in the community.

Finding a position in a community, or in a neighborhood, through a group, an organization or a commune can provide a sense of belonging.

Esteem Needs.   Everyone has a need for respect from others and from themselves. In our society, many people achieve such respect or esteem through accumulating money, possessions or through success and fame. Esteem can also be achieved through wisdom or self-development.

When the individual gains self-esteem it is accompanied by a sense of confidence, as though all things are possible. The person may become productive, with many successes at work and home.

Deficiency Motivation.   We have seen that people are less likely to be self-actualizing if they are starving or lack self-esteem. The individual who has not satisfied the hierarchy of needs is moved by deficit motivation. *Deficit motivation* means the person is driven to act to satisfy basic needs such as hunger or thirst. In contrast, with self-actualizing or growth motivation the individual chooses to do something for self-expression. The person moved by deficit motivation tends to seize whatever is available, seeking to gratify basic needs for self-esteem, belonging, love, safety or physiological needs.

The self-actualizer is not psychologically or phys-iologically dependent on others for survival. He or she has achieved a certain amount of personal foundation through satisfying the hierarchy of needs and through self-development and is ready to deal with issues such as being true to the self. One will find it easier to do such things as lose weight, quit smoking, exercise, be truly concerned for the welfare of others in a self-actualizing mode rather than in a deficit motivation.

Self-Actualization.   Self-actualization is the final stage of development, the realization of one's potentials and capa-bilities. The self-actualizing tendency may not occur until midlife, if at all. The individual must have some measure of satisfaction and fulfillment of lower needs for higher needs to materialize. The higher needs, such as love and self-actualization, can be postponed longer, for they're not crucial to survival. However, meeting these higher needs produces the greatest sense of happiness and fullness in life.

Self-actualization requires a free environment includ-ing nonrepressive economic and political conditions. It's easily interfered with by a poverty-stricken environment which may hold or redirect a person's attention to the lower needs. An environment with excessive coddling or, in another vein, with extreme permissiveness, can disrupt the process. Maslow says that if a child is given too much freedom too quickly, the youngster may be anxious. It is freedom within expanding limits which can hasten the self-actualization process.

Self-actualization takes courage, strength, self-control and discipline. It takes the courage to give up the comfort-able, predictable, controllable way of life one has grown accustomed to in favor of fulfilling one's potentials. It takes the strength to leave one's former securities and emotional props, the old ways of thinking about oneself. It requires the discipline and self-control to forge a new way alone. This deliberate growth and self-challenge is not always a comfortable state. Yet the reward includes happiness, fulfillment and peak experiences.

Maslow's desire to determine the highest human potentials led him to study people whom he thought were self-actualized. He combed through contemporary and historical figures, seeking the best examples of humanity, people who actualized their greatest potentials. He found certain patterns and characteristics in common among some great figures including Thomas Jefferson, Albert Einstein, Aldous Huxley and Eleanor Roosevelt. From such studies Maslow described the qualities of self-actualizers.

Characteristics of Self-Actualizers. Maslow says the self-actualizing individual is more mature, more fully human, motivated by higher needs. The person has a sense of belonging and rootedness, love from friends, status—all in all, a place in life.

The self-actualizer does not, for any length of time, feel anxiety-ridden, unsure, unsafe, ostracized, uprooted, unlovable, rejected or unwanted. The individual does not feel despised or looked down upon; nor are there crippling feelings of inferiority or unworthiness. Self-actualizers can be described as expressing themselves in life rather than merely coping. Maslow estimates that very few people achieve self-actualization; in fact he draws a figure of about one percent or less, although there are many degrees of approximation.

The following list notes the qualities of a self-actualizer and gives direction to the goal of becoming a fully

Abraham Maslow wanted to study what it is like to be human, when we're functioning at our very best. *Courtesy of Archives of the History of American Psychology, University of Akron.*

functioning person. These are the character traits Maslow found in common among self-actualized individuals:

1. The ability to freshly appreciate an experience and enjoy it as though it was the first time.

2. Self-actualizers are open, spontaneous and not afraid of making mistakes.

3. They follow values which are primarily based on their own feelings rather than in agreement with someone else. They tend to be ruled by their own character rather than by the rules of society.

4. Such people have democratic character structures which includes sympathy and empathy for humanity in general, kinship and understanding for others.

5. Self-actualizers have peak experiences which can occur in the context of virtually any activity. The person experiences power, the occurrence is intensified and colors seem more vivid.

6. The person has a clear perception of reality and is able to see other people and the world objectively.

7. The individual doesn't focus on the self but rather on issues which are to be resolved. There is a sense of purpose about the person's life.

8. Self-actualizers need time for solitude and independence, time to reflect and find satisfaction in being by themselves.

9. Such people accept themselves and others. They accept their weaknesses as well as their strengths.

10. They make strong, deep, fulfilling friendships.

11. They are creative and innovative in their approach to life.

12. They avoid falling into cultural norms. Rather than behaving according to what the culture says is appropriate, such individuals follow what they feel is true and just.

The Jonah Complex. What keeps people from self-actualizing, from realizing their unique potentials? One reason, says Maslow, is fear of success, "of our best side . . . our talents, . . .our creativeness."[10] The fear that performing at our maximum ability will bring with it unknown responsibilities and duties that we might not be able to handle is called the Jonah complex. As a consequence, many choose the comfort and security of routine over the challenge of the unknown.

Maslow says that many women fear the best in themselves and as a result hold themselves back from intellectual achievements. Maslow notes that some women have been trained socially to believe that achievement is unfeminine, so they may restrict themselves from the self-actualizing process, from expressing all their potentials, in order to maintain their role model. In a similar vein, men who have been taught to fit the strong, unemotional male image our culture values, may restrain themselves from revealing a more feeling, tender side, also important to the self-actualization process.

Conclusion

What kind of environment is conducive to the self-actualization process? The individual must first satisfy the lower needs. If the person is continually trying to defend him- or herself, one cannot concentrate on higher needs. Environments which threaten the person are detrimental to growth. Self-actualization takes place in a supportive, caring environment of positive regard in which experiences are clearly perceived in order to make the best choices for personal growth.

Both Maslow and Rogers are great believers in free will. Our lives are not so much determined by our pasts as they are by how we choose to actualize our needs in the present moment. While childhood experiences are important, we are not so much victims of them if we take an active role in the present. If we can distinguish between the lower deficit motivations on the hierarchy and actualizing motivations, rather than seizing things we can look at the broader perspective of establishing a personal foundation and developing mutual trust with others. This can occur through

growth-promoting experiences such as building relationships based on unconditional positive regard.

If we can change our self-concept from expecting
perfection of ourselves, to include process, change and
mistakes, then we can feel good about ourselves now.
We've seen from the developmental psychology chapter
that process and change are part of growth. If the idea of
change and error is incorporated, then we can maintain self-
esteem and accept mistakes. The aim is to be who one truly
is; to trust one's own intellect and to derive security and
strength based on personal competence. Personal satisfaction is less dependent on approval from the outside world;
rather, it is based on listening to one's inner self. This is not
a life for those who want comfort, it is a life of challenge,
stretching and growing.

CHAPTER FOUR

Behavioristic Psychology

Understanding Conditioning for Self-Direction

A. Classical Conditioning
  1. Social Learning Theory
    a. The Need for Maternal Contact
  2. Can Fear Be Instilled and Generalized?
  3. Extinction and Spontaneous Recovery
B. Operant Conditioning: Are We the Product of Rewards?
  1. Prejudice
  2. Superstitious Behavior
  3. Resistance to Extinction and Partial Reinforcement
  4. The Socialization Process
C. Controlling Aggression
D. Conditioning and Stress
  1. Stress Overload: Experimental Neurosis
  2. Prolonged Stress: Do We Really Ever Adapt? The General Adaptation Syndrome
  3. Stress and Early Aging
  4. Efficiency and Stress: Optimal Performance
  5. Biofeedback
E. How to Apply Conditioning
  1. Changing Type A Behavior
  2. Improving Study Skills
  3. Weight Loss
  4. Using Conditioning to Stop Smoking
F. The Power Of Classical Conditioning in Advertising
G. The Pervasiveness of Conditioning

Understanding Conditioning for Self-Direction

*H*is thoughts whirled as he lay in bed. Wires running down from his chest led to a black box strapped to his waist. Inside the box each beat of his life was being recorded along with any irregular flutters. His mind focused on the patterns of his life which had brought him to this edge. Would he be able to back away? What would he have to give up? Money? His profession? Security for his family? His future? Future! What future? That was what was in question.

Bill is a prime candidate for a heart attack, exhibiting what San Francisco cardiologists Meyer Friedman and Ray Rosenman call "Type A" behavior, exemplified by a strong competitive drive, aggressiveness, and a sense of continual pressure which leads to doing many jobs at the same time. Although Bill may be praised at work, his lifestyle may shorten his life by 20 years.

Are we allergic to modern life? Some refer to such illnesses as diseases of adaptation, the result of keeping up with the competitive pace of modern life. In contrast, in more traditional societies cycles of activity are balanced with relaxation periods included in the daily routine: villagers pause to pray, Easterners begin the day with yoga or meditation; and in Latin culture workers stop for an afternoon siesta. In contrast to the United States, some European towns close so completely for a month's vacation that it can be difficult to mail a letter. Such breaks are means of getting in touch with the self and the biologically based need to pause.

Let's look at a modern lifestyle. Up to now, Bill has been a real go-getter. He's condensed his morning routine to 15 minutes. When he awakens he rushes into the bathroom to shave. He reads the newspaper at the same time. Then he throws on his clothes and grabs his breakfast to eat on the way to work. His driving has developed into a fine art, moving in and out of the fast lane dodging other cars. At work Bill is hard-driving and ambitious, able to do many jobs at the same time under pressure. He never takes a sick day and often skips his vacations.

"Yes," his boss has told him many times, "you're made of the kind of stuff that's sure to succeed."

Bill has always beamed at the attention. After all he has excelled and earned promotions. Up to now he has been only mildly aware of the cost to his body of the tension with which he lives. In stressful situations his body responds with an outpouring of adrenaline to handle the emergency— resulting in what is called the fight or flight response. However, because he often can do neither, the constant presence of stress hormones can wear down his body's immunological system or cause damage in the gastrointestinal tract such as ulcers.

A growing number of people suffer the modern afflictions. A U.S. Department of Health, Education and Welfare report says that, for other than young people, the main causes of death in this country are heart disease, cancer and stroke. What's behind this epidemic? Is there any hope? What can be done?

The report says, "A distinctive feature of these conditions is that most of them are caused by factors that are not susceptible to direct medical solution." These would include the individual's psychological well-being, life patterns and the environment. Further advances in curing these diseases involve individual responsibility for health and changes in lifestyle for the majority of Americans.[1]

Drs. Friedman and Rosenman estimate that while more than 50 percent of Americans suffer from Type A behavior, this complex of emotional reactions can be altered. One can become freed from this "hurry sickness." In fact, Carl Thoresen, a Stanford University psychologist, reports in a study of 1,000 heart attack victims that those who change their characteristic behavior have reduced by half the chances of recurrent heart attacks.[2]

In trying to understand behavior how can we explain why Bill acts in such an unhealthy way? *Conditioning* gives us a perspective to understand such behavior. When his boss praises Bill or gives him a promotion, he is rewarding Bill for being competitive. This has become a powerful motivating force behind Bill's behavior.

Exactly how much of our behavior is the result of social approval or disapproval? Our culture consists of a built-in set of rewards and punishments for certain beliefs, actions and levels of performance. Enculturation, as we will see, is a very subtle process. Many of the values which we assume to be our own, we've actually learned from our culture. Those things that seem to happen automatically in us are often a result of conditioning.

Classical Conditioning

The study of conditioning originated quite by chance, no more in the beginning than an annoying side effect of serious research. The discovery was made by a Russian scientist, Ivan Pavlov. Pavlov had won the Nobel prize for originating a method to measure digestive secretions such as salivation. He was engrossed in his studies of how much saliva dogs secreted at the taste of food when his experiment was disrupted. Initially the dog salivated shortly after food was placed in its mouth, as expected. But as the experiment progressed, the animal began to salivate sooner and sooner, at first when harnessed in the experimental apparatus, then upon sight of the laboratory assistants entering with food, then later whenever the laboratory door was opened and eventually as soon as the animal heard the experimenters' footsteps.

As you might have guessed by now, it became very difficult to measure the onset of salivation, confounding Pavlov's experiments. Yet the physiologists came to recognize a far more important discovery.

Pavlov expected the dog to salivate at the taste of food. Food is an *unconditioned stimulus,* which means that the organism automatically responds to it without any prior training. Food, drink, warmth, pain and loud noises are all unconditioned stimuli—one's reaction is automatic, built into the nervous system. For example, a loud noise will cause an infant to give a startle response. In Pavlov's study the dog's initial reaction to food, the unconditioned stimulus, was an *unconditioned response.*

Yet what surprised Pavlov was that the animal would salivate at something which seemed irrelevant to the unconditioned stimulus of food—at the sight of laboratory assistants or at the sound of their footsteps. Since these were

Finding money can illustrate the power of a conditioned stimulus. If you found this object on the street, you might have an emotional response and get excited, while a one-year-old baby would treat it no differently than any other piece of paper, as a neutral stimulus.

not unconditioned stimuli, Pavlov reasoned that the animal must have learned to associate these cues with food. He decided to test his theory. Could the dog be taught to salivate at something totally unrelated to food? A neutral stimulus shall we say? He chose a bell which was sounded in the dog's presence just before food was presented. Just as the physiologist expected, eventually the dog salivated upon hearing the bell ring alone without the arrival of any food. Pavlov had gained some control over the animal's behavior by manipulating a *neutral stimulus.* Well, reasoned Pavlov, the bell originally had been a neutral stimulus; however, when it was paired with food, the dog began to associate the bell with food and it became a *conditioned stimulus.* It is called a conditioned stimulus because its power is conditional on pairing it with an unconditioned stimulus such as food. He called the animal's learned reaction a *conditioned response* because its occurrence depended on previous associations of the conditional and unconditional stimuli.

DIAGRAM 1
Classical Conditioning

UCS ━━━━▶ UCR
(food)   (salivation)

An unconditioned stimulus (UCS) automatically elicits an unconditioned response (UCR).

NS (bell)

UCS ━━━━▶ UCR

In Classical Conditioning the UCS is preceded by a neutral stimulus
(NS) which becomes associated with the UCS.

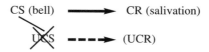

CS (bell) ━━━━▶ CR (salivation)

UCS ╌╌╌▶ (UCR)

The neutral stimulus gains power through association with the UCS to
produce a response in the absence of the UCS. The neutral stimulus becomes a conditioned stimulus (CS) and the response to the CS is called
a conditioned response (CR).

This process of pairing an unconditioned stimulus with
a neutral stimulus to evoke a conditioned response is called
classical conditioning. To appreciate the importance of
Pavlov's finding we must realize that until his research no
one had been able to demonstrate the psychic processes involved in learning or how to specifically control the learning process. For the first time there was real scientific
evidence and a procedure for studying learning. Learning
was conditional upon certain associations taking place. He
had hit upon a method which could be generalized to

learned behavior in human beings to account for pleasures, fears and habits. How else could you explain students' mouths watering when the lunch bell rings although there's no food in sight?

Social Learning Theory. The experiences which form the basis of learning begin in infancy when a child learns to associate food and warmth with Mother. When the infant cries, Mother's face appears just before nursing, so that Mother (who will become the conditioned stimulus) is paired with food (the unconditioned stimulus). As a result, Mother is associated with eating and other pleasurable activities such as warmth and relief from pain. As time passes, Mother's presence alone soothes the child. Eventually these warm feelings are generalized to other people. This forms the basis of the child's trust and desire to be with others.

With this model it's possible to clearly understand why a child has such a fond attachment to his blanket, as attested by the cartoon character of Linus of "Peanuts." It begins in infancy when a baby associates the blanket with warmth, rest and comfort. In psychological terms the blanket becomes a conditioned stimulus for such pleasurable feelings. The author's toddler doesn't want to take a nap until he has his blanket in hand; he begins to cuddle it, looks sleepy and talks about bed, because the blanket has become a conditioned stimulus for sleep.

In summary, according to social learning theory, an initially neutral stimulus, such as Mother, gains its power to affect us through association with unconditioned stimuli. Social learning theory says that many of our responses to the world are conditioned; the child learns to associate Mother with food, warmth and comfort, attaching the same strong feelings for these basic needs to human beings.

The Need for Maternal Contact.   Following this assumption, what would you guess would happen to the child
who lacks such associations? Since the results of experi-
menting on children could be disastrous, researcher Harry
Harlow and his colleagues did a study with rhesus monkeys
to see how they would develop without maternal contact. At
birth the monkeys were separated from their mothers and
placed with artificial surrogate mothers. When they were
frightened, the infants would run and cling to a substitute
mother made of wire covered with sponge rubber and terry
cloth. The young animals nursed from a wire mother which
had a bottle attached to it. As the monkeys matured they did
not form normal relationships with other members of their
species. In fact, they were not sexually competent and most
of them were eventually artificially inseminated.

Without the maternal experience the youths were not
good mothers themselves. The first to become a mother
ignored her baby and sat very still on one side of the cage,
staring. Harlow explains:

> As the infant matured and became mobile, it made
> continual, desperate attempts to effect maternal con-
> tact. These attempts were consistently repulsed by the
> mother. She would brush the baby away or restrain it
> by pushing the baby's face to the woven-wire floor.[3]

What are the implications of such an experiment?
Children who grow up with little maternal contact, who are
not conditioned to associate people with food, warmth and
other pleasurable activities, may have difficulty with interpersonal relationships. Social behavior is not automatic, it
must be cultivated. Human contact conditions the child to
associate pleasurable feelings with people and to become a
member of society.

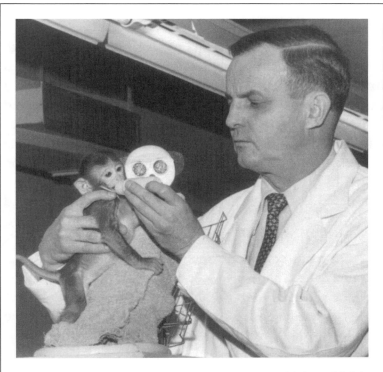

Harry Harlow feeding an infant rhesus monkey with its artificial, terry cloth mother. *Courtesy of the Archives of the History of American Psychology, University of Akron/Harlow Primate Lab, University of Wisconsin.*

Can Fear Be Instilled and Generalized? Let's turn to a famous experiment to test conditioning on a child. A study by John Watson on Little Albert, a well-adjusted eleven-month-old infant, illustrates how fear can be instilled. Two months before the experiment began, Little Albert was shown a white rat and a rabbit. He looked at them with keen interest and reached over to play with the creatures. Albert, like other infants, was afraid of loud noises and would cry when the experimenter clanged a bar.

In the experiment a white rat was presented to Albert, but just as he reached for it a steel bar banged. He stretched for the rat once more and the bar sounded again. As you'd expect, Albert began to cry. A week later the rat reappeared and Albert withdrew his hand before the white furry creature could touch it. Seven times the rat was paired with the loud clang of the steel bar so that a strong negative emotion would be created in the infant. Finally, when the rat alone was present, Albert began to cry; he fell over and crawled away.

This experiment had far-reaching effects, for Albert's fear encompassed not only the white rat, but anything white and furry. The following week he was frightened upon the sight of a friendly white rabbit. He even responded negatively when he saw a Santa Claus mask. Albert left the hospital the day these tests were made so we can only wonder whether he grew up afraid of Santa Claus. Albert's fear of anything that resembled the white rat is called *stimulus generalization*. This means that anything that is similar to the original conditioned stimulus can evoke a response. The effect of such conditioning is very powerful since it causes an automatic response while the person may not even be aware of the source.

Even one interaction can have a dramatic effect on the child, conditioning a fear response. Imagine four-year-old Sherry. She and her parents are at Yosemite National Park, gazing over the edge of a cliff. Sherry bends over to get a better view. She can see what look like little toy cars below and starts to reach for them. All of a sudden Dad, frightened at how close she is to the edge, swoops her up, begins to scream at her and spanks the youngster. Sherry is startled by the sting of his hand on her bottom. The pain and the loud noise are both unconditioned stimuli which become associated with looking down. In this lone experience the perspective of looking down from a height may become a conditioned stimulus for fear. Sherry may become afraid of heights, hesitant to even climb up on a ladder, unaware of what's behind her fear, for her response is automatic.

While in this example the child is spanked, we can see why in psychology physical punishment is not a preferred means of teaching children. It teaches them fear, as well as to hit, and creates emotional conflicts, without clarifying alternatives or giving information about how to do things correctly. Yet spanking is still prevalent. In 1995 Dr. Rebecca Socolar found that forty-two percent of 204 mothers surveyed had spanked their young children, under the age of four, in the week before the survey. The spankings occurred more often in inner cities than in suburbs and among those who had been spanked as children by their mothers.

It is not surprising then that conditioning is responsible for many of our fears. Sarah sits contentedly on the park lawn, letting a snake crawl around her arm. It is only when she brings the reptile home and her mother screams that Sarah too becomes afraid of the animal. Or, in another instance, Sarah may sense her mother's apprehension whenever they see a dog on the sidewalk as she anxiously hurries her daughter to the other side of the street. Whenever Sarah spots a dog she too may cross the street as a result of her mother's uneasy response to these canine animals.

Such fear conditioning can shape a child's life, limiting exposure to the world. The unknown or the unusual can become a conditioned stimulus. Children may grow up afraid of new ideas or people because their parents rebuked them loudly when they strayed away to approach new people. As you can guess, these youngsters may associate unpleasant feelings with adventure and expansion, never knowing that their early conditioning stands in the way of success.

So, we can see how conditioning is a very powerful motivating force in the individual's life. Based on the biology of pain and pleasure, classical conditioning forms much of the person's emotional basis. It is responsible for the power behind certain words to move us. Advertisers take advantage of this fact. Commercials for banks describe them as "big, friendly institutions" or as the "Rock of Gibraltar," phrases which instill a sense of security in the viewer because they are conditioned stimuli to evoke positive feelings. A sense of nationalism can be thought of as conditioned. How can a piece of cloth which differs for each nation throughout the world stir people to such depth? One generation may enculturate the next away from reading. If a father doesn't read, he may condition his son by telling him that reading is for eggheads. The boy may grow up avoiding books, limiting his chances for college and professions which require reading. On the other hand, a youngster whose family enjoys reading may learn to associate pleasurable feelings with books.

Prejudice is passed on from generation to generation largely as a result of conditioning. Disparaging remarks about Blacks, "honkies" or any other group may condition the child to feel negative about such people. For example, Danny walks home each day from school arm in arm with Pete, a child of a different race, until one day his mother sees him and looks shocked and yells at him. Later that night he hears his father using racial slurs. His parents' biases may eventually condition him to associate negative feelings with other races.

Extinction and Spontaneous Recovery. As we've seen whenever the individual gets close to a negative conditioned stimulus—whether it's new ideas, books, heights or snakes—he has a negative response. The easiest way to minimize such negative feelings is to avoid the stimulus. This is called *avoidance conditioning*. For instance, John associates going to the dentist with memories of having his teeth drilled as a child. Today he handles this fear by avoiding the dentist. Sally hates to give speeches. Just the thought of giving a speech in her Friday morning Spanish class makes her hands clammy. She may decide to skip the class.

When a person avoids giving a speech or going to the dentist, or anything unpleasant, he or she feels better, no longer afraid. Avoidance is reinforced. A *reinforcement* is anything that makes it more likely a response will occur again. A reinforcement is often a reward or it may involve escaping or avoiding pain. In this case, as the individual escapes the unpleasant task, physiological responses to fear such as clammy hands are reduced. Breathing slows down and heart rate decreases so that one feels calm again.

But by continually evading the situation the individual never overcomes the fear. By dodging the dentist, John's only association with it is his childhood apprehension. The problem with avoidance is that the person never stays long enough, whether it be in the dentist's chair or in front of a class giving a speech, for the fear response to vanish or be extinguished. *Extinction* involves the weakening of the association and eventual disappearance of the conditioned response because it is no longer reinforced. Avoidance conditioning is difficult to extinguish because of the secondary rewards of escaping unpleasant feelings.

While in the process of extinguishing behavior, positive reinforcement can be used to develop a new response.
This is done by presenting a stimulus which evokes positive
feelings in place of the one that caused negative emotions.
To understand this better let's take the child's apprehension
of snakes. The snake might be presented at the same time
the youngster sits down to eat, or when she sees Mother,
who is associated with pleasure. Or perhaps the girl handles
the snake with someone who has good feelings about rep-
tiles in lieu of hearing someone scream at the sight of the
creature. By providing the child with positive experiences,
she is conditioned to associate such feelings with snakes.

Actually, it was Pavlov who first had a notion of extinguishing behavior which he demonstrated in experiments
with dogs. He found that if the bell, which had been associated with food, was sounded over and over without being
followed by food, eventually the dog stopped salivating.

However, even the process of extinction can have its
exceptions. Long after the dog no longer salivated to the
bell an attendant accidentally rang it and the animal began
to salivate once again. This reversion to old behavior patterns which seemed to have been extinguished is called
spontaneous recovery.

It is through the process of spontaneous recovery that
old habits suddenly re-emerge. For instance, Diane, a young
woman who was once intimidated by authoritative voices,
had learned to be assertive when confronted by others. Yet,
one day without warning, she becomes afraid of an aggressive individual. The conditioned stimulus, authoritative
voices, which she dreaded as a child, may spontaneously
recover some of its strength. This reappearance of an old
response is part of the process of extinction but it is only

temporary. In a short time the conditioned response may recede again and become more completely extinguished.

Although spontaneous recovery can disrupt an individual's motivation to surmount old habits, remember that it is limited. For example, Tom, who is on a diet, seems to be doing a great job losing weight. Yet, unexpectedly one day he slips back into old patterns, gorging himself when he's frustrated. Later, discouraged, convinced he lacks the willpower to take off the extra pounds, he deserts the reducing plan. However, according to spontaneous recovery, if he would stay on the diet, in a short time he would probably overindulge less frequently. The breakthrough occurs when the individual doesn't give up in the face of old impulses. Every time you succeed at replacing an old habit with the response you want, it makes it easier to do the next time.

Operant Conditioning: Are We the Product of Rewards?

Have you ever had the feeling that your life was slipping into a rat race? Let's follow the imaginary story of Harry the mouse and consider the impact conditioning has on his life.

The alarm sounds. Harry is jarred from his sleep, driven from the bed. He turns off the alarm, staggers down the hall maze to the bathroom, then to the kitchen, where he finds a reward of coffee cake. Some mornings he gets in his car, others on mass transit, and travels through the freeway maze, arriving at work bleary-eyed. He hops up the stairway network, hoping to get some reinforcement during the day. He winds his way through the intricate pathways between desks in the office pool to his corner, where he proceeds to sit down and work through piles of paper. He moves a pen in between lines on sheets of paper which he promptly deposits through a maze of in and out baskets and mail chutes. Finally 10:30 arrives and Harry runs down the hall for a reward of a few sips of coffee. At lunch he walks down the corridor, nodding "Hello," as he's been reinforced for doing in the past, by a greeting or a pat on the back. He gets a few pellets to munch on at his local eatery. At 5 p.m. he runs down the stairway maze and hops in his car to find his way back to his cubicle. He scampers into the kitchen for a few licks of sweetened water or alcohol. Finally he sits down in the living room, pets his little mice and watches T.V. He's back in his nest. He creeps down the hall and sets the alarm for the next day. It's easy to see that Harry is a product of rewards. He has learned through reinforcement to follow a relatively narrow path.

Fantasies aside, can our behavior be shaped as is a rat's behavior in a maze? Have you ever wondered how our culture reinforces us to maintain continuous movement: to accumulate more possessions, another car, to get to the top, to where the reward is? It's a sort of fictional finalism: once we achieve such and such our lives will be complete. Such conditioning can be very impersonal, taking little account of individual needs.

To get a better appreciation of our culture's rewards, let's turn to some observations made by an American psychologist, B. F. Skinner. He focuses on overt behavior which he can see and measure in the laboratory with no reference to internal motives. Skinner maintains that behavior can be largely determined by the use of rewards, which he demonstrates in studies of animal behavior in a *Skinner box,* a cage equipped with a bar. When a rat presses the bar, it is rewarded with a pellet of food, which drops down to the animal. Before the rat hits the bar, the animal will probably go through a series of random responses: it may jiggle the

UC Berkeley Animal Laboratory Skinner box. The rat is pressing the bar which automatically releases a single food pellet from the container.

cage door, scratch the floor, perhaps roll over, and then sniff each item in the cage, until it finally hits the bar which results in food. It may wander around the cage before eventually managing to rap the bar again. Thus the rat learns that a certain behavior—pressing the bar—results in a reward, food. The food pellet reinforces the animal's behavior.

What was the unconditioned stimulus behind the rat's behavior? Why did the rat initially press the bar? It's very difficult to say; in fact it appears to have happened randomly. The rat was rewarded for his behavior, yet the food pellet came after his response. It did not initially produce the bar press.

Here we must draw a distinction between classical conditioning, as in the case of Pavlov's dog, and operant conditioning, which is demonstrated with the Skinner box. The reinforcement differs from the unconditioned stimulus which motivated Pavlov's dog because it does not elicit the desired behavior but rather follows it.

The Skinner box is used to demonstrate *operant conditioning*. It involves getting the subject to perform a certain activity and then rewarding the animal. Through reinforcement one is able to shape behavior, first by getting the animal to make the desired response, and then by reinforcing it, which makes it more likely to occur again.

Have you ever wondered how animal trainers can teach seals to blow horns, dogs to ride bikes or rats to lift more than their body weight? They use operant conditioning to teach animals to perform such elaborate tricks. Dolphins can be taught to whistle at specific frequencies and durations. A bird can be conditioned to pull a toy fire truck and climb the ladder attached to it. A rat can be trained to climb a spiral staircase and a ladder, cross a narrow drawbridge, pull a toy car over by a chain and jump into the car.

Such performances certainly make us think that the animal must be very intelligent. Yet such complex tricks are based on reinforcing the animal's behavior each time it approximates the desired response. This entails breaking the task into smaller units and rewarding each accomplishment. For example, since it is unlikely that a rat will walk over and climb a spiral staircase on its own, the trainer first rewards the animal when it strays close to the staircase. Then the reward is delayed until the rat's response is closer to the desired sequence of responses, for instance, until the animal puts one foot on the stairway.

Conditioning was used to train these animals to do things which would not occur in their natural habitat. *Courtesy of Marine World.*

Operant conditioning can have some useful lifesaving applications. The U.S. Coast Guard in San Francisco has a training program for birds. Their Air Rescue Station uses pigeons trained to spot life boats. The birds are first conditioned to peck at a disc when they see a yellow or orange spot. Three birds at a time are put in a helicopter compartment so that their vision is 360 degrees. Out over the ocean they go to it, pecking at a disc when they see a yellow or orange spot, however this time the spot is a life boat at sea waiting to be rescued. The Coast Guard reports that the animals are more than twice as accurate as people. The pigeons are bright enough to learn the task yet not smart enough to be bored.

Sometimes we unwittingly shape behavior in undesirable ways. For example, children may learn to cry for attention if they find that their parents ignore them when they're quiet and talk to them when they become annoying. The child's whimpering is reinforced by parental attention. One alternative to extinguish fussiness would be to give attention when the child behaves well and ignore the whining.

Operant conditioning can result in abnormal behavior that can persist throughout a lifetime. Why would a person stutter or continually blink when trying to speak in a tense situation? What is the reward involved? For Frank it started when he was a child. One day his father was admonishing him; he picked up the boy and started shaking him. His father's friend, who noticed that Frank was beginning to blink excessively, touched his friend's arm and said, "I think the boy has had enough." As time passed, whenever Frank was being reprimanded and started to blink repeatedly, his father would stop scolding him. In such a fashion Frank learned that when he had a tic in his eye people would immediately stop pressuring him. In a similar vein, the young child who stutters may be treated more gently by adults who realize the youngster is having difficulty expressing himself. Although both the tic and stuttering offer short-term relief, in the long run they limit the individual's success in life.

Prejudice.   Aspects of prejudice can be demonstrated in the laboratory through operant conditioning. Rats are placed on a cage floor, half of which is painted black and the other half white. When a rat steps on the black side, an electric shock automatically goes off. The rat can be taught to stay off the dark side to avoid being shocked. In this case the animal escapes the situation to avoid the negative reinforcement. In a similar fashion children may not associate with other races to avoid their parents' hostility. Their prejudice may be reinforced through a derogatory joke about another race, which is rewarded by laughter or approving smiles.

Conditioning can be very subtle. Studies by Crowne and Strickland show that head shaking and verbal reinforcements of "uh-uh" can affect some people's choice of words. Through selective reinforcement the experimenter shaped the subject's behavior. We learn how to communicate with people according to what they reinforce.

Superstitious Behavior.   Conditioning has extensive effects on our lives. Operant conditioning can help explain superstitious behavior—why some people swear by a rabbit's foot or a certain item of clothing, which is sure to bring them good luck. For instance, whenever Martha goes gambling, she consistently wears a particular orange blouse and plays three certain slot machines located at the west end of the casino. Why, you wonder? A few months ago, while she was wearing her orange blouse, she was playing those three machines when lights started blinking and $50 in coins tumbled out of the machine. The curious thing is that although she's played many times since without winning, without being reinforced, nevertheless she unswervingly attributes her victory to that orange blouse. Although no logical relationship exists between the reward (hitting the jackpot) and the response (wearing the blouse), she is convinced one does. Such accidentally conditioned responses are called superstitions.

Some baseball players exhibit superstitious behavior before a game, swearing they won't play unless they use a certain mitt or wear a particular piece of clothing because they've won in the past when that article was present. Now they're sure it's crucial for victory. If you ask them to prove their hypothesis by switching the piece of clothing, they may well refuse, anticipating disastrous results; that they would lose the game. Or, if they do oblige, they may lose the game anyway, because they've lost confidence. In this manner they unintentionally prove to themselves that they need the "lucky" item.

Such inadvertent conditioning can be demonstrated in the laboratory. In the pigeon's cage there is a light mechanism that can be programmed to go on whenever the food mechanism is operating. One day the animal is scratching and the light comes on. The next day his trainer notices that the bird seems to be acting peculiar, walking around the cage, scratching, and then looking up expectantly at the dull light, waiting for it to flash on. The animal has been conditioned to associate scratching behavior with the light coming on. In each of these cases, because the response precedes the reward, the organism behaves as though the response caused the reward. Such superstitious behavior leads people to spend energy on activities that don't pay off. For instance, a baseball player may go through extra moves before hitting the ball to increase his luck rather than saving his energy and attention for responses that pay off.

Resistance to Extinction and Partial Reinforcement. Skinner made a dramatic discovery in the laboratory quite by chance. He was running out of food pellets and decided he would only reward the animals every other time as they learned to press the bar for food. To his surprise he found that the subjects who learned under *partial reinforcement,* that is, reinforced intermittently, learned just as well as those who were reinforced every time they performed an act. In fact, it was actually harder to extinguish the behavior of animals who learned under partial reinforcement. After the pellets were stopped, the subjects' behavior was more resistant to extinction than the behavior of those animals who were reinforced for every response while learning.

The concept that behavior persists long after a partial reinforcement has ceased helps explain why Martha, undaunted, drives to the casinos, weekend after weekend, playing the slot machines until four in the morning, sure that she will win, just as she did a few months before. From Skinner's discovery we can surmise that the person who is rewarded only occasionally, as in gambling, will actually stay at it longer, even when there aren't any more rewards. Presumably this occurs because the conditioning experience has incorporated playing without winning all the time.

The Socialization Process. Now that we understand the mechanics of conditioning, let's look more closely at how it affects us step-by-step in human growth and development. According to social learning theory, values and beliefs are largely the result of the culture's reinforcements.

From infancy the child learns to respond to the world in terms of rewards and punishments. Mother scolds Julie when she pushes over the lamp and later praises her when she says, "Thank you." At first this process is completely externalized: the punishments and rewards come from one's parents. Slowly the child begins to incorporate her parents' values. She learns to respond in anticipation of certain rewards and punishments. She may walk around the house pointing out all the "no-nos" and in the beginning even push the lamp over, all the while saying, "No, no."

There's a certain amount of uniformity, which becomes the basis for Julie's value system. Let's see how she arrives at a sense of right and wrong. At the grocery store Julie takes a cookie, her mother rebukes her, patiently explaining that these are not their cookies. At this point Julie concedes, although she wonders what's wrong with taking this particular cookie. Her question becomes clarified the following week. She begins munching on a banana at the store and her mother tells her that these bananas, which don't look at all like cookies, are not to be eaten either. A similar scenario is repeated many times before the abstract concept of stealing emerges for Julie. In a parallel fashion the parent teaches the concept of "two" by varying the concrete objects while keeping the number constant—two pencils, two dogs, two books. By altering all dimensions except the concept, the child arrives at such abstract understanding. As the child learns to anticipate certain rewards and punishments, he or she internalizes society's values. For example, if the small person knocks over the lamp, he or she may expect a slap on the hand. As time passes, how the youngster lives up to the culture's values becomes part of the self-concept. Now in place of parental authority is self-praise and self-criticism, which determine how one feels about the self. This is how children develop a conscience.

Conditioning is a very subtle process that accounts for many social attitudes, motives and behavior; in short, conditioning is largely responsible for the socialization process. As we've seen, social learning psychologists trace social behavior back to relieving those very basic drives we spoke of earlier in the chapter—hunger, thirst, pain and pleasure. They maintain that parental fulfillment of the child's most basic needs determines how the youngster feels about people in general and how important human relationships will be throughout life.

Yet, if such behavior can be explained in terms of relieving our most basic needs, one may ask, why do people

do extraordinary things to help one another with no visible
reward? Why would a person endanger his or her life by
rushing into a burning building? Wouldn't the desire to preserve life, or at least to stay away from heat, be stronger?
Do we need to assume there is some greater force driving
the individual?

Social learning theory suggests that conditioned responses can eventually become independent of biological
drives. For example, after the author's father retired from
carpentry, he continued building cabinets and making toy
chests. Why would he continue his work when he was no
longer being paid money? A social learning theorist would
explain that his response of sawing wood was reinforced so
much over the years by paychecks and compliments from
his boss that now the stimulus of moving his arms as he
saws the wood has become conditioned to be pleasant in
itself, providing its own motivation.

Controlling Aggression

As a child, I remember adults describing a particularly rau-
cous fight, saying, "They were fighting like cats and dogs."
Images of animals, who were natural foes, chasing, growl-
ing and hissing, attacking each other came to mind. But, do
cats and dogs have to fight? Can they be taught otherwise?
In fact, today I have a pet dog and cat that are the best
of friends. What determines these animals' attitudes?
Psychologist Zing-Yang Kuo decided to challenge our assumptions and test his conviction that behavior is learned.
He raised animals that would normally fight in three different situations. He chose kittens, chow and terrier puppies
and cockatoos. In the first set of pens were kittens, puppies
and birds, who were taught not to fight with one another.

The second group of animals had no training. A final group were raised in isolation.

In the first set of pens Kuo, using a specially designed glass-walled feeding center, taught the animals to wait patiently for food, while the animal ahead of them finished eating. They learned to eat one at a time. Any animal that "cut" was taken to the end of the line. He knew males would fight over females for dominance in mating, so he removed females from the group during estrus or the mating period. He interrupted good-natured play fighting, which began to get too rough, with a spray of water in the face. The animals were exposed to visitors, such as canaries and rats, for 10 minutes every day to reduce their hostility to strangers.

Results of the study illustrate that socialization does work. In the first group, after training, none of the animals would interrupt one another while the food dish was occupied. While the untrained groups initially fought over food to establish dominance, they were otherwise friendly towards each other outside of feeding times. At 10 months of age all the animals were tested for their response to visitors. None of the trained animals were hostile towards strangers. In contrast, the untrained animals were antagonistic, often attacking and fighting strangers "like cats and dogs." However, the response of animals raised in isolation was extreme: there were ten cases of cats killing and eating small birds and rats and dogs chasing and killing rats, birds and rabbits.

From these studies Kuo concludes that fighting and social dominance are not necessary evils and can be prevented in some animals. He finds hope for human beings, suggesting that the means for creating a peaceful society may lie in using learning techniques to prevent the development of aggressive behavior.

Zing-Yang Kuo, an important comparative psychologist from China, who did his graduate training in the United States, had a strong conviction behavior is learned. He demonstrated with scientific experiments that much aggressive behavior between animals such as cats, rats and dogs, usually assumed to be a result of inborn instincts, is influenced by learning. *Courtesy of the Archives of the History of American Psychology, University of Akron; and Dr. Gilbert Gotlieb, University of North Carolina at Chapel Hill, Center for Developmental Science.*

Conditioning and Stress

Using our understanding of conditioning, let's look at how
it interacts with stress. Just how many difficult and crucial
decisions do you face every day? On occasion do they get
to be too much, do you feel overwhelmed, unsure of which
way to turn?

Stress Overload: Experimental Neurosis.   In the laboratory, Pavlov made a discovery that advanced our understanding of how conflict affects the ability to discriminate.
His assistants found that too much stress could drastically
alter an organism's ability to make any kind of decision.

The experiment went like this: Pavlov's assistants
conditioned a dog to distinguish between an ellipse and a
circle through a series of trials in which the circle was followed by food and the ellipse was not. The experimenters
changed the shape of the ellipse so it began to resemble a
circle with one side only slightly flattened. The dog continued to salivate exclusively at the sight of the full circle.
Then the scientists proceeded to confuse the animal by
changing the ellipse again so it resembled the circle even
more closely. At this point not only could the animal no
longer distinguish between the two, but when shown the
original ellipse and the circle, the dog could no longer make
the earlier discrimination. Instead, dramatic changes took
place in the dog's behavior. It became agitated and upset,
barked, tore at the apparatus and became inhibited. Studies
with rats, cats and sheep have yielded similar results.
Indiscriminate stimuli or inescapable conflict produce what
is called *experimental neurosis,* a condition in which the animal loses its ability to discriminate.

Such studies can help us understand neurosis in
humans. When the individual is pushed beyond his or her

capacity, one's ability to differentiate may totally break down, leaving the person functioning at a lower level than initially.

The conflicts of modern life may be enough to elicit neurosis. For example, Sam, an office worker, may be working under pressure to complete what each one of his cohorts insists is top priority. He is faced with choosing between a number of equally engaging alternatives, with answering the phones and responding to new assignments within an ever diminishing time frame. Eventually, unable to cope with too many competing stresses, he may no longer be able to make what were initially easy decisions such as

Is this an unconditioned stimulus or a conditioned stimulus? Is it a stimulus for "hurry up" or "slow down and relax"?

where to file a folder. We must remember that this is not the only pressure point in his life. As soon as he steps out the door of the office and into his car, he is forced to instantaneously make a number of life-and-death decisions on the crowded freeway. At home the evening news further agitates his tired being with reports of nuclear leaks, fighting in the Middle East, murder and rape. After dinner, in a moment of quiet, he tries to reason out how to spend the rest of the evening. Yet under such prolonged stress with so many seemingly unresolvable choices, he may no longer be able to judge what's best for him, since his level of functioning has been reduced.

Prolonged Stress: Do We Really Ever Adapt? The General Adaptation Syndrome.   A Swiss physiologist, Hans Selye, found that although an animal may initially appear to have adjusted to a considerable amount of stress, in reality the organism may be dangerously close to illness or even death. In fact, under prolonged stress, the body begins to manifest symptoms such as ulcers, skin discoloration, deteriorating organs and other severe illnesses.

Selye set about to find out how experimental animals physiologically would cope with stress. He found the animal's response took place in three main stages. In the first stage, the *alarm stage,* the animal's body handles the stress by increasing the production of hormones and certain sugars and salts. These chemicals, which increase one's strength and endurance, appear to be designed to cope with short-term emergency situations. Problems occur when the stress is prolonged, as it was in Selye's experiment. The animal's bodily functions begin to deteriorate, leading to bleeding ulcers, diseased adrenal glands and other illnesses.

One of the most fascinating aspects of Selye's study is that in the second stage, what he calls the *stage of resistance,* the animal appears to have adjusted to the strain and to have recovered most of its former strength. The ulcer is recovering as are other body organs. If you saw the animal at this stage, it would seem healthy. Superficially it's difficult to tell the difference between the animals under stress and those not subjected to it. However, the animal is less able to take on new stresses at this point. If the stress is strong and persistent, the animal breaks down as we see in stage three, the *stage of exhaustion.* Selye found that the animal's apparent "recovery" lasted only a few weeks. Then the production of essential body chemicals fell dangerously low, the organs became diseased and the animals began to die. The animals could only maintain defenses for so long until their resources were exhausted. Their physiological response to prolonged stress is called the *general adaptation syndrome.*

How serious are the ramifications of these studies for human beings? It appears that although a person seems to have adapted to stress, all of one's resources may be mobilized to handle the present load, so that a new stress can break down the whole system, overwhelming the individual and resulting in illness or an emotional breakdown. For example, Sue has a high-powered job. She and her husband just moved into a new home. She recently made a trip to the East Coast to visit relatives. Together, these items present a significant number of changes to which she must adapt. Nevertheless, she appears to have coped with them. Her body has responded with the alarm stage and stage of resistance. Yet, she's being challenged to deal with even more: her boss is hard on her. She has already used up her resources. She becomes distressed by her employer's attitude, breaks down, reaching the stage of exhaustion, which may manifest itself in physical symptoms such as a cold or more serious illness.

So although we may appear to be handling a stress, that's not the final indicator of whether we are up to taking on more. There is a need to separate appearance from inner reality, to stay in touch with our resources, assessing how much we're committed and whether we're ready for new challenges.

Stress and Early Aging. A study in 2004 from the University of California, San Francisco, has demonstrated that stress actually ages the immune cells of the body. The researchers say they have found the first direct evidence that severe and chronic emotional stress can age people biologically: it can trigger premature aging of immune system cells. The cells of mothers who were subjected to the day-to-day stress of their severely ill children and who perceived they were under stress aged on the average ten years more compared to the cells of mothers of healthy children. Scientists examined tiny segments of DNA and protein called telomeres. Telomeres cap the end of the chromosomes and are shortened as cells reproduce, a measure of age. When they reach a minimum they can no longer reproduce. That's when the risk of disease increases. It is interesting to note that this shortening did not take place for some mothers with sick children who did not report feeling stressed according to the authors of the study, Professors Elissa Epel and Elizabeth Blackburn.[4]

Efficiency and Stress: Optimal Performance. Conditioning can work to our advantage as well as our disadvantage. How can we use this power to shape and direct behavior to control the stress and tension in our lives?

First, under how much stress do we function well? A certain level of stress increases our efficiency. In fact, some

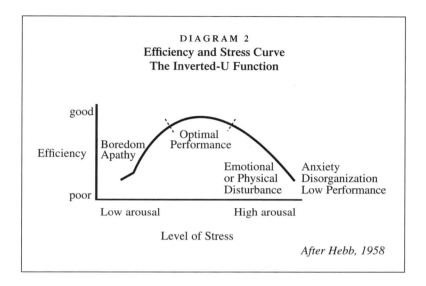

DIAGRAM 2
Efficiency and Stress Curve
The Inverted-U Function

Efficiency

good

poor

Boredom
Apathy

Optimal
Performance

Emotional
or Physical
Disturbance

Anxiety
Disorganization
Low Performance

Low arousal   High arousal

Level of Stress

After Hebb, 1958

pressure contributes to functioning at *optimal performance.* Try to ascertain just how much stress contributes to increasing your efficiency. Too much stress results in anxiety and lowered performance while too little also results in low performance. (See diagram 2.)

Dr. Thomas H. Holmes devised a scale to measure the impact of change on the individual's well-being. From studies of more than 5,000 people he found that patients would become ill when major life changes took place in clusters. For example, death of a family member, combined with a pregnancy, a new job or moving into a new home, could result in illness. He found that life changes such as divorce, death of a close family member, personal illness, a jail term and marriage create the most stress. His work suggests that pacing ourselves whenever possible can reduce the risk of stress-related illness.

If we apply the concepts of experimental neurosis, the general adaptation syndrome, the efficiency-stress curve and the life change scale together, we can see that our abilities for effective decision making and for handling stress are limited. Under too much stress, not only is the person unable to deal with new challenges, but incapable of making good decisions about which stimulus to respond to. Our resources for effective decision making are challenged by the high-pressure urban lifestyle which most of us participate in. At times it may be wise to limit activity, acknowledging that we are not always in a position to make good decisions about how much we can do. We may have difficulty gauging others' capabilities as well, because they appear to have adapted, although all of their resources may already be committed. These four concepts also demonstrate the importance of *self-direction,* for the individual is in the best position to control stress if one learns to monitor the self inside out: psychologically, biologically and socially. Becoming aware of the dynamics of stress and how much one can safely handle is important to maintain good health and the quality of one's life.

The person we read about at the beginning of this chapter has been able to turn his life around by learning to monitor his physiological and psychological resources; making conscious decisions about how many new tasks he can take on and when to conserve energy. When he is confronted with anxiety-producing situations, he has learned to trigger a relaxation response such as slow breathing. He has realized that he has limits and has shifted his priorities, reducing the need to get everything done today. He schedules "quiet time" for himself, where there are no demands. By taking care of himself he can live a longer life.

He knows that responding inappropriately to everyday situations, as though they were life threatening, causes unnecessary wear and tear on the body, which itself may ultimately be life threatening. He's learned that he can alter Type A behavior and reduce the risk of having a heart attack.

Biofeedback. For those who like to see how animal research eventually may contribute to the lives of people, let's turn to a recent breakthrough in psychology based on the fundamentals of conditioning.

As we've seen, people can be conditioned into positive behavior. One of the most exciting breakthroughs is biofeedback, learning to voluntarily control involuntary bodily processes that had been previously thought to be beyond the individual's control. Just as the individual is conditioned to live at a hurried pace, he or she can be conditioned to slow down by decreasing blood pressure and heart rate. To practice biofeedback the person is connected to a machine which measures responses such as heart rate. The key to the technique's success is that it gives the individual "feedback," a visible indication of minute body responses. A light flashes, for example, when heart rate slows down below a specified level to reinforce such behavior. The subject tries to recognize the thought or emotion associated with the slowed heart rate and repeat it. In this manner the person learns what it feels like to be relaxed and how to give direction to the body. The subject is given feedback for small changes in behavior that create a desirable physiological state and reinforced by the flashing light.

Some biofeedback monitors can be operated by placing one's fingers on a machine to measure what is called galvanic skin response. When a person is under stress, electrical conductivity of the skin varies. By listening to the humming tones which the machine emits, a person can vary the electrical conductivity of the skin by learning to relax.

The application of biofeedback is amazing—with practice the person can learn to control headaches and the secretion of stomach acids which can produce ulcers.

How to Apply Conditioning

Conditioning can be used for positive growth, to change old habits, to learn to stop smoking, to improve study skills, to lose weight or to reduce stress. First, set a goal, keeping in mind your own best interest. This requires acknowledging that we don't have to see ourselves the same year after year, we have the freedom to change. Determining your own best interest calls for some self-reflection—evaluating old modes of thought, emotion, action, and your self-concept. How do they all fit into a changing direction? Once a conscious plan and goals are established, break the project into small, attainable steps. Operant conditioning demonstrates that a new behavior pattern is learned more effectively if the task is broken into smaller units and accomplishments are followed by rewards. Regularly monitor and evaluate yourself so that you get feedback. Acknowledge any progress you make.

Our understanding of the dynamics of stress can help to more effectively apply conditioning. Change requires setting aside time and energy in order to perform at an optimum level of efficiency. Avoid introducing a new mode of behavior during stressful periods, such as finals, when resources are already committed.

For optimum performance, monitor and control the stress level. This would include scheduling in relaxation and leisure time, which may lead to more efficiency and self-direction.

Recognize that this is a period of transition, with some inherent discomfort while extinguishing old responses which have been reinforced for years. To consciously change old habits requires determination. Be patient, realizing that the habits being extinguished are strong. The studies in this chapter indicate that learning takes time and an acceptance of the discomfort of making mistakes which accompanies the process of change.

The best method to extinguish an avoidance response may be to stay in the situation, developing new habits until old feelings pass. Avoid being too discouraged when old habits, which you're trying to eliminate, suddenly gain some of their former strength, for this reappearance is only temporary.

Changing Type A Behavior. Earlier we mentioned results of a study by Carl Thoresen[5] and Meyer Friedman[6] which found that altering Type A behavior can cut the recurrence of heart attacks and the death rate in half for people who have already suffered a heart attack. The five-year study was aided by a grant from the National Heart, Lung and Blood Institute. Similarly, Dr. Dean Ornish[7] has found that changes in lifestyle can begin to reverse coronary heart disease in a year. In both of these studies people are taught to change a number of learned responses. The changes in life style included a low-fat vegetarian diet, moderate aerobic exercise, stress management training, changes in certain belief systems and restructuring of various environmental situations. For many of us, adopting such goals may help reduce stress. How can we apply this to our lives? Consider these possibilities:

1. Learn how to relax. Set aside 20 minutes a day for a quiet meditative type experience in which there's nothing to be accomplished but to slow down one's body by deep regular breathing, to stop worrying.

2. *Try a different approach to driving the car;* rather than driving competitively, drive slower (55 mph); stay in the right lane.

3. *Learn to listen.* Focus one's full attention on the other person. Listening makes a person pay more attention to others and slow down. A less frenzied pace will create less hostility from others and result in more environmental support.

4. *Reevaluate the work environment and its demands:* ask, "How can I rearrange it to make it a more pleasant environment, interacting better with peers and subordinates?" People find that, out of habit, they may be in routines that are not very productive. For example, a utility company manager encouraged associates to give him work on Monday. With all of the assignments, he felt overwhelmed and struggled through the rest of the week. By altering the way he approached others, delegating more work to associates and getting assignments throughout the week, he was much more satisfied and productive.

5. *Monitor how your body feels.* Minimize food high in fats and heavy or large meals. Eat more often during the day instead of having one meal at the end of the day.

6. *Learn to wait.* Practice waiting with more patience in restaurants, at the bank, in supermarkets, in traffic jams, and use waiting time to reflect or meditate on life.

7. *Restrict television watching.* Reduce watching violent, highly competitive or disturbing events (the 11 p.m. news).

8. *Reevaluate and restructure your priorities and resources as your circumstances change.* Life is fluid, continually changing. British psychologist Kerry Chamberlain found that difficulties in daily life which contribute to psychological distress and affect one's well-being may change from one life stage to the next.[8] For example, Chamberlain found that health is a daily concern for the elderly. In contrast, college students and mothers with young children in his study placed a much greater importance on time pressure, citing it as a highly rated area of hassle. Be aware that as circumstances change, it may be necessary to reevaluate one's priorities and the allocation of personal resources.

9. *Exercise.* Do moderate aerobic exercise regularly. Jonathan Brown measured subjects' heart rate on an aerobic exercise bike. He found that those who were more physically fit were less vulnerable to adverse health effects from life stress.[9] According to psychotherapists exercise is one of the most effective ways to reduce tension and reverse a bad mood, especially combined with relaxation, putting one's feelings in perspective and controlling one's thoughts.[10]

10. *Become more aware and consider changing how you think.* A hostile personality type with cynical attitudes of consistent mistrust of others and frequent anger is associated with heart disease says Dr. Redford Williams at Duke University Medical School in North Carolina.[11] In many situations it's how one perceives things that is the problem to be solved. "How do I respond to the way others treat me? If someone criticizes me, can I examine my feelings of anger to evaluate my beliefs?" Notice how you talk to yourself and how it fits certain beliefs or fears. Practice positive self-talk. Reduce seeing what happens in life as a direct challenge or threat, especially to one's sense of control or esteem.

Practice controlling your thoughts and putting your feelings and events in perspective. In *cognitive psychology,* Albert Ellis says your thoughts, perception, interpretation or appraisal of a situation are often more important in

determining its effect on you than the event or situation itself.[12] Have you ever seen a minor event become blown out
of proportion, perceived as an irreversible catastrophe, creating overwhelming stress? Become aware of irrational
beliefs which can exaggerate negative consequences. The
power of these overwhelming negative emotional responses
can limit the person's awareness of other alternatives. Dr.
Lynda Powell, a professor of preventive medicine at Rush-
Presbyterian St. Lukes Medical Center in Chicago, found
that by using the tools of cognitive psychology, patients in
her study cut the recurrence of heart disease by 44 percent.
Basically they learned not to "bite the hook." Imagine you
are a fish swimming in serene waters. Suddenly you get
stuck in a traffic jam and blame the people in front of you—
that's the hook. Don't bite it. Dr. Powell taught patients to
replace the negative thought with the word "hook." They
became less reactive and could choose not to "bite it" or
respond to the stress.

*11. Become more active in resolving stressful situ-
ations.* The perspective we take on the events in our life is
so important that researchers have measured how a positive
attitude can help one remain healthy in the face of stress.
Suzanne Kobasa of the University of Chicago has found
that a set of personality characteristics, which she calls
hardiness, seem to deflect or moderate the negative effects
of stressful life events.[13] Hardy individuals make commitments, get involved, believe they have some influence and
control of events and see change as a challenge or stimulus
for personal growth. They find life's activities interesting,
not just a means to an end. Such attitudes may result in a
more positive and active involvement that transforms stressful life situations, thereby reducing stress in the future. In
contrast, less hardy subjects who reported feeling powerless

may be more passive. Kobasa discovered that those who were high in hardiness were more likely to stay healthy when under stress. On the other hand, those who were less hardy and high in Type A behavior suffered the greatest deterioration of health in stressful life situations. Hardiness can even affect elite athletes. Sports psychologist Judy Goss, of the Canadian Olympic Association, found hardy athletes had less depression and anger during extensive training as elite athletic swimmers than those who were not hardy.[14]

12. Cultivate personal relationships. Strong social support may make an individual less vulnerable to disease. Results from a twelve-year study by C. Stout of Italian-Americans in Roseto, Pennsylvania show that the death rate from heart disease was less than half that in neighboring communities.[15] Although the population had a high intake of animal fat, and other risk factors such as obesity, smoking and lack of exercise were similar to other communities, the social structure was much more supportive. Researchers found Roseto to be an unusually close community; members have strong family ties and support one another in time of trouble. The study suggests that emotional support may reduce the risk of heart disease and even counteract the harmful effects of known risk factors.

Improving Study Skills.   As a child, Bob grew up in a household in which no one read. He was not rewarded for his reading attempts. Now in a community college, he would like to be a good student, so he devises a plan which includes scheduling study time. When someone wants him to do something, he evaluates whether he can afford to take on new activities without jeopardizing his studies. With a schedule in hand he can monitor how effectively he maintains study periods rather than losing time to less important demands of his environment. He takes a study-improvement class to further clarify his strengths and weaknesses. He attends a reading lab where he receives positive reinforcement for his progress from his instructor. Next, he alters the environment at home to make it more conducive to studying, remembering that he will study best in an atmosphere where he is conditioned to perform a particular task. Rather than propping himself up on the bed where he is conditioned to sleep, he decides to clear off his desk, to do nothing else there but studying, so that in a few days he will have a strong habit of studying as soon as he sits there. He's patient with himself, keeps track of his progress, recognizing that his grades will improve slowly with some ups and downs. He is rewarded by the knowledge that he is developing skills which are important to the goals he has chosen.

Weight Loss.   Jan begins to change her habits which lead to overeating by keeping a log of what she eats for a day, the calories in the food, where she is and what she's doing while she eats. Now she analyzes her behavior to determine which conditioned responses she wants to change. Is turning on the television a stimulus for opening the refrigerator and snacking? While doing the dishes does she feel prompted to relieve boredom with a junk food break? What are the habits she wants to eliminate? Rather than watching television she decides to invite friends over to visit and to join a health club where she goes after dinner to exercise. She starts to make the extra effort to keep healthy food at home and carries something healthy in her purse to eat so she's not tempted to buy a candy bar. She keeps records of her weight loss, giving herself feedback to evaluate small increments of progress.

Using Conditioning to Stop Smoking. Irene analyzes what feelings and situations prompt her to reach for a cigarette—for example, when she starts the car or when she talks on the telephone. To cut across the habit chain, she makes the cigarettes less accessible—wrapping each one carefully in aluminum foil with a rubber band around it, packing them in the car trunk when she's driving and, at home, removing them from convenient locations such as the kitchen counter where the telephone sits. Irene finds that if she waits about ten minutes, the urge to smoke will often pass. She is prepared to reward her successes with something healthier that makes her feel good, perhaps a walk in the garden, a bike ride or a movie. Cigarettes are no longer relied on as the main way to take a break. In time, she experiences the personal rewards of feeling better physically and psychologically, more confident of her ability to be self-directive.

The Power of Classical Conditioning in Advertising

The influence of classical conditioning is revealed once again in the power of advertising. John Watson did more than do experiments with Little Albert, the baby who became afraid of furry animals after they were paired with loud noises.

Watson was a pioneer who laid the groundwork for modern advertising, applying the principles of classical conditioning. He saw the market place as a laboratory in which the customer was to be deliberately controlled by the advertiser.

To assure a reaction from the consumer, Watson instructed advertisers to ". . . tell him something that will tie him up with fear, something that will stir up a mild rage, that will call out an affectionate or love response, or strike at a deep psychological habit or need."[16]

Watson intentionally tried to stimulate anxiety in young mothers with an ad for Johnson and Johnson baby powder in the 1920's. The headline read, "Oh dear, I wish my baby wouldn't cry so much," creating doubts about whether the mother knew how to care for her infant. He also stimulated anxiety in order to sell Pebeco toothpaste to newly independent young women who smoked by telling them not to worry about "smoke-stained teeth and tobacco-breath," since they could still be lovely if they would just use Pebeco twice a day.

His techniques for testimonial advertisements are still used in beauty magazines to promote beauty and status that come from using particular cosmetics and wearing particular brand name clothing. Today ad campaigns pair products (the neutral stimulus) with images of adorable babies, happy families, attractive women and beautiful natural settings to elicit positive emotional responses. So we can see that another important element in becoming more self-directive is to be aware of how conditioning is used to manipulate consumers, leading to over-consumption and debt.

The Pervasiveness of Conditioning

As we've seen, conditioning pervades our lives. Up to now we may have been only partially aware of the attitudes and values which we have been teaching or conditioning in our children through rewards and punishments. Their preju-dices, fears and pleasures are largely a result of condition-ing. And what about ourselves? At times we may feel limited by our responses to the world, as though our be-havior is automatic, like a robot. Indeed, if behavior is con-trolled exclusively by past experiences, one may feel predetermined, responding to a new situation with an old conditioned response.

Conditioning helps explain how people can revert to behavior which is not always in their best interest. For instance, they may be conditioned by cultural reinforcers to drive themselves or be reinforced against the potential enrichment available from reading books and going to college. Even Freud's ideas of early childhood fixations can be explained through avoidance conditioning and experimental neurosis. The young child, pushed beyond his or her ability to control bowel movements, may respond to control in a rigid, fixed manner as an adult, avoiding situations associated with negative experiences.

How many times a day do we behave in ways which have been conditioned by the culture? Are there some of them that we would like to change? For example, are we judging another person objectively or acting according to an old conditioned response? What about fear, of facing a classroom of students or an authority figure? We can use our understanding of conditioning to shape our behavior and make us more effective at self-direction.

Unlike many other areas of personality theory, most of this material has been substantiated by scientific demonstrations in the research laboratory, often using animals as subjects.

There are two ways of looking at ourselves, both inside and out. While the previous chapter on self-actualization emphasized inborn human tendencies, conditioning theory emphasizes that we are molded by the environment. The emphasis is on external references such as material rewards. The next chapter stresses the interaction of both internal and external forces and shows how the individual can be overwhelmed by outside forces. The final chapter focuses on our inner resources for the development of individuality.

CHAPTER FIVE

Social Psychology

Subtle Tyrannies of Society—How Social Forces Influence Personality Development: Erich Fromm's Theory

Subtle Tyrannies of Society: How Social Forces Influence Personality Development

"It's almost like a prison that you create yourself...
You want to break out ... and tell everyone "this isn't
really me at all."

Zimbardo's Stanford Prison Experiment

What motivated thirty-eight well-educated men and women in 1997 to leave families, friends and successful professions and join a cult called Heaven's Gate where, under the influence of its leader, Herff Applewhite, they would commit ritual suicide in order to board a spaceship they were convinced was trailing behind the Hale-Bopp comet?

How do you explain the Branch Davidian followers in 1993 doing battle with military tanks and federal agents and dying in a fiery inferno with their leader, David Koresh, whom they believed was an angel protecting them from the end of the world?

What motivated nearly a thousand members of the People's Temple back in 1978 to leave family, friends and country and with their leader, Reverend Jim Jones, journey to a commune in a remote section of jungle in South America where later, at his command, nearly all would commit mass suicide?

Why do individuals give up their independence and turn to cults for the security they can't find in themselves? Why do seemingly normal people follow the dictates of an Applewhite, Koresh, Jones or back in the 1930's and 40's, a Hitler? What is their vulnerability? Is it the leader's strengths? Do all of us have this same potential to follow a madman? What is it about human nature that allows us to seek control or to be controlled by others? With some 5,000 cults in existence in this country what are the chances of knowing a cult member?

Why do people who have functioned in society for years become destructive? How, for example, can a San Francisco city supervisor—formerly a policeman and youth leader—murder the city's mayor over a perceived slight? Or, how can a former University of California, Berkeley professor turn from teaching mathematics to allegedly murdering and maiming people with letter bombs in the name of struggling against modern industrial social forces? Are these people inherently evil or possessed and simply pretending otherwise? Well, what then?

Erich Fromm asked these same difficult questions as he watched the extermination of more than six million Jews by the Nazis before and during World War II. Why, he asked, would the German people support Hitler, a deranged leader, or "Mein Führer" as he was called? Why in recent times would cultists blindly do the bidding of such madmen as Jones, Koresh or Applewhite and, at their command, engage in murder or commit mass suicide? Even after surviving the holocaust of Nazi Germany, Fromm, a Jew, still believed that human nature was good. After pondering the German national character, he concluded it was not individuals who were bad, but the forces of society that shaped behavior. Fromm maintained that to understand human behavior one must look at the society in which people live.

Why, Fromm asked, did the Germans support a tyrant? They looked to Hitler, he concluded, as someone to take care of them, to make their decisions for them. In other words, Hitler relieved them of the burden of freedom. They no longer had to decide what to believe or what to do with their lives. The Nazi Party made all decisions.

You may wonder how freedom can ever be a burden. How can people seek to be free but yet so readily surrender their liberty and responsibility? Well, being free can be very lonely. Have you ever had a day when you could do whatever you wanted? You may have felt desperately alone, with nothing to do, and no one to see. In such a case freedom may be a burden. Some adults experience a similar lack of direction and anxiety on Sunday afternoons. This "Sunday neurosis," as psychologists call it, occurs because the individual doesn't know what to do with free time outside the structure and routine of the normal work week.

In *Escape From Freedom*, Fromm says that, in many modern cultures, people find freedom a burden because their societies have discouraged them from developing themselves. Freedom makes them feel lonely and insignificant. He maintains that in order to significantly reduce human misery, society must be changed; individual counseling or therapy is not enough.

Have you ever felt that forces outside of you were determining the way you would act? Have you ever come

Erich Fromm believed if we want to understand the human
personality, we have to consider the impact of social, political
and economic institutions. *Courtesy of Library of Congress.*

away from a situation having said things that weren't "really you" because you felt pressure from friends, family or a boss?

In this chapter we'll look at how great an influence the environment has on our behavior. Contemporary research in social psychology has found that destructiveness, for example, is not simply a characteristic of the person, but often can result from a destructive environment. This section examines how social forces influence human behavior and how, in some cases, they cause human beings to go against their own identities and morals to carry out destructive acts. We'll explore the relationship of the individual personality structure to the environment and how, if the personality is not given an opportunity to develop, it becomes vulnerable to subtle intimidation and manipulation by negative social forces. We'll look at how to achieve our own freedom and live more effectively by minimizing the effects of outside pressure and developing the ability to choose in light of our best interests.

The Stanford Prison Experiment

What would it take to turn normal college age people into "brutal prison guards" or withdrawn, emotionally upset prisoners? The Stanford Prison Experiment was designed to demonstrate the psychological effects of imprisonment on volunteers and the conditions under which role playing ceases to be a game and becomes a reality. In a study conducted in a mock prison, Stanford University professor Philip Zimbardo found that students became so absorbed in playing their roles they lost track of their own identities. Role assignments became influential in shaping behavior far beyond individuals' definitions of themselves.

The study involved 30 college-age males randomly assigned to act as prisoners and guards in a simulated prison on campus. Zimbardo sought to learn how people adapt when they lose their liberty, civil rights and their privacy, while those who are "guards" gain power and social status. The project, initially set to run for two weeks, had to be terminated after six days because it was too successful! Four of the prisoners, unable to cope with their confinement, developed extreme emotional depression and acute anxiety attacks. From the start the prisoners' identities were undermined. They lost the freedom to dress and comb their hair the way they wanted, they had to wear nylon stocking caps and smocks. Rather than being called by name they were referred to only by number. The prisoners were forced into dependent relationships; they had to ask for permission to use the bathroom or to smoke cigarettes. They were subjected to continual harassment, and every few hours during the night the prisoners were awakened and made to recite the prison rules.

The guards were "deindividuated," as Zimbardo says. They wore identical khaki uniforms and silver reflector sunglasses that made eye contact impossible. They carried billy clubs and handcuffs. For their part, the guards did more than carry out their jobs; they began to use domineering and abusive methods. Guards used psychological tactics to isolate each prisoner from fellow prisoners by undermining trust and making each one suspicious of the other. Over a third of the guards were hostile and cruel, humiliating and degrading the prisoners, which further weakened their self-respect. They became infatuated with their power. As one guard admitted, he derived great pleasure from dominating the prisoners. The guards found themselves treating the prisoners as something less than human. Zimbardo notes that even the several compassionate guards eventually went along with the more power-oriented guards. Every guard at some time followed abusive, authoritarian behavior since everything was defined in terms of power. Not to use power was considered a sign of weakness.

Meanwhile, the prisoners were faced with a growing sense of powerlessness and hopelessness as their privacy and freedom were taken away. Zimbardo says, "As the guards became more aggressive, prisoners became more passive; assertion by the guards led to dependency in the prisoners."[1] Instead of protesting, the prisoners began to act depressed, institutionalized. Some became hysterical; others did whatever they were told, finding that the safest strategy to avoid insult and punishment from the guards was to withdraw, to "toe the line." By doing nothing, they were not singled out and harassed by the guards. Zimbardo notes, "By choosing instead to behave in ways that help de-individuate them, powerless people can at least seek the security of anonymity and non-existence in the eyes of their oppressors."[2] As the prisoners became more helpless the guards' sense of authority and mastery grew.

A few days into the study, Zimbardo, who acted as the prison warden, gave the prisoners the choice to give up the $15 a day they were earning in order to be paroled. All but three prisoners said they would gladly give up the money to get out of the prison. But the participants were so programmed to think of themselves as prisoners, that when their request for parole was denied, they quietly returned to their cells, oblivious to the fact that they were free to leave the prison and end the study. Even Zimbardo, who had designed the experiment, said the prison had a life of its own and could have continued without him:

It was remarkable how readily we all slipped into our roles, temporarily gave up our identities, and allowed these assigned roles and the social forces in the situation to guide, shape and eventually to control our freedom of thought and action.[3]

The experiment had become real in the minds of the participants, it was no longer an intellectual exercise. Four prisoners were released because of extreme emotional depression. The study was terminated early out of fear the prisoners were being undermined psychologically. Students in the study conformed so much to their roles that they lost their individual identity and became overwhelmed by the environmental situation (the mock prison).

One of the most important findings of the experiment was that the subjects were so absorbed by their assigned roles they could no longer differentiate between role playing and the self. Overtaken by the oppressiveness of their environment and by the irrational authority exerted over them by the guards, they lost track of their options. Rather than discuss their lives on the outside they spent 90 percent of their time talking about how to escape or to survive in the prison.

Prisoner #416 says:

I began to feel that I was losing my identity, the person I call [name], the person who put me into this place, the person who volunteered to go into this prison. . .was distant from me, was remote until finally, I wasn't that. I was #416—I was really my number and 416 was going to have to decide what to do. . . .

One prison guard summed it up:

It's almost like a prison that you create yourself. You get into it, and it's just, it becomes almost the definition you make of yourself, it almost becomes like walls, and you want to break out and you want just be able to tell everyone that, this isn't really me at all, and I'm not the person that's confined in there. I'm a person who wants to get out and show you that I am free, and I do have my own will, and I'm not the sadistic type of person that enjoys this kind of thing.[4]

Zimbardo, in summarizing the experiment, said that in less than a week, the prison experience undid what it had taken the participants a lifetime to learn. It brought out the worst side of human nature. Some, who served as guards, took pleasure in being cruel, while others, who were prisoners, became dehumanized robots.

In the end Zimbardo called off the experiment not only because of the prisoners' and guards' behavior, but because he himself felt absorbed in the role of prison superintendent, losing a grasp of reality and, as he put it, "I could have easily traded places with the most brutal guard or become the weakest prisoner full of hatred at being so powerless . . . I could have been Calley at My Lai, George Jackson at San Quentin, or one of the men at Attica Prison."

Frightening as it was, Zimbardo had found a quality in his own personality that could be swayed to conform to the environment. He concludes that this tendency exists in all of us and that individual behavior is largely determined by social forces and environmental pressures rather than personality traits or character since psychological tests had not predicted such extreme behavior. Zimbardo says that assigning labels to people and then putting them in situations in which the roles are meaningful is enough to cause pathological behavior and that many people can be made to do almost anything when put into psychologically compelling situations—regardless of their morals and values.

The harassment and insult used by the mock prison guards on the prisoners is similar to the psychological tactics used in cults to break people down and separate them from each other, destroying relationships and forcing allegiance to a leader. Cult members may become alienated from other family members and deindividualized through coercion and manipulation. Conversion to one's role in a cult often takes place when an emotional crisis is manufactured and the person is in a panicky, disoriented state. Cults can induce rapid behavioral changes with such tactics; in a matter of days a person can disappear from family and change drastically.

Cult recruiters look for normal people in transition, a freshman at college and alone for the first time; a divorcee without a mate. UC Berkeley Professor Emeritus and cult expert Margaret Singer says cults initially use deception. A presumed meeting of new, potential members turns out later to have been composed of seasoned members of the cult. Cult leaders obtain allegiance one step at a time, very subtly pressuring new members to drop relationships with friends and relatives. Offering recruits a way to cope with their loneliness and alienation, the cult eventually ensnares all in an authoritarian structure.

From the Stanford Prison Experiment, one could conclude that the roles society assigns can sometimes determine behavior more than individual feelings. So, although inside we may feel kind and humane and fair, on the outside we may find ourselves acting in a completely different manner because of environmental pressure. Positions of power such as the guards enjoyed, for example, being a boss or a member of a dominant group, can persuade a person to make unjust decisions. Conversely, a sense of social and psychological oppression can take away the individual's sense of dignity and lower his or her feelings of self-worth. One can get to know oppression through many different avenues—through prejudice, through imprisonment, through being treated unfairly or irrationally by others. We must not underestimate the power of social forces.

Freedom and Aloneness

The importance of freedom is better understood in a historical perspective. Fromm suggests that throughout time human beings have been intent upon breaking the primary bonds that tie them to nature and moving toward independence. To begin with, people are free of the instinctive biological mechanisms that control animals and are therefore more flexible. A key to independence lies in the development of tools that gave primitive people freedom from what had previously been natural restrictions. With spears and knives they could kill larger and faster prey more easily and make clothing and shelter to protect themselves from the elements.

Though we have overcome many of our biological limitations—building houses to protect us from the cold, harnessing energy to produce large amounts of food, using medicines to prevent disease and to extend life—we know this transcendence is only temporary. Human beings are no match for the natural forces that can generate molten lava spewing from volcanoes or earthquakes that devastate entire cities. Eventually grass grows over the buildings people construct. Humans cannot overcome nature nor their own tragic fate, death. We realize that ultimately we are powerless, yet daily we must transcend nature if we are to live creative, productive, satisfying lives.

Throughout life we face the dilemma of being one with, yet separate from, nature. We are separated by our knowledge and through the buildings and structures we create to protect us. At first infants do not perceive themselves as being separate from the environment. They have no sense of their own identity; they are simply one with the world. So, when infants drink orange juice they experience "wet," "cold," "orange." The experience is not separate from an awareness of themselves. There is little differentiation between the orange juice and the child.

But the struggle soon begins to overcome dependency on parents and others. As children grow, they learn to distinguish themselves from other people and eventually to separate their individual identity from culturally defined roles. Eventually they learn they are more than the roles that society assigns. In contrast, a man living in a village centuries ago might define himself by his role, as a male, a warrior, a member of a certain tribe. Just how much have these definitions changed? Go into your college cafeteria and pose the question to someone: "Who are you?" The person you ask may reply, "I'm a student, a mother of two, I live in such and such a city, I'm Hispanic." Yet that's not sufficient; she is more than the sum of these roles. In fact, she may think that if you treat her only in terms of such pre-defined roles, the relationship will indeed be limited. These thoughts may pass through her mind because the modern, urban world emphasizes freedom from traditional culturally defined roles. A prime example is the Women's Movement where women are encouraged to step out of traditional roles. Only as a woman sees herself as separate from her own mother and her children can she think of herself as something more than the role of a wife, homemaker, mother and reach out to express something different that is uniquely hers.

Although discomfort accompanies this sense of separateness, there is potentially much personal reward; we grow by coming to grips with our uniqueness. Fromm says that as we experience and express ourselves emotionally, intellectually and physically, we develop aspects of the self that we were not aware of before, and individuation results. What's more, we learn that we are unique, separate from nature, from our parents, from our country. This separation results in at once the development of the self and feelings of aloneness. We learn that no one but ourselves will ultimately take responsibility for us. We are faced with finding security in ourselves, in our own competencies.

Residents in the vicinity of Three-Mile Island in Pennsylvania, for example, where in the 1970s a nuclear power plant "melted down," came dramatically to realize that they cannot rely on social institutions for their safety or security. Similarly, a study in that same decade showing that in one year 10,000 deaths resulted from over two million unnecessary surgeries prompted Americans to become more personally involved in their own health care and accounted for a surge in the practice of holistic, preventive health care. A whole self-help movement has grown up in which individuals, now aware of the weakness and dangers of institutions, seek to exercise their personal competencies and to take responsibility for themselves.

The way things are, who can we count on to take care of us? Our parents? That only worked when we were children. Our government? What about the toxic substances which people are exposed to? Can we count on doctors to keep us healthy? Isn't anyone out there looking after us?

Well, then, if we're on our own, at least we'd better have an opportunity to develop our own resources.

Unfortunately, modern society doesn't always provide optimum opportunities for self-development. Cultivating the self is a very difficult and delicate task, requiring supportive social, economic and political conditions.

It takes tremendous resources and conditions—absent in much of modern civilization—to cultivate a human being. Fromm says aspects of modern societies are not designed to meet human needs. Several studies, for example, have clarified the effects of modern social forces on the family. To enjoy the quality of life lived by people in the 1950s and 60s, for example, it takes the combined incomes of both parents—and working more hours per week. Twenty-five years ago, one income sufficed for the two required today, and Mom or Dad could stay home with the kids. Today, only 19 percent of children in the U.S. live in two-parent families with only one parent working says Judith Brewer (1995), of the U.S. Population Council.[5] Additionally, marriages are dissolving with increased frequency. In the period 1970–1990, divorce rates doubled in many developed countries.

What are the ramifications of these changes for children? Children in single parent homes are much more likely to be poor and live in impoverished conditions. Steinbury found that latchkey children have more susceptibility to peer pressure and the influence of gangs. When children have less time with parents it is more difficult to learn social skills and loneliness can result.

Many children today say the computer has become their best friend, says Zimbardo, who has been studying shyness for 25 years. "The increasing numbers of shy people mean Americans are lonelier, more alienated and in worse shape, both mentally and physically . . . hardly a prescription for a healthy society," says Zimbardo. He says society needs to reemphasize that the human connection is important.[6]

Where children live in single-parent families, in impoverished conditions, and have little time with responsible parents, or where parents are working multiple jobs just to support themselves and their families, society obviously places little value on human development.

In fact, society's virtues may be contrary to human fulfillment. There are many examples of socially successful people who die personally unfulfilled. Marilyn Monroe became a model of sex and beauty, yet she felt used, became depressed and eventually committed suicide. Howard Hughes—once one of the wealthiest persons in America—died a lonely recluse.

If there is no one ultimately taking care of us, and if we haven't developed our own resources, we're indeed vulnerable, on our own, unprepared for what's in store for us. Yet we are free. But the concept of freedom doesn't really apply if we're lonely, overwhelmed and frightened. Lyrics of a popular song some years ago noted that "freedom's just another word for nothing left to lose." The singer was referring to life without meaning.

What happens to the individual who has not had the opportunity to develop his or her potentials? Freedom makes this person uncomfortable because of an underlying sense of powerlessness. For such a person freedom becomes identical with self-doubt, with a kind of life that lacks meaning and direction; it becomes something from which to escape. Freedom is then experienced as an unbearable burden. By fleeing, a person tries to escape the feelings of powerlessness and aloneness. Fromm describes this negative freedom as "freedom from." He would say the bonds of the past, which once tied the person to friends and family, are broken, yet the individual may not have developed the capabilities to productively use this new-found freedom.

Take the case of fledgling robins. A newborn bird becomes aware that it has been sitting in a nest that is confining. It begins trying desperately to get out. Finally it hops over the edge, free at last from the past, only wide open spaces. It jumps. But wait. Something is wrong. The robin doesn't know how to fly. Its freedom ends abruptly as it falls to the earth, to its death. In this example, the robin achieved "freedom from" the nest, yet did not have "freedom to" fly because it lacked the ability. Anyone can have *freedom from,* which is based on awareness, but *freedom to* is based on competence.

We may express "freedom from" by saying, "no." For example, an individual may declare: "I'm not going to listen to the same music my parents listen to. I'm not going to wear my hair according to society's dictates. I'm not going to be the same kind of person as my father." We now have a clear picture of what this person won't do. "But what *will* you do?" "I don't know," the person may answer. In contrast, when one experiences "freedom to," he or she is able to express—and further develops—the self emotionally, intellectually and creatively.

There is an impulse to try to escape "freedom from," the negative form of freedom, and the accompanying feelings of insignificance and powerlessness. The escape is attempted through submission to people, to institutions or to ideologies. Each promises relief from the uncertainty of being alone and vulnerable. Through complete submission the individual feels secure, no longer overwhelmed by choices that are difficult to evaluate. Nevertheless, submission is costly, for, as Fromm points out, the person loses

Freedom, Aloneness, and Self Growth

Freedom and Aloneness

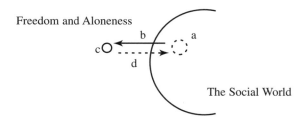

The Social World

In the above diagram, the circles represent the individual. The arrows indicate movement away from, and then toward, the social world.
a. An undifferentiated person who has not distinguished the self from others or the surroundings
b. The person becomes aware of being separate from nature/culture. This is the first step towards freedom of thought and action.
c. Position of person who is undeveloped but now is aware of being a unique, separate entity, alone, and vulnerable in comparison to the world.
d. The impulse to escape the feelings of aloneness by giving up one's self through submission to become one with the world again.

Freedom To Be Oneself

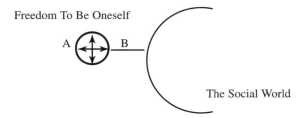

The Social World

In the above diagram, circle A represents the developing self and B represents the relationship between the self and the world.
A. When the society contains adequate social supports to help the person fully develop, the self grows more competent, reducing by comparison the overwhelming powers of the world.
B. The developed individual becomes one with the world again by maintaining the integrity of the self and through consciously expressing the self in personal relationships and work.

individuality, the opportunity to be true to the self—to think and behave independently.

Fromm argues that submission to outside authority ultimately fails because we are irreversibly separate from others. When people become submissive to authority they become angry at having reduced themselves to a childlike dependency. Caught, they project their anger towards the very persons or institutions upon which they are dependent, blaming them, for obviously, "They are the reason I'm crawling on my knees." The leader of a cult may try to deflect this anger by promoting the belief that the group is being threatened by the outside world. But being angry at one's source of security is not a very stable situation. So eventually the person may attack the authority or a substitute. This could help explain the motives behind the murder of San Francisco Mayor George Moscone. His assailant, a city supervisor, became enraged when the mayor failed to reappoint him, although he had previously withdrawn his name from the race. The supervisor had been a supporter of established authority all his life, serving as a policeman and a youth leader. Yet when he eventually found his career at odds with an authority, he became enraged, marched into the mayor's office and, with a gun, shot and killed the mayor. Within two years of being paroled, after serving five years in prison, the former city supervisor took his own life.

Surely the solution to separateness doesn't lie in lashing out at someone else or in giving up one's identity. You overcome a sense of isolation and become one, says Fromm, by participating in the world without giving up yourself. The only productive solution to resolve the feelings of separateness from the world is by expressing oneself through authentic work and relationships. In the long run, says Fromm, the only solution is to become more personally developed.

Belonging

A sense of belonging or unity with others is obtainable through sustained efforts by the individual who is being true to himself or herself; the consequences of being untrue to one's self are personal and social destructiveness such as exploitation, hate, gangs, violence and cults. Taking this responsibility for truth requires personal awareness, development and the continuous cultivation of these qualities. The danger lies in seeking security through others (rather than just enjoying them), which results in the person giving up himself or herself, including the rational capacity to question matters that go against the authentic self.

Fromm says we have a basic conflict between the desire for security and freedom to be ourselves. Traditionally, the need for security has been satisfied through belonging. Infants are one with their parents, seeing themselves through their parents' eyes. As the child grows older their allegiance shifts to their peer group. The security they gain from belonging, being part of the "in group," is usually at the cost of leaving other people out; in other words, an "out group" is needed to define the "in group." Yet consciousness of the self can be muted by a sense of belonging. Fromm observed that the peasant would think of "we" instead of "I," and answer the question of "Who are you?" by describing his or her lineage or group. However, this sense of belonging went so deep, sociologists Snell and Gail Putney say, that it obscured the person's sense of individuality and choice. This happens to the young child who might think of him or herself as mother's little boy or daddy's little girl.

Historically, a sense of belonging was achieved simply by functioning within the society. In fact, traditional society fulfilled the needs of the self though belonging. What the

individual was, they were born into. The individual inherited a sense of community, a place, a vocation. Villagers
would farm the same land for generations. In contrast, modern individuals are intensely aware of creating their own
lives through the choices they make, in terms of career,
community, family.

This change came with the industrial revolution. With
the migration to the city and the advent of the technological
society, one no longer had the same sense of community or
vocation. Now there were so many new possibilities.
Granted, labor saving devices satisfied basic physiological
needs but there was a void in human emotional fulfillment.
The industrial revolution broke down the traditional sense
of extended family, of belonging and ultimately of security.

Many normal, adjusted people in modern society are
still trying to find security through belonging. Seeking
security through belonging can lead to less freedom of
choice. If a person's main motivation is to fit in, this may
prevent candid open associations with people. This lack of
intimacy may result in a sense of isolation. The person may
experience emptiness, loneliness, despair, leaving the individual vulnerable to irrational forces in society, such as
cults. It's almost as though one is in an existential crisis and
left hanging on the edge of an empty universe. One may
give in and conform, yet by doing so obliterate a sense of
self integrity and the opportunity to develop the personal
competencies needed to function in the world.

Irrational Authority

Now suppose that society could get people to give up their
own will and the struggle to be themselves in favor of society's will? What could interrupt the individual's development of growth and competence? Why would anyone

continue to work hard if not to be more fulfilled and happier? Here, Fromm's brilliance illuminates what comes between individuals and their well-being, leading them to reduce their ultimate feelings of fulfillment and happiness by not being true to themselves. The key, says Fromm, is *irrational authority* which is first imposed on us as children by our parents and continues to shape our behavior into adulthood. The child is overcome by guilt based on not pleasing people who are feared. This subtle form of guilt is used to break the youngster's will and to drive the child into submission. The result: the person gives up his or her own will for society's dictates and gives up the struggle to be true to his or her own thoughts, feelings and values. Keep in mind that this guilt is not a genuine moral guilt, which the individual might experience as a result of not living up to one's potentials, but rather is derived from the fear of displeasing someone in authority.

The child may eventually buckle under the authority, giving up the struggle for freedom to be oneself and self-development. Because the individual has not had the opportunity to grow and to strengthen the self, self-confidence is lacking; and so the person may turn to others for security, to feel better about him or herself, and so becomes easy to manipulate.

With such eagerness, Fromm points out, the individual is unlikely to distinguish whether the outside authority is rational, just as the German people failed to distinguish how irrational Hitler was. It was secondary, for he gave them a sense of security.

Let's look at the difference between rational and irrational authority, for this is central to understanding Fromm's theory. An ideal example of *rational authority* is the teacher-student relationship, to which the student chooses to submit in order to become more competent. Eventually the student, with hard work, may become as good or better than the instructor at playing tennis, or whatever skill is being mastered. The student becomes strengthened with the skills, reducing the distinction between the teacher and the pupil. On the other hand, with an irrational authority, such as a slave owner, the slave does not profit from the relationship. The slave grows weaker, less able to break away, while the master is strengthened, intensifying differences between the pair. What's more, the slave does not choose the position, whereas the student does, in order to learn. Once the student has learned a skill the authority relationship automatically dissolves. If the relationship continues, it is based on something other than authority, such as friendship.

Now that we understand these two obvious examples, let's apply them. Are there more subtle forms of irrational authority in everyday life? What about the people with whom we choose to associate? Have you ever wondered why you were drawn to a certain person although, whenever you leave, you feel inferior, incompetent, uncomfortable and less yourself. Was the other person subtly dominating you, manipulating you? Irrational authority can be imposed by individuals or institutions that tell us what to do or believe without keeping our best interests in mind. How can we avoid or at least minimize our contact with irrational authority?

Social Adjustment: At What Price?

Societies may require that people submit to irrational authority. We can suspect, then, to be socially adjusted in Fromm's system, the person may have submitted to irrational authority. If so, the socially adjusted person has given up the fight to be true to the self, saying, "Just give me peace and I'll do whatever is considered normal in my society." If the society is Nazi Germany in 1941, then the socially adjusted person is able to walk innocent people to their deaths in the gas chamber. If the society is urban, competitive and materialistic, socially adjusted members compete with one another for jobs, or for a lane on the freeway, or for dominance in personal relationships, even at the cost of intimacy. Here, Fromm draws an important distinction between the social definition of mental health, which is to be adapted to participate in and help maintain the society, and the individual definition, which involves contributing to one's own ultimate growth and happiness. Therefore an individual may be well-adjusted to society, but not necessarily healthy if the society does not encourage his best interests.

To be *socially adjusted,* the society or group may require its members to incorporate socially patterned defects into their behavior, faults that become socially acceptable because everyone practices them. Socially patterned defects are present when the majority of a society or group does not attain the goals of freedom and spontaneity. If everyone has the same defect, it will not be recognized as such. For example, greed, isolation, detachment, competition and aggressiveness, qualities considered defects in some cultures, are acceptable in our culture. In fact, such defects may help the person fit in and may even be raised to a virtue by society. They may give the person an enhanced feeling of worth and protection from the profound sense of inadequacy and isolation the individual would have otherwise experienced in another time or culture, in which the defective behavior may have been recognized as neurotic. For example, ambition (which our culture values), along with greed, were called forms of insanity by the 17th century Dutch philosopher Benedict Spinoza.

Snell Putney, co-author of *Normal Neurosis,* uses a humorous illustration of a socially patterned defect so engrained in the culture that even a therapist overlooks it. A patient, late for an appointment, proceeds to explain to the therapist that the delay was due to counting lamp posts along the way. The therapist nods in agreement, and says he's often late for the same reason. He can understand that counting lamp posts is important. Our imaginary therapist could well go on to say that he doesn't have time for his children because, besides counting lamp posts, he's busy buying things—bigger TVs, computers and new cars. He wonders why they are unhappy. (Perhaps they need a prescription for drugs.)

What about people fighting to be themselves? How difficult can the struggle be? For some, it may result in *neurosis.* The neurotic hasn't given up the fight against irrational authority to be true to the self, to be independent and exert free will. This person hasn't succeeded yet at developing individuality, but still refuses to submit, unwilling to give up the struggle to maintain integrity. Such a person may seem confused, perhaps destructive, often battling against all authority, unable to distinguish the rational from the irrational. The difficulty is that by fighting rational authority, he or she may delay the development of personal competence. For the neurotic, the cost of not being submissive to society is a tremendous sense of isolation and feeling of inadequacy. We can see that the neurotic and the socially adjusted person are both unfulfilled, but thankfully there is a third choice. Where the socially adjusted person buckles under and the neurotic keeps fighting, the healthy person wins. Remember, Fromm defines *healthy* people as those who contribute to their own optimal growth and happiness. They have achieved some degree of fulfillment and are able to distinguish what's good for them. They are inner-directed. This sense of purpose is not limited to self-absorption but includes a concern for others that contributes to one's quality of life. The importance which Fromm attributes to the personal cultivation of a concern and love for others is reflected in his book *The Art of Loving*. Healthy persons are free to exert their own will, to be creative, to make and cultivate personal commitments and through this self-expression to transcend their culture and their past. They have clearly defined the self to minimize participating in activities that would undermine their self-esteem and development.

The first thing that may become obvious to people working to be themselves is the subtle pressure from friends and relatives who find their cultural assumptions being questioned. For example, you may question materialism and defer from buying a new car or the latest clothes or furnishings. Even all the cooking apparatus being marketed (separate machines to knead bread, to cook hot dogs or popcorn while many people have cooked with just a few simple pots), an example of the culture's preoccupation with material, doesn't appeal to you. So, you assert yourself, refusing to buy the latest gadget everyone is using and you're not even enthused about microwave ovens, beepers or cellular telephones. Suddenly you're doing things that aren't considered normal: serving meals to the homeless, taking a course in yoga or traveling to another country. You throw others off balance, your plans make them think about their lives and some of their own unfilled wishes that they've put aside in order to fit in the culture.

Defense Mechanisms or the Means of Escaping From Freedom

In a society that discourages self-development, individuals don't learn how to creatively express themselves. Rather,

they are in a constant state of anxiety, reacting, overwhelmed by the magnitude of the problems the world seems
to hurl at them, in contrast to their limited resources. How
do people cope with such feelings that seem very common
in our society? Fromm says there are three defense mechanisms a person may develop to escape the anxiety of freedom: the first is based on authority and power, the second
on destructiveness and the third on conformity.

Authoritarianism.   The first defense mechanism is authoritarianism, a blind obedience to authority. The *authoritarian
personality* gives up individuality in favor of fusing with
someone or something in order to gain the strength which is
lacking. Such a person might lose him or herself in a political party, such as the Nazis, and give up personal will for the
will of the party. The goal is to escape feelings of insignificance and aloneness that come from experiencing the negative side of freedom.

The Sadist and the Masochist.   The authoritarian
personality has two aspects: the masochist and the sadist.
Both qualities emphasize power: the *sadist* tries to dominate others while the *masochist* seeks to submit to someone
or something powerful. For the authoritarian, there are two
groups of people in the world: the powerful and the weak.
The powerful are automatically to be loved and submitted
to, whether or not they are just. The sadist feels contempt
for the weak; they are to be attacked, dominated, humiliated, exploited. The weak may include the poor, the handicapped, children, the elderly and minorities. The sadist may
strive for absolute rule and, in the most extreme cases,
wishes to make others suffer. Meanwhile, the masochist
seeks someone to submit to, and takes pleasure in being
dominated.

Yet for all their differences, these two characters are much the same. Both seek to unite the self with an outside power; to give up their individuality. The masochist uses submission and the sadist uses dominance as a means to escape the unbearable isolation they feel. They are both dependent on another person or a social cause to feel good about themselves. To escape feelings of insignificance, the masochist lets others swallow him or her up, while, in the second case, the sadist does the swallowing or incorporating to enhance the self and consequently lose the integrity of the self.

Some people use marriage to escape feelings of aloneness and powerlessness. In fact, in certain relationships, the masochistic tendencies of submission and the sadistic tendencies of dominance become the overriding theme. A husband, for example, may try to be a "big man," resourceful and powerful, dominating and taking care of the "little woman" to inflate his own image while "the little woman" wants to be controlled to gain the strength she lacks.

In the following case, a sadistic husband really needs his wife to feel powerful: Bob, a domineering type, beats his wife Sally, telling her, "I don't need you; I don't need anyone." One day Sally decides to leave. Suddenly Bob is transformed. He begs her to stay, trying to convince her he loves her, he tells her he'll change. He exhibits a surprising dependency because he needs his wife to dominate so he won't feel alone and anxious. If she stays with him, he may, of course, revert to his previous behavior. Actually, physical strength is not the only means to dominate someone. A sadistic wife can dominate her husband emotionally by belittling him, telling him he always does everything wrong.

Cult Appeal. Let's apply Fromm's theory to try to understand why people join cults. In a cult, members are submissive to a leader who promises security and relief from feelings of anxiety and aloneness. Both the leader and followers escape isolation at the cost of being true to themselves. Let's see then how well this model fits three major cults of modern times.

In cults such as Heaven's Gate, Branch Davidians or the People's Temple, leaders promised their followers a better way of life, a way out of their difficulties. Marshall Herff Applewhite promised his followers a higher plane of existence. Former followers who dropped out of the Heaven's Gate cult, for example, recount how the group thought earth was becoming increasingly inhospitable.

According to Dr. Singer's research, cult members are slowly persuaded to give up freedom of thought through programs of coercive behavior, thought control, and isolation. Violations of the rules in the Heaven's Gate cult included judging for one's self and becoming personally involved with others. This isolation included giving up contact with the outside world. Their computer business web site, called "Higher Source," allowed them to support themselves in relative isolation. In its early days, members were told to wear black hoods, to speak only a cursory "Yes," "No," or "Maybe" to one another, and to associate with only one other person. Later they dressed uniformly and in a unisex fashion, with baggy jeans and short hair cuts. Members were discouraged from any sexual activity. According to Singer, in 1978 Applewhite told his followers to be prepared to face murder and suicide in order to follow him, and to be beamed up by a spaceship. The current interest in science fiction shows may have contributed to Applewhite's success at convincing his followers to join a spaceship he said was following the comet Hale-Bopp. Each had $5 in his or her pocket and a small suitcase packed for the "journey." All had died from poisoning and asphyxiation in a mansion outside of San Diego, their bodies lying neatly on their individual beds, covered by purple shrouds.

Only four years earlier in Waco, Texas, members of the Branch Davidians believed their leader, David Koresh, to be an angel, who predicted they must defend themselves from the end of the world. To make members more dependent on his authority, he separated family members, forbidding mothers and daughters from talking to one another, and requiring further submission by controlling the group's sexual activity.

Everyone outside the cult was considered an "outsider" and a potential enemy—particularly family members. Calculated isolation took over cult members. Koresh developed a crisis mentality among followers by depriving members of food and sleep, as he spoke for hours about the impending end of the world.

Believing the end to be imminent, he convinced 100 followers, and their children, to hole up inside a compound with enough guns and ammunition to wage a small war against federal agents. Koresh's alleged arms buildup and abuse of children prompted the Treasury Department's initial attack. It ended when fire swept through the building during a raid by federal agents. In the aftermath there were 86 dead cult members and four dead federal agents.

Now consider the most tragic cult of modern times, the People's Temple, which led to the largest murder-suicide of 913 people in the jungles of Guyana. In San Francisco, the Reverend Jim Jones had attracted a group of people who were inspired by his idealism, his appeal to brotherhood and social justice. His charismatic leadership gave church members the hope that they could change themselves and the world. To achieve this they put Jones' idealism ahead of themselves—individuals and families became submissive to his authority. His congregation surrendered their possessions and money to Jones in exchange for security and direction.

What happened to the ideal world People's Temple members set about to build, first in their church in San Francisco, and then later in a commune called Jonestown in Guyana? What went wrong? One contributing factor may be that once members went to Guyana they gave up all contact with their former daily lives and the outside world. The members' lives were completely controlled, they were told when they could eat, work and sleep. Jones' authority was absolute; it could not be questioned even if irrational. Initially inspired by his idealism, People's Temple members gave their total allegiance to Jones, even when he was at odds with truth and freedom.

In Guyana, the sporadic incidents of Jones' abuse of his power multiplied. He sexually exploited women in his congregation, had members beaten and called himself God. In Jonestown, there was no other authority but Jones. Like the guards in the Stanford prison experiment, he became absorbed in his role, pulled into the world he had created, where he eventually succumbed to an inflated view of his own powers. According to Fromm's theory, Jones had sadistic tendencies, striving to dominate and incorporate his following to enlarge himself.

Jones manipulated his followers, pretending specifically he had poisoned them to test their commitment. Initially they were terrified, but then became desensitized to the thought of taking their lives.

When authorities came to verify reports that Jonestown members were being held captive, unable to return to their families in California, Jones ordered both the murder of a congressman who was investigating his church and the mass suicide of his followers telling them that the world was too corrupt for them to stay in it any longer. As the ultimate act of submission to his irrational authority, members went against their instincts of self-preservation and drank cyanide, even going so far as to order their young children to follow. Those few who refused suicide were murdered by other cult members. A few days later authorities found over 900 bodies stacked in the hot Guyanese sun. The members' submission to Jones had allowed them to momentarily find meaning in life, escaping feelings of powerlessness and anxiety over being alone in the universe, but ultimately, it cost them and their children their lives. Today, some of the deaths in Jonestown are being called a mass murder rather than suicide.

What leads people to give up thinking for themselves? Similar to the prisoners in Zimbardo's study, who defined themselves by their roles and were unable to walk away from the mock prison, cult members could not separate themselves from the roles assigned by their leader.

According to Fromm, people may give up their own thoughts, feelings and will—the struggle to be oneself—to conform to the dictates of society or a group. If the overriding motivation to join a group is to get away from the loneliness and lack of meaning in life, then members are not in a position to question, to risk no longer belonging, and to be out on their own.

What are the common elements of these three cults? They are led by an inspiring leader who gives hope, meaning and group membership to overcome feelings of insignificance and a life without meaning. Cult members believe they are part of something important from which they draw the strength that is lacking individually. In exchange for security and direction, absolute submission, conformity in thought and behavior, is required by all members. The leader, as well, strives to escape similar feelings of alienation and insignificance, to achieve a sense of wholeness by dominating his followers. He requires that the members show total allegiance, by separating from family members and giving up all contact with the outside world. By increasing the isolation of the members, their dependency on the leader to feel good about themselves becomes more complete. When a "crisis" emerges the person has little recourse but to follow the direction of the leader.

Fromm says submission is costly, for cult members lose their individuality, the opportunity to think, behave independently and be true to the self. Having given up control of themselves, we can see why cult members submit to the dictates of their leader, even giving up their lives.

Destructiveness. The second defense mechanism is destructiveness. Fromm says that destructiveness occurs when the person is unable to creatively express the self. The more satisfied the individual is with life, the less likely the urge to destroy. But what about the reverse? A thwarted, isolated individual may become destructive to escape the feeling of powerlessness. Fromm explains destruction as the last, desperate attempt to save the self by removing all objects with which individuals can compare themselves. Through violent revolution and terrorism, an individual obliterates ideals, people and institutions that might otherwise form a basis for comparison. An extreme example is the doctrine of nihilism, which maintains that social organizations are so bad that destruction is desirable for its own sake. If a person cannot establish a successful relationship, he or she may try to destroy it. Through destruction, the person feels superior, in control; free of the challenge of the relationship.

Let's apply Fromm's theory to the growing wave of terrorism. For example, consider the case of Timothy McVeigh. Trying to gain a sense of importance and overcome a feeling of powerlessness, the veteran of the Gulf War blew up the Oklahoma City federal building in 1996, killing 168 people. He said he thought revenge should be taken for the government's actions in Waco, Texas. What motivates a person to indiscriminately murder people? Building on Fromm's theory about destruction, the terrorist is responding to a sense of alienation. As terrorists see it, the world pushes them around, they feel powerless, with no creative channels open. To retaliate, they destroy the things, including people, that make them feel worthless.

Similarly, the defense mechanism of destructiveness can help us understand another terrorist, the Unabomber. For more than 17 years the Unabomber was on a killing spree annihilating people via letter bombs that exploded when opened. Three people were killed and 23 injured by his bombs.

Theodore Kaczinski, the Unabomber suspect, formerly a University of California, Berkeley professor, lived in extreme isolation, writing that he never made a friend during his entire adult life. "For 37 years I've desired a woman. I've wanted desperately to find a girlfriend or wife but have never been able to . . . because I lack the necessary social self-confidence and social skills."

He wrote, "This fear of rejection, based on bitter experience both at home and at school, has ruined my life, except for the few years that I spent alone in the woods, largely out of contact with people." Kaczinski, like McVeigh, was raising his sense of self importance, overcoming a sense of isolation, by seeing himself as a hero battling against modern social forces for the benefit of others. Kaczinski believed he was struggling against technology to protect people and McVeigh thought he was avenging the lives lost in Waco, Texas and hoping others would join him in a revolution.

Lacking the opportunity to develop social skills, Kaczinski seemed overwhelmed by his fear and loneliness and may have become destructive to destroy the comparison between himself and others.

According to Fromm, a person who missed the opportunity to become a fully developed human being may have only the awareness of "freedom from," the freedom to negate, but lack the competencies of "freedom to," which is necessary to contribute constructively. Destructiveness is one defense mechanism a person may use as a result of experiencing the aloneness of being separate in the modern world without the opportunity to develop the self.

Conformity. The third means of escaping freedom is through conformity. People try to escape the sense of loneliness and alienation they feel by conforming, by minimizing the differences between themselves and others. After all, the more we seem like others, whether it be the way we wear our hair, our clothes or the way we act or think, the more we feel part of a group and less alone—but at the cost of our individuality. People try to protect themselves from freedom by conforming. When they conform, they blend into the social landscape, camouflaged like a chameleon that changes color to protect itself.

Conformity is encouraged in our culture. What are some of the mechanisms that encourage it? The mass media—especially television—give us instantaneous images of not only how our peers across the country, and even across the world, are dressing and acting. It makes it very easy to find and fit into a mold.

Even the education process can encourage conformity by suppressing critical thinking. In school, a teacher may ask a child, "What do you think about this?" The child responds, "I think such and such." The teacher says "No, that's the wrong answer." Yet the teacher asked for the child's thoughts. The child used the power of critical thinking which, in this case, the teacher discouraged. Or, consider what happens when a girl named Tina one day decides to stay home from school. Her grandmother says children should always want to go to school. Yet, all of us know that, even though we may like school, no one always wants to go to school. The child learns to act as though she always wants to go to school and to repress her real feelings. She is pressured into thinking she wants something, mistaking society's will for her own. How often do we feel pressured to "want" something because others tell us so?

Consider who uses the power of critical thinking in the following case. Curious about the weather, you ask two different people whether they think it will rain. First, a crusty, old man sitting by a lake responds, "My arthritis has been bothering me in one knee. The birds have been flying in circles at the end of the lake and there's a breeze." You say, "Never mind, I want to know if it will rain." He says, "I'm getting to that. Yes, the way the birds have been acting I think it's going to rain." The second person you ask says, "There's a low pressure area moving in with winds reported at about 25 miles per hour. The barometer measures 29.3 and there's an 80 percent chance of rain."

Although this person can spew off the latest television weather report as though he was a tape recorder, it is the old man who is thinking, feeling, using his own life experience. The other person's thinking has conformed to the electronic media's interpretation of the weather.

A subtle kind of conformity can take place when an individual is pressured into thinking he or she wants something, mistaking society's or a group's will for one's own. Fromm describes a premed student who entered therapy because he was failing his medical courses, yet passing other equally difficult classes unrelated to his major. Through counseling, he discovered that he didn't want to become a doctor, that he had mistaken his family's wishes for his own.

The cost of conformity is losing touch with the real self, with one's individuality. The individual who conforms—acting, thinking and dressing like members of a group—is unable to express his or her personal self. Conformity blunts the original thoughts and feelings that distinguish people from one another and make them unique. Conformity prevents the kind of experimentation that is necessary for the development of the self and for developing a sense of security based on competence. At some level, an individual who conforms may become increasingly insecure by relying on stereotyped answers rather than developing the personal skills necessary to arrive at real solutions.

Would You Electrocute Another Person?
Stanley Milgram's Obedience Study

Do you think there's much chance you would electrocute a stranger if you thought it was for science and were paid $4.50 to do it?

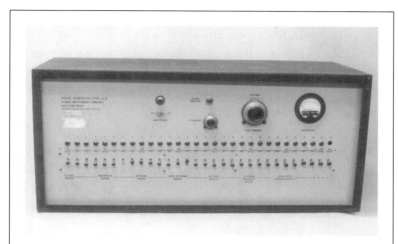

This is the shock generator Milgram built. The subject used it to "shock" a victim when the latter made an error. Depressing a switch illuminates a bright red light. Subjects were caught in a situational force, continuing to depress switches at increasingly higher voltage levels, sometimes all the way up to 450 volts. *Courtesy of Archives of the History of American Psychology, University of Akron.*

Stanley Milgram, a social psychologist at Yale University, wanted to find out just how many people were willing to electrocute a subject who screamed and protested in pain. The motivation for his study was to test obedience. Milgram, who is Jewish, also wanted to find out why the Germans had blindly obeyed Hitler's instructions to incinerate millions of people. He thought it was a character flaw in the German people, a blind obedience to authority, and set out to prove that people were different in the United States—at least that was the plan.

So he took out an ad in a local newspaper for paid volunteers to help administer a learning experiment. Since

Milgram had only limited resources to start with, a $300 grant, he built his own authentic-looking electric-shock generator complete with a graduated scale ranging from 15 to 450 volts and written descriptions of shock intensity ranging from "Slight Shock" to "Intense Shock" to "Danger: Severe Shock."

The experimenter told the subjects they were taking part in a study of learning and memory and that they would be "teaching" concepts to others. The "teacher" was told to give the learner an electric shock of increasing intensity when he made a mistake on a learning test. The "learner," who actually worked for the experimenter, would gasp and groan when the shock buttons were pushed, although no shock was actually given. The learner's screams increased as the shock supposedly became more intense and he even pleaded with the "teacher" about his heart condition. Even so, more than 50 percent of the subjects obeyed the experimenter and pushed the current all the way to 450 volts in spite of the victim's protest and his eventual silence indicating his presumable death from the shock.

Why did some subjects continue to apply shock? There were no threats or force used, no guns pointed at them, no handcuffs; there was no great financial gain; in short, no rational reason. They appeared to be normal, nice people who had empathy for the victim. When the victim screamed that he couldn't stand the pain, the teacher was up and out of the chair, protesting, telling the experimenter they shouldn't continue. Yet, when the experimenter said "The experiment must go on," many subjects yielded. Amazingly, out of compliance, subjects presumably shocked other people to death rather than defy authority.

What defense mechanisms did the subjects exhibit? First, authoritarianism, a blind obedience to authority, even if it was irrational. Second, conformity. They conformed to the experimenter's expectations.

Milgram says that it was much more difficult to get the teachers to disobey than he anticipated. He had the learner loudly protest and scream as he was being shocked so that the teacher would disobey.

"We didn't get disobedience," explains Milgram. "It really was the first finding: that obedience would be much greater than we had assumed it would be and disobedience would be much more difficult than we had assumed."

Sixty-five percent of the subjects—American men between the ages of 20 and 50—showed absolute obedience and shocked the learner all the way up to 450 volts.

How does Milgram explain such obedience?

He says that the subjects are locked into a structure from which they do not have the skills or inner resources to disengage themselves. Such people are transformed. They see themselves as carrying out someone else's wishes rather than acting on their own.

The structure of a situation can lead people to do unexpected things. Milgram's explanation is key to understanding how people can get caught up in the moment. As the subjects continued delivering more shock, they found it even more difficult to separate themselves from the situation by disobeying. Once they had shocked the learner with 75 volts of electricity, why not go all the way and deliver 90, 150 or 450 volts, as they were instructed? This is an example of a *situational force*. Situations can develop their own momentum in which the dominant motivating force is not within the person, but within the environment. In Milgram's study, even though the subjects didn't want to continue to shock the learners, their behavior was determined more by external pressure than by the internal authority of their own

Stanley Milgram used a shock generator to demonstrate obedience to authority. *Courtesy of the Archives of the History of American Psychology, University of Akron.*

values. They were more concerned with obeying the experimenter than they were about hurting the learners. As Zimbardo said about the Stanford prison experiment, psychologically compelling situations can lead many people to do things they don't really believe in, in spite of their convictions.

This can help us to understand how the Nazi authorities held such power over the German people, who stood by while innocent people were murdered. In the early 1930s as Hitler's power base grew, the situation gained momentum, so that when the Nazis finally demanded outrageous acts of submission from their countrymen, they had already gained total compliance. From his experiment, Milgram learned that blind obedience to authority wasn't unique to the German character. This experiment was later repeated with women and undergraduate students and yielded similar results.

In an experiment using Milgram's teacher-learner model, Brant, demonstrated that racial discrimination may interact with situational forces, by showing that white subjects had a greater willingness to shock a black rather than a white victim. However, in a later study, Rogers and Prentice-Dunn discovered this relationship was more complex. Initially, they found the opposite, that unless there was a threat involved, white college students actually gave lower levels of shock to black students. But, when white students felt insulted by either a black or white student, they tended to give the black student the stronger shock. So even with changing social norms, people can revert to racism, when they feel threatened.

Believing that one is only slightly shocking a person may, by small steps, draw the subject into compliance, just as cult leaders slowly gained the trust and allegiance of their followers. In Milgram's study the participants' cooperation was obtained by beginning the experiment at a low voltage and presumably increasing the shock 15 volts at a time.

What impact could situational forces have upon the deaths of cult members? Could situational forces have been a factor in the tragedy at Waco, Texas, where Branch Davidian cult members refused to leave their compound while federal agents, intent on saving children and adults from Koresh's leadership, eventually stormed the compound? After almost two months of waiting, did the agents feel pressured to gain control of the compound and its members? Was it situational force that prompted the Federal Bureau of Investigation to attack with tanks and tear gas to end the 51-day standoff? Authorities were later criticized by the government for aggravating the situation.

It's interesting to think of situational forces in terms of our own lives. Have you ever been caught up in a situation? For instance, people sometimes get absorbed by their career, caught in the momentum of their job and the potential upward mobility. As they become engrossed in fulfilling their job role, they may neglect other aspects of their life, such as their children, because, as the boss says "the job has to go on," much as in the Milgram study where the experimenter emphasized "the study must go on." If we look back at Zimbardo's prison experiment, we can see that the guards were caught in a situational force. They had a job to do—to maintain a prison—the prison had to go on. There are times in our lives when a situational force may make us feel that we are being swept away, that we've lost control. In such instances, a break such as a vacation from one's environment, is particularly helpful in allowing one to stand back and reevaluate choices.

Also, participation in destructive activity can actually reduce the level of personal functioning. In a thought-provoking study using Milgram's shock model, Buss and Brock found that subjects who delivered shock when they didn't believe in using it were diminished in their ability to remember information about the destructive effects of shock. In other words, in terms of ego strength, their impaired memory reduced them as people.

From Milgram's study we can predict human behavior and understand, for instance, how a few destructive people can surround themselves with obedient people and can exercise great power. The Reverend Jones, for example, encircled himself with guards who would carry out his commands, much as the subjects enforced the experimenter's commands in the Milgram study. Through the guards, Jones was able to control the members of his group who were unwilling to kill themselves; the guards forced them to drink the cyanide. Lacking an acceptable image of themselves as separate from their leader, the guards were incapable of walking away no matter how bad the situation became.

Milgram concludes that, if the request comes from a seeming legitimate "authority," many people will do what they are told, regardless of the consequences. This means that government, for example, with its prestige and power, has a great deal of authority over citizens.

Milgram raises the issue of whether, at a certain point, people have a moral responsibility to disobey if obedience means giving up one's convictions. In Fromm's context, one way to resolve such a conflict is to think of the situation in terms of irrational or rational authority. Does it contribute to the overall good of people or is it destructive?

Obedience to irrational authority is not dependent on education or professional skills. Members in both the Heaven's Gate cult and a Japanese cult whose members killed 12 people on a crowded Tokyo subway in 1995 were well-educated. Japanese citizens, in fact, were troubled that the Aum Shinri Kyo Cult had attracted some of Japan's most brilliant students, as well as Ikuo Hayashi, a distinguished heart surgeon who trained in the United States and who actually released the deadly nerve gas.

Conclusion

Let's summarize. In this chapter, we've seen that the environment can have a significant effect on how we feel about ourselves and treat one another. Human behavior is determined not only by internal factors, but also by roles in which we find ourselves. The social environment may not always encourage our growth; in fact, irrational authority may hold us back from developing our potential. For example, dominating friends may not encourage us to expand in directions different from their goals. We may think of ourselves according to how others perceive us, whether they tell us we're intelligent or slow, attractive or homely. It's not always easy to separate who we are from our social environment.

If the personality is denied the opportunity to develop, it becomes vulnerable to subtle intimidation and manipulation by negative social forces that may further reduce the level of personality functioning. According to Fromm's theory, freedom can become a burden from which the undeveloped personality seeks to escape through conformity, submission to outside authority or through destructiveness.

Zimbardo's prison experiment and Milgram's obedience study illustrate that in certain social environments destructive behavior can be produced. Such studies are converging to redefine our view of human nature. No longer can we look at people as being evil or possessed. According to these social psychologists, destructiveness, to a large extent, is a reflection of the environment. Fromm therefore would say that in order to reduce violence in our environment social institutions must be changed.

What can we do to avoid getting caught up in the roles and pressures exerted on us by our social environment? A central concept for Fromm is to develop the ability to distinguish rational from irrational authority. If we can differentiate the competent leader from the manipulating would-be leader who maintains power by merely deceiving, intimidating or dominating us against our interests, we can make the world a better, more rational place for human development. In other words, we do not reflexively reject all authority, for if we do, we lose an avenue of growth.

Feelings of anxiety and insecurity make us vulnerable to irrational authority. Cults appeal to many who want to overcome feelings of aloneness. Jonestown followers turned to the People's Temple for security. Applewhite relieved his followers' anxiety by promising a transformation to life in another world. The subjects in the Milgram study went along with the authority to avoid anxiety. Yet, turning one's life or one's freedom of choice over to someone else, as in Milgram's study, only temporarily relieves the feelings of anxiety and aloneness.

Where can we find security? It's easy to be part of a group. We can find a sense of belonging at any time as long as we give up our allegiance to ourselves. Yet, we've seen the weakness of exchanging the development of personal competence for a temporary security based on submission to authority. Rather than giving up one's individuality in a relationship or to a group, Fromm says the solution to aloneness lies in becoming one with the world; through participating in meaningful activity and deep relationships with others, which give us the opportunity to express and develop our authentic self. In short, Fromm encourages us to see freedom as an opportunity to meaningfully direct our lives.

As we develop our own self-concept more clearly, we can better evaluate our roles, determine whether they limit our growth and, if necessary, redefine them to more fully express ourselves. With an accurate self-image, we're less likely to unwittingly do things against our own growth and fulfillment. The healthy person is defined in terms of optimal growth and happiness, rather than simply what society expects. Fromm says this individual growth requires that society make human development its priority.

What does this chapter mean to our individual lives? According to Fromm, as healthy individuals:

1. We would only participate in activities that are rational, or in other words, that contribute to our self-concept, personal well-being or relationships.

2. We would be in touch with our own feelings to a greater degree and be less vulnerable to being intimidated. As a result, we would have a greater opportunity to experience, be aware of, and develop what is unique in each of us.

3. We would have a more constant sense of being true to ourselves and the joy that comes from it.

4. We would be in a better position to pull out of relationships or groups that become destructive because we would be more conscious of our unique self.

5. It would be easier for us to more spontaneously express our individuality and to be ourselves in deep and meaningful relationships.

6. We wouldn't be so easily caught up in fads that waste our time and resources.

7. If we became a leader or employer, we might be able to get more constructive work from people because they'd feel their interests were being considered and that they were being treated with respect. Similarly, one's spouse and children would feel they could express themselves because they were being treated in terms of their uniqueness and individuality.

CHAPTER SIX

Jungian Psychology

The Universal Language of the Unconscious: Carl Jung's Theory

A. The Collective Unconscious
B. Dreams
C. Opposites
D. The Four Functions
    1. Thinking
    2. Feeling
    3. Sensation
    4. Intuition
E. Archetypes
    1. The Anima and the Animus
    2. The Persona and the Shadow
    3. The Wise Old Man and the Wise Old Woman
    4. Archetype Summary
F. Compensatory Guide
G. Symbols
H. Myths
    1. The Hero Myth
I. Fairy Tales
J. The Individuation Process

The Universal Language
of the Unconscious

A young lad named Carl Jung growing up in Switzerland in the late 1880's used to wonder why he felt as though he were two different people inside. His number one personality was the boy who did what society expected of him, was polite and courteous, attended school, took on the roles and values of his society. Yet he had a growing awareness that there was someone else inside of him besides his social self. He called this entity his number two personality. Number Two lived outside of time and space. He wasn't concerned with going to school, or fitting into Swiss culture. He was immeasurably wiser and greater than young Carl. The number two personality possessed uncanny knowledge, he had great dreams and visions of the world. His imagination produced beautiful, profound images which Carl had never seen before in his life. There was no question of right and wrong for Number Two; somehow he was in touch with eternal values. Number Two wasn't bothered by being slighted by society as was the number one personality of Carl. Number Two had such a sense of well-being that young Carl longed to penetrate this side of his nature. In fact, he chose, as his life goal, to bring these two personalities together.[1]

The psychiatrist Carl Jung is thought by many to be one of the greatest thinkers of the twentieth century. For those who feel a sense of alienation in the modern world, that material success, money, possessions and status don't answer a deeper, more spiritual need, he speaks clearly.

"The meaning of life is not exhaustively explained by one's business life, nor is the deepest desire of the human heart answered by a bank account."[2]

Rather than searching the outside world for meaning, Jung says that the answers are within each of us, just below consciousness, in our number two personality.

The number two personality dwells in the unconscious. In Jung's view the unconscious contains a great guide, friend and advisor to the conscious, the number one personality. The unconscious is one's internal world. It represents the soul. It knows far more than we see in our rational world. It is the source of psychic wisdom and insight.

So the unconscious is much more than a refuse bin for unresolved childhood experiences as it was for Freud. Jung says it also includes the positive aspects of human nature, of a more spiritual, universal self.

Remember the song, "I want to be me, to do or to die, I want to be me"? The songwriter speaks to us of a very personal search to discover what is one's own unique personal scheme for life.

Jung embarked on this search through getting to know his number two personality. He learned that within the psyche is an individual plan for each of us, a "secret design for life" as he calls it.

It is not surprising then, that central to Jung's work is the idea that each person is one of a kind—with his or her own direction. By getting to know the unconscious we can learn how to fulfill our own unique destiny, to maximize our personal development.

When the individual says, "I want to be me," at some level the person becomes aware that something more than the conscious "me" exists, something more than one's everyday motives of sociability, materialism and power. In order to discover the number two self one must try to get to a deeper, more basic form of existence and yield to the power of the unconscious.

The Collective Unconscious

There is within the unconscious, says Jung, a source of great wisdom, a memory of human experience called the *collective unconscious*. Just as the body design we've inherited from our species is thousands of years old, so are aspects of our personalities. Instincts, urges, predispositions, are all inherited, as is the collective unconscious. Jung believed that if we listen to the wisdom of the collective unconscious, which has insights and understandings gained through thousands of years of human evolution, our lives will be far richer.

The collective unconscious manifests itself in symbols. Jung explains that these recurring symbols emerge in cultures around the world which are isolated from one another. For instance, the cross has been used not only by the Christians, but by the Greeks 4000 years ago.

Dreams

Jung once had a patient involved in dishonest business who had taken up rather dangerous mountain climbing. He recounted to Jung a recurring dream he had of walking off a mountain top. Jung asked him to stop mountain climbing immediately. The patient refused. A few months later the

Symbols recur throughout many cultures. Although variations of
such figures are found in different historical times and cultures,
their symbolic meaning is similar. This cross-shaped figure was
made by Greeks 4000 years ago, 2000 years before Christianity.
Notice the crucifix around the neck of the stone figure.

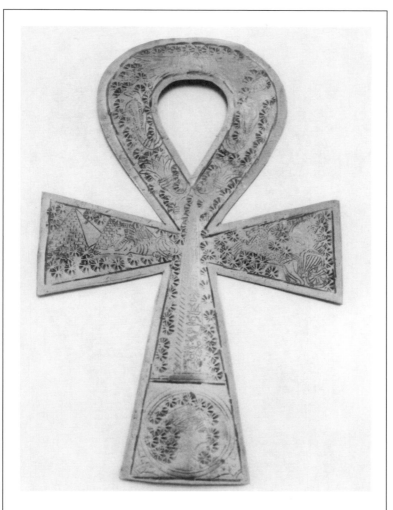

Note the similarity of both these figures (the Greek cross-shaped figure and the African fertility doll on the next page) to the ankh. The ankh is an ancient Egyptian symbol designating the divine power that supports both life on earth and life after death. It is often found in relief on temple walls, tombs and inscriptions, often in the hands of a god or goddess. Ankhs were one of the objects most frequently placed in tombs.

Fertility dolls in the shape of the cross are used in Africa today.
These dolls are given to young girls as toys to learn of motherhood. When a woman becomes married she carries a doll in the
small of her back wrapped in her clothing in order to help her
become pregnant and to assure a healthy and beautiful child. If
she never bears children the figure is buried with her to assure
better fortune in the next life. *Courtesy of African Museum,
Washington, DC.*

man died in a mountain climbing accident. His friend described how he let go of the rope "as if he were jumping into the air."[3]

According to Jung the unconscious knows far more than we see in our everyday lives. This man's dreams had great meaning for him. His disregard cost him his life. He took up mountain climbing to literally "get above" or transcend his shady business dealings. His dream warned him of the danger in his present lifestyle. Jung says if the warnings of dreams are disregarded, real accidents can take place.

The unconscious does much of its communication with us in our sleep while we are free of the restrictions which our conscious mind imposes upon us. The dream is a very personal expression from the person's unconscious—a direct and meaningful communication to the dreamer. Dreams are not only significant to the immediate life of the dreamer. They are part of the internal regulating process which directs psychic growth, part of the great lifetime plan of individuation. They can help the dreamer develop attitudes and wisdom which will help throughout life. Through bringing dreams into consciousness the conscious learns to know and respect the unconscious so that the individual becomes whole, integrated, calm and happy. Gradually a wiser and more mature person emerges.

The number two personality, which Jung refers to as the *Self,* is very different from the conscious personality. It is an inner guide which can be grasped best by studying one's dreams. The Self brings about continuous personality growth. At first this aspect of the psyche may appear as merely an inborn possibility:

> It may emerge very slightly, or it may develop relatively completely during one's lifetime. How far it

develops depends on whether or not the ego is willing
to listen to the messages of the self.[4]

The Self is the organizing center, the totality of the
whole psyche. It is the inventor and source of images in
dreams. As the individual becomes more receptive to listening to dreams, the dreams get better and more helpful, the
inborn Self becomes more real and the person becomes a
more complete human being.

Among the main reasons the unconscious design for
our individual lives seems unavailable is because society
discourages cultivating the number two self. The trouble
with listening strictly to the conscious "me" is that its sense
of itself and its potentials has been limited by socialization.
The child is taught how to feel and how to respond to life,
to fit into culturally defined categories.

The youngster's feelings are often capped by a society
which looks at life very matter-of-factly in terms of an impersonal language of scientific data. The adult world gives
names and statistics to what were once uninterrupted emotional experiences. In this process civilization strips events
of their vitality and power to move us. The intense experiences of ecstasy which the youngster knows, playing on the
beach or petting an animal, are controlled and diluted.
Gazing at the beauty of a peacock is no longer purely an
emotional experience. It is interrupted with information
about the bird: "It is called a peacock; it weighs about 35
pounds." Yet this description does not convey the excitement and awe one feels when the bird displays its plumage
or a sense of its spirit.

Normally we fail to acknowledge the spirituality of an
experience, relying on objective data. Many of the would-
be uninterrupted emotional experiences are boxed up and

buffered by society. Without this emotional energy events and people in our lives may not make a deep impression. So our one-to-one interaction with the world has been objectified.

Our immediacy of contact with nature has gone and with it the "profound emotional energy that it supplied," says Jung. For example: "We refer to the world as 'matter,' a dried intellectual concept with no great meaning such as Mother Earth. What was the spirit is now intellect and ceases to be the Father of us all."[5]

What is an intense experience in the wild, the kill, becomes emotionless, bland and matter-of-fact in the city. The stalking hunter knows excitement, fear, a sense of survival and sacrifice through the loss of an animal's life. In contrast, the urban children who go to McDonald's to eat a "Big Mac" or a "Quarter Pounder" may not even know they're eating an animal. They may not realize that the hamburger came from a steer or that an animal died in the process, in summary how important the natural world is to their very survival. Even prepackaged meat in supermarkets bears few reminders of its source. This is very different from traditional European open markets where half a steer carcass, a cow or pig's head stands in full view of the butcher's stall.

To a certain extent socialization requires letting go of one's awareness, a narrowing of consciousness. To operate a busy telephone switchboard requires not only a tremendous amount of concentration, but a split from the rest of one's consciousness. Modern people have developed willpower and the ability to work efficiently, but at the cost of losing touch with what Jung calls "the original mind," the psychic power available to primitive people who were emotionally involved with nature and had not been socialized to ignore the inner self.

Socialization directs us into a narrow, controlled, artificial, less spontaneous way of life. Conscious waking life is full of prejudices. We are exposed to all kinds of influences and social pressures which seduce and reward us into following ways unsuitable for developing individuality. Jung explains:

> Other people stimulate or depress us, events at the office or in our social life distract us. Whether or not we are aware of the effect they have on our consciousness, it is disturbed by and exposed to them almost without defense.[6]

Gossip, a compromising work situation, all interrupt us from coming to grips with our own individuality. This is especially true for extroverted people and for those who have feelings of inferiority.

In the course of civilization and an advancing technological society people have learned to repress their emotions, relegating them to the unconscious. In contrast, primitive people still maintain touch with this energy, with spirituality and with natural phenomena which they see in their daily contact with nature.

Unlike modern people who consider dreams nonsense, primitive tribes may depend on dreams for their very survival. Among the Naskapi Indians of the Labrador peninsula, who live in isolated family groups as hunters, the major obligation of the individual is to follow the instructions given by dreams and then to manifest them in art. The Naskapi believe that a "Great Man" who dwells within each person sends them dreams. The Naskapi follow the advice of their dreams for hunting, which the Indian's life depends on. These primitive people, untouched by modern civilization, maintain that generosity and love attract the Great

Man, while lies and dishonesty drive him away from the inner being.

In a dream state we depart from the controlled thoughts we normally maintain by day to the striking imagery of the unconscious. The unconscious speaks to us in symbols which are charged with feeling to make a strong impression on the dreamer. Because our conscious thoughts have been stripped of their emotional energy, it's difficult for us to be moved by a notion. Similarly, if the unconscious simply advised us to make a change, it might not have the same impact.

An extroverted woman, preoccupied with what others thought of her, dreamed about herself at an elegant party, trying to make a good impression. There was one thing to mar this image though; she was wheeling around a wheelbarrow filled with excrement. The unconscious' message to her was bold, equating her concern with her impression on others with a pile of feces.

Opposites

Dreams often compensate for a lifestyle which over-emphasizes one aspect of the personality. In the previous dream a pile of excrement brought the woman back to earth, compensating for her haughtiness. A person all wrapped up in intellectual activity may dream of bestial sexual acts, as the unconscious draws attention to the need to integrate the physical side along with the intellectual in waking life.

Jung found that balancing opposites is essential for a person to achieve a sense of completeness. Two such opposites are *extroversion,* a tendency to concentrate on the external world, on outside events, and *introversion,* to study one's own reactions and experiences.

Ideally one needs to be free to alternate between action and introspection. Sometimes the world requires participation; in other situations it calls for reflection. Growth entails flowing back and forth. How well the person has integrated these opposites can be measured by whether the individual can successfully reverse a personal orientation to life. Many people tend toward an extreme. They may be extroverted, concerned more with the social and physical world, with how others see them. Or they may think more about their inward impressions of the world, and contemplate existence.

The Four Functions

Jung classified the human personality into four psychological functions: thinking, feeling, sensation and intuition. One or two of these traits normally stand out. They exist in opposition to one another so that while most people tend to cultivate one or two of the functions, the others remain inferior. Thinking is in opposition to feeling and sensation is in opposition to intuition. In the process of socialization one function may be emphasized and as a result its opposite remains undifferentiated and inferior. Yet none of these traits is superior to another; the individual needs all four to be complete. Our growth lies in the conscious development of our inferior functions.

Thinking.   Thinking involves using one's intellectual faculty. The thinker seeks to analyze and order facts to evaluate the world. Thinkers are logical and may try to adapt themselves to life by intellectualizing their feelings. Such people may neglect the feeling side of themselves.

Feeling.   Jung refers to feeling not in the sense of emotion, but as an opinion used as a rational function for weighing and evaluating the world. The feeling person would say, "I

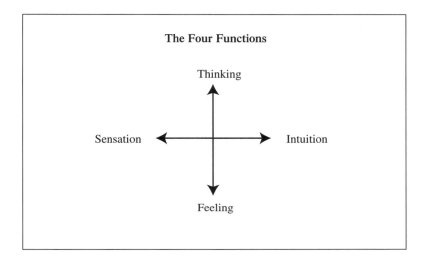

The Four Functions

Thinking

Sensation ←——————→ Intuition

Feeling

like such and such." Decisions are based on value judgments—whether something is agreeable, disagreeable, good or evil. This individual may not have developed impersonal reflective thinking.

How do you approach life? Are you known for your sharp thoughts? Do you move according to your feelings, saying, "I feel this is a good thing"? Remember, the ideal is to balance these two functions, to use them both, depending on the situation.

Sensation.   While the individual uses either thinking or feeling to evaluate the world, sensation or intuition is used to perceive or know the world. The person dominated by sensation would say, "I only believe in what I can see and touch. That is reality." The sensation function is oriented toward action; yet it often lacks imagination. Jung describes sensation-dominated people: "They live as if the state they have arrived at today is final with no possibility of change, as though the world and the psyche were static. They're completely dependent on what they see."[7] The future is not

important since it doesn't exist in concrete form. They may
be only slightly conscious of the need to deal with philosophical questions about the meaning of life and death.

Intuition.   The intuitive type relies heavily on hunches,
fantasies, on what could be. These are the people with visions and insights. Intuition is directed by the unconscious.
Whenever a decision is made in the dark, intuition comes
into play. Intuition has a capacity to inspire people. It's
crucial for scientists and physicians.

The great heroes of our time, Robert Kennedy and
Martin Luther King, were intuitive. "I have a dream," said
King.

"Some men see things as they are and ask why; I
dream things that never were and say why not," said
Kennedy.[8]

In some cases the intuitive individual may see the underlying significance of an idea but may not be good at carrying it out. The person may be fantastic to listen to,
inventive, even have an idea for a non-gas engine but may
not get down to working with the greasy nuts and bolts to
put it together.

To recapitulate the four functions: Sensation tells me
that something is; it does not tell me what it is. Thinking
tells me what an object is; it gives it a name. Feeling tells
me the value of an object, whether it's acceptable. Intuition
is concerned with future possibilities.[9]

You can rank these functions in your own personality
by first determining which trait stands out. If you can identify with being a thinker, then the opposite function, feeling,
is the most inferior of the four. Then choose between the
other two functions, in this case sensation and intuition.
Whichever is first, its opposite ranks number three in the

Martin Luther King's "I Have a Dream" speech is an example of the intuitive nature of heroes of modern times. *Courtesy of Library of Congress.*

personality. So for instance, if you pick sensation as the second strongest personality characteristic, then intuition would rank third.

Jung notes that growth requires a continuous effort to bring the inferior function into consciousness, first by recognizing it and then by steadfastly applying it in daily life. Incorporating the opposite trait can help improve not only one's mental, but one's physical health. Intuitive types who downplay sensation may not devote enough time to exercise and maintaining health. These categories help explain how we evaluate the world differently from one another. For example, your mate may make decisions by saying, "I like such and such," according to feeling, while you tend to respond to the world by thinking. Neither method is superior. The goal is to balance all four functions to meet the complex and unique situations of life.

Archetypes

Sue couldn't believe how it happened to her. Just like in fantasy the first time she saw Ron rockets went off, bells rang, and she fell head over heels in love. It was no wonder, he was the perfect man. He was so much in control of himself, so cool, so organized, so intelligent, so rational and so powerful. She knew sharing her life with Ron would be a dream come true. That wasn't enough. Sue could hardly believe how Ron immediately professed his great love for her and found her almost flawless. Amazingly, he seemed to overlook all her faults—he thought she was the most beautiful woman he had ever seen—he loved her long hair. He spoke so highly of her tenderness, her gentleness, enthusiasm for life and creative side. No wonder they felt there was nothing else to do but to get married as soon as possible.

"But I guess people see each other differently after marriage," she thought. "Ron isn't in control like I thought. I've been reminding him for a week that we have to get our taxes in. He just seems like a little boy, he hadn't even thought about it. I feel like I'm the one that makes things work."

Now that she's married, Sue begins to question how accurate her view of Ron was before they married. Why didn't she see his flaws?

For centuries poets have told us how blind love is. A man gazes upon his woman through a lover's eyes which do not see shortcomings. William Wordsworth, in his poem "She Was A Phantom of Delight," says that his love "was a phantom of delight, when first she gleamed upon my sight." He describes her as "a dancing shape, an image gay, to haunt, to startle, and waylay."

Why do men fall so helplessly for women? Jung might attribute some of love's nearsightedness to the fact that a lover fulfills a partner's ideal image of the opposite sex.

These images of the opposite sex within us are important components of our personality. They are part of our number two personality which is made up of a cast of characters Jung calls archetypes. *Archetypes* are inborn images of men, women, parents, heroes, a wise old man and a wise old woman within us. Jung found these archetypes recurring in dreams and mythology. Archetypes are innate predispositions in the unconscious, a way in which we respond to the world that is not based solely on our conscious life.

The Anima and the Animus. While the *anima* is an archetype of women which is found in men, the *animus* is the masculine component of women. The anima personifies feminine characteristics in men such as gentleness, sentiment, intuitiveness and creativeness—a more emotional side.

In our culture men are taught to be tough, to think ahead, to be unemotional and to ignore the more feminine, tender side of their natures. In order for a male to establish himself in such a highly technological, competitive society, he concentrates on developing intellectual abilities and career skills, ignoring the more "feminine," spiritual and emotional side of his nature. Once he lands a job, he may neglect his personal needs for comradeship and emotional outlets in favor of cultivating masculine qualities such as willpower, objectivity and forcefulness, to achieve power and position.

When a man refrains from expressing a more tender, soft side, his personality is out of balance. The anima will seek expression, trying to right his personality. It may emerge in moodiness and other such feminine qualities which he takes on, or it may take a woman to bring a man in touch.

Stan, a powerful businessman, after years of concentrating on his rational, intellectual abilities, has forgotten how to feel, how to listen to his emotions. He's attracted to Diane because she's so full of feeling, spontaneous, her face is so warm when she speaks. She animates his life, stirs him and helps him get in touch with his intuitive side, in short, with his anima.

The first and most powerful influence on the anima is the male's mother. Depending on the nature of their relationship, his anima may be positive or negative in character. If their association is riddled with strife he may be dominated by the negative traits of his anima such as moodiness, inconsistency and chaos.

The anima also represents a collective image of women throughout the ages which exists in each man's unconscious. This means that the figures of womanhood which have been passed on through art, literature and dance of the fair maiden, the madonna, the temptress leading the stranger to doom, or the Greek goddess, exist in each male's psyche.

Although a man may not be consciously aware of them, they may emerge in his fantasies, particularly when he meets a woman to attach such feelings to. He may find her, as did Wordsworth, "a dancing shape, an image gay, to haunt, to startle, and waylay." In other words the young woman Wordsworth spoke of may not have personally possessed all these qualities. Yet he saw them in her. What he really saw were images of his own mind.

This is not something a man controls; he doesn't make up these projections, they happen to him. It is not surprising then, that men may treat women with preconceived notions instead of relating to their individuality. A man may put a woman on a pedestal as though she were a Greek goddess or alternately treat her as though she were a temptress with little basis for his behavior. In the first case she may complain that she wants to step down off the pedestal, to be treated more humanly. Further, if a man ignores his feminine nature, it can take control of his personality. He may become irritable, unpredictable and disorganized, not even recognizing these qualities in himself, projecting them on others.

If a man projects these undesirable qualities on his wife, it can spell disaster for the marriage. Matt has thought seriously about separating from Martha because he feels dominated by her. Yet what he thinks is Martha's doing is the neglected feminine element in his own personality which controls him. So we can understand how he feels captured by his wife when, in fact, it is his own anima. He may divorce Martha to elude her control, only to discover these feelings still plague him even on his own, until he comes to grips with his own unconscious.

The anima often comes to a man in his dreams, personifying a mythical character such as a fair maiden, witch or a goddess. It is through listening to the anima's message that a man can achieve balance. If a man is able to recall his dreams and fantasies and consciously relate to his anima it will increase his insights, intuitiveness, creative abilities and the beauty in his life. On the other hand, if a man is afraid of his anima, he may not get married, for such an intimate relationship might force him to deal with his own feminine component.

At its best the anima can transform a man. This involves taking seriously the anima and bringing it into the conscious world through writing about her, painting or sculpting forms resembling one's dreams. Through this deliberate effort the anima becomes conscious and fixed in one's mind, so that it can be examined. The most valuable role of the anima is putting a man's mind in tune with inner values which opens the way to spirituality and wisdom. The anima represents a guide or mediator between this world and the inner world of the Self.

On the other hand, for women, the animus represents the masculine element generally, the thinking side of the personality. It lays down rational judgments, it is organizing, objective, aggressive and controlling. The animus can give women the courage and strength to carry out a search for truth and direction in their lives.

Diana is drawn to Stan because he's so forceful and in control, so well organized, he brings her in touch with these elements in herself. While she has been following her feelings which flow in all directions, like a stream with no banks, Stan has helped her rediscover her abilities to set boundaries through using her intellect.

Women may experience their animus alternately in men whom they admire or fight, in the first case falling in love as a result of trying to get in contact inwardly with parts of themselves which they haven't acknowledged. Sue attributed power, strength and clarity of thought to Ron—her inward image of masculinity. When she sat listening to Ron, entranced by what he said, she was listening to her animus. It was as though she were looking at a movie in her mind, instead of her partner. While she dealt with her husband as though he were in control, what she really felt was an aspect of her animus. Through marrying Ron she unconsciously tried to get in touch with her masculine traits.

Such projections can lead to misunderstandings in relationships when the partner doesn't meet the mate's inner image of the opposite sex. When Sue married Ron, she learned to her surprise that he wasn't as controlled or rational as she had perceived him before marriage. Sue and Ron may continue to have misunderstandings, wondering why their partner doesn't fit their expectations. Or they may try to separate their image from the real person.

This differentiation is part of the process of individuation. For Sue it means detaching herself from the man she's in love with, distinguishing the real person in the outer world from her archetype.

The animus may have destructive elements. In women the animus can account for strong convictions. A woman may speak with unquestioned opinions, which she extolls in a loud masculine voice. Her opinion is sacred and there are absolutely no exceptions. She may be right in a general sense but not in a specific way. It is the father who endows his daughter with undisputed convictions. She accepts them as general truths, yet they don't account for individual differences.

The Persona and the Shadow.   As a child we're taught to behave a certain way—to be sociable, gregarious, amiable, talkative, ambitious, successful. These qualities or similar ones become part of the personality we project to society in order to be well-liked. This sociable part of ourselves, this role we take on, Jung calls the *persona*. In essence it is a mask we put on every morning, a way of putting "our best foot forward." It is the number one self that serves to conceal our inner feelings—in extreme cases even from ourselves.

Furthermore, this social self is fragmented. We're taught to accept the good part of ourselves but not the evil. Western culture discourages us from integrating opposite qualities— we are told to be masculine and ignore our feminine qualities, or to be feminine and neglect the masculine side. A strong person is taught not to reveal any weaknesses. In contrast, in Eastern culture, male and female, good and bad are expected in the same person. In our society the social self, the self that personifies all the ideal qualities, is substituted for the real self. The difficulty arises in this fragmentation, for the social self is not the whole self and may be contrary to the real self with its own life story to unfold. The process of individuation then is to rediscover the lost elements, to reunite all aspects and make the person whole again.

In direct opposition to the persona is the *shadow,* the dark side of the personality, the self that wants to do all the things that we do not allow ourselves to do, the one who represents our weaknesses and failings. The shadow personifies the person's uncivilized desires and emotions which are incompatible with social standards and the ideal personality. After acting out the dark side the person may say, "I was not myself," or "I don't know what came over

Meeting with the Shadow. This is Jung's drawing of his own shadow, in an attempt to give form to and make conscious what was unconscious. *Courtesy of the Estate of C.G. Jung.*

me." The Shadow can represent lustfulness, irresponsibility, laziness, slothfulness—qualities which the person learned were bad as a child. The more restrictive and narrow the society or subculture, the larger the shadow.

Rather than admit to the dark side of ourselves, there is a tendency to project these qualities on others. Whereas we experience our repressed opposite-sex characteristics through projections on the opposite sex via the anima or animus, the shadow is projected on the same sex. So if we have a difficulty in a relationship with someone of our own sex, it is a result of our shadow. This projection is understandable since we are still experiencing these negative qualities unconsciously. A woman who is greedy may talk about a female relative's stinginess. Jung says we can learn a great deal about ourselves from people we despise or hate, for they represent many of our own weaknesses or failings on a personal level. Such an idea is popularly summarized in the statement, "What Peter says about Paul says more about Peter than Paul." The shadow may be collectively seen as a devil or a witch, or a country may project unacceptable qualities in their culture on another nation. During the 1980 hostage crisis, Iran and America may have become each other's shadow. In demonstrations and political cartoons the people of both countries thought the other was evil, powerful and underhanded.

However, the shadow can also represent good parts of the personality which the child learned were socially unacceptable. For example, a happy-go-lucky youth sent to a rough school where he is required by peer pressure to defend himself physically may learn to be serious and tough for self-preservation, relegating his carefree side to his shadow which he projects on others.

The Wise Old Man and the Wise Old Woman. The wisdom of the unconscious is often personified in dreams through the image of a wise old man or woman. The wise old man may emerge as a great father or an Indian guru, for example. He possesses great wisdom, prophetic powers and the gift of healing—in short he has superior insight. The wise old woman could be portrayed as Mother Earth, a priestess, a sorceress, a goddess of nature and love. This image is timeless, seeming in dreams to be simultaneously young and old. The wise old man and wise old woman are representatives of the Self, their wisdom the voice of the unconscious, which should be subjected to conscious criticism to be of value in one's life.

Archetype Summary. As these archetypal forces come forth in dreams, their purpose is to restore a balance to the personality. For example, a competitive and aggressive man may dream of a feminine figure as his anima tells him to rely on feeling once again. An important aspect to appreciate concerning archetypes is that they express a knowledge beyond the individual's personal experience and awareness.

Part of the individuation process is acknowledging the existence of archetypes and integrating them into one's conscious life. This does not mean that one becomes an archetype. In fact, if the individual believes he or she possesses the power of an archetype, the ego becomes inflated and the person acts beyond present capabilities. For example, a woman may take on the archetype of the Great Mother. She becomes possessed by it, believing she is endowed with an infinite capacity for loving, understanding, helping and protecting others. This individual may eventually falter, wearing herself out in the service of others. Or she may make others feel demoralized by insisting that they are dependent on her. There is danger in seeing herself as the Great Mother for she may be compelled beyond her strength and capacity. Jung calls this *inflation,* the conscious is blown up out of proportion through identification with the archetype.

Compensatory Guide

Jung saw life as a process of alternating between opposites. To achieve a sense of harmony within and wholeness requires that the individual accept success with humility, that one alternate a dynamic exertion with a retreat. The individual develops through experiencing both sides of an issue. Courage is gained not simply through charging the enemy, but by incorporating an awareness of one's fears. Growth occurs through seeking to balance one's potentials—assertiveness with humility; tentativeness with certainty; and action with self-reflection.

Unfortunately Western culture encourages a rather lopsided development, emphasizing power and material achievement, while neglecting the spiritual side. Yet even though a person may not be aware of possessing any spiritual inclination, this repressed element still exists and will seek expression to set the personality in balance. The more one aspect is neglected, the more out of balance the personality is. For those who ignore the spiritual side there is a sense of meaninglessness and lack of direction in life. The inner guide tries to restore equilibrium by reminding the individual of the abandoned function through dreams, fantasies and activities. When the powerful businessman dreams of a soft, feeling woman, his inner guide is reminding him of the gentle side of his nature. In the case of the mountain climber mentioned earlier, he tried to compensate for his materialism by climbing mountains, rising above his everyday financial dealings. In dreams the compensatory guide spoke to him of walking off a mountain top, an extreme to balance the shady side of his personality which dominated his conscious life. A woman caught up in intellectual activity may dream about wild sexual encounters to remind her to "get out of her head."

The ego may refuse to incorporate the opposite function, as the mountain climber refused to deal with his inner values. The unconscious, in its attempts to balance the person, may become more negative, demanding and even dangerous when continually ignored. Jung says neurosis and psychosis are reactions to not living out our true stories, being true to ourselves. Symptoms themselves are desperate attempts to put the person in psychic balance again.

Symbols

Symbols are the language of the unconscious as it strives to balance itself and to achieve wholeness. Up to now most of us have probably given little thought to symbols in our lives because Western civilization is based on rationalism, a concept that everything can be explained according to reason. *Symbols,* on the contrary, include an image with energy and cannot be completely defined verbally but must be experienced.

Jung surveyed cultures around the world to learn about symbols. He found that in various primitive tribes as well as modern cultures there were recurring symbols and myths: symbols of the sacraments of life, of birth, marriage, wholeness and death; and myths of the universal life struggles to achieve bravery, of beauty and the beast, of the ugly duckling. For him their recurrence demonstrated that the collective unconscious and its symbols were shared by people of all places and all times.

Furthermore, he found that symbols served specific purposes. Symbols have the power to help the individual transcend one's situation, to rise above limitations. While the individual contemplates a symbol, the person's energy is aligned to direct him or her through certain life stages. So, for example, in modern Christian culture, the marriage ceremony focuses and channels the bride and groom's energy toward a lifetime commitment to another person. In contrast to vows before the Justice of the Peace, a religious ceremony contains more symbols which bring to mind the virtues required for a successful marriage. The white veil and dress symbolize purity; the church, the presence of God in the marriage; the congregation, making a commitment in front of society. Many religious symbols such as the cross, incense, the Virgin Mary, are external forces to channel energy. The cross helps focus the Christian on Christ and on personal sacrifice and the promise of rebirth.

Symbols in a sense make the unconscious conscious. Symbols which emerge in dreams, in dance, in art—in many different forms—help the person experience instinctive energy which would otherwise be beyond their conscious experience and to direct it toward a common cultural interest. In short, symbols are charged with emotional energy. For example, throughout civilization stones have been used as a symbol of that which is complete, unchanging, immortal, the eternal Self. They are central to the meaning of life and death. Most obvious is the tombstone, a symbol of death in our culture, a permanent memorial to the eternal spirit. The ancient Germans believed that the spirits dwelled in the tombstone. Similarly, Michelangelo Buonarroti, the Italian sculptor, said of his powerful and moving pieces, that his job was simply to release the spirit in the rock, rather than carving a figure of his own imagination. The Australian Aborigines have sacred stones which they believe contain the spirits of the dead. In Western culture we project emotional energy into precious stones which represent the sacraments of life—the birthstone represents one's birth and wholeness, and the wedding ring serves as a symbol of an eternal relationship.

The rituals which employ symbols, such as the sacrament of baptism, the marriage ceremony and the funeral, are powerful emotional experiences. Through their energy Jung believes such rites bring the individual in close contact with the inner self or with the image of God within which leads to *wholeness.* This concept of wholeness is related to the traditional sense of holiness in which the individual is in touch with the Self, with God within, with inner grace and with all mankind.

We can see in primitive cultures how rituals or rites of passage serve to transform the individual from one life stage to the next. For example, in the Masai tribe of Kenya, the young men, called Moran, perform a ritual dance of manhood, jumping high, symbolically transcending their fears and ambivalences. The dance channels the young men's energy and focuses it for the tasks of manhood.

At holidays we use symbols, many of which have survived from ancient cultures. For example, the Easter rabbit is connected with ancient spring festivals, representing abundance, life, purity and innocence. A basket of colorful eggs was used in the spring celebrations of the ancient Persians, Egyptians, Greeks and Romans. In Babylonia, eggs were offered to Astarte, the goddess of fertility. The egg symbolizes the beginning of new life. The Greeks and Syrians exchanged crimson eggs representing Christ's blood.

In art, architecture and rituals there are symbols of cultural transcendence, of breaking out of human containment. Skyscrapers, seemingly reaching to the heavens, airplanes

Skyscrapers are modern symbols of escaping the limitations of earthly bonds.

and space travel are modern symbols of escape from earthly bonds, while in primitive tribes birds, feathers and dances are used to portray breaking the tie of gravity and rising above everyday problems. Hawaiian, Masai and Native American chieftains wear beautiful headdresses made of bird feathers to denote their elevation above everyday matters to a position of leadership. Birds, which fly near the heavens, are often regarded as messengers of the Gods and associated with the supernatural. Bird feathers are used in ceremonies of many societies to call upon supernatural spirits for assistance to cure illnesses, to develop awareness or new perceptions and to solve life's problems.

Jung found an important symbol of wholeness occurring in cultures throughout the world to which was attached great meaning. It is the *mandala*, a circle or any four-sided figure such as a square. Mandala is an ancient word meaning

The use of feathers in headdresses of chieftains has been widely used as symbols of special powers in North America, Africa and the islands of Hawaii. This Masai chieftain of Kenya wears an Ostrich headdress to denote his position of leadership.

Mato-Tope, a prominent Madan chief wore this headdress of
eagle feathers in 1834. The honor of wearing such a headdress
was reserved for only the most distinguished leader. As a
warrior, he can also be seen as a powerful masculine archetype.
*"Mato-Tape (Four Bears)" Watercolor on paper by Karl
Bodmer, courtesy of Joslyn Art Museum, Nebraska.*

The ancient Hawaiian chieftains had full length robes, as well as headdresses, made of bird feathers. This cloak is made of red and yellow feathers. *Courtesy of Bishop Museum Archives.*

magic circle with a central point. It is one of the oldest religious symbols and is found throughout the world. The mandala motif appears in Christianity; the cross is a mandala, as is the cross in the center of a circle which appears in some civilizations as a sign of wholeness. The mandala represents the center of the self, integration and balance.

Jung found the mandala appearing in dreams of many of his patients, accompanied by a strong feeling of harmony and peace. When a mandala is present in dreams, it is a statement that there is an element in the individual's personality moving toward wholeness. It expresses the individual's desire for completeness. It is almost as though within the circle or square the Self is protected from the outer world.

This is Jung's painting of a mandala created in 1920. He was inspired by a dream he had in January 1914, anticipating the outbreak of World War I in August 1914. It represents the Sacred in a ring of flame above a world of war and technology. *Courtesy of Estate of C.G. Jung.*

The mandala is expressed in art and even in dance. There are ritual dances and folk dances which include a circling round a central point, a withdrawal to the four corners and an advance to the center.

Contemplation of the mandala figure is meant to bring a sense of inner peace, that life again has meaning and order. Great benefit can be derived by drawing the mandala and reflecting upon it. As one contemplates, fantasies and hunches will emerge as the messages of the unconscious surface, leading to a renewal of the Self.

Myths

A *myth* is a story, the origin of which is forgotten, which may express in symbolic language a natural phenomenon, event or belief such as how the world came about or why a person is in a situation that must be overcome. But a myth is something more than a prescientific, naive interpretation of the world. Jung considered myths to be fundamental expressions of human nature which symbolize how people experience natural events in their lives. For instance:

> The rising of the sun then becomes the birth of the Godhero from the sea. He drives his chariot across the sky and in the west a great mother dragon waits to devour him in the evening....he is born again in the morning.[10]

Primitive people don't separate the experience of the inner world from the outer world. What happens to them also happens to the sun. This myth is an expression of how a person experiences a sense of rebirth each morning at sunrise and conversely at night feels swallowed up in darkness as the sun sets and the individual is overcome by fears and doubts.

Myths, like dreams, are emotionally charged, intense experiences, expressions of the unconscious and imagination. Myths are direct expressions of the collective unconscious and so they are similar throughout the world. According to Jung the characters we read about in mythology exist within each of us—the conquering hero, the innocent pure child, the wise old man. Part of our nature, they live within us as archetypes which are activated when we read mythology. Certain archetypes such as the conquering hero, who overcomes the forces of evil and liberates people from death, occur over and over again.

The energy in the myth can empower and energize people. In other cultures these myths are acted out through rituals, ceremonies and dances which seem to grip the audience as if in a magic spell. In the myth the individual is glorified, he or she has great power. Such myths inspire the spectator, who identifies with the hero. The spirit of the myth gives people a feeling that they themselves possess superhuman qualities and can transcend their everyday limitations. Mythology in Greece inspired a whole society, setting a tone for exalting the worth of the individual.

The Hero Myth. This archetype represents the unfallen hero who is capable of everything, the shining knight who slays the dragon, overcoming evil so that good may prevail. The dragon represents the evil in the outside world and ultimately evil within us, the seductive enemies such as pride, self-absorption, anger, cowardice, the desire to gossip, and laziness. The developmental task of the hero is to overcome these inner deficiencies in order to grow into the next stage. Slaying the dragon represents sacrificing the ego to a higher good.

The hero myth is central to becoming an adult. The hero myth empowers the person with the energy necessary to overcome childhood dependency on parents and to focus on mastering the adult world.

A young man may have an inflated view of himself as the conquering hero, capable of all great things. The idealistic youth believes that he can subdue all evil in the outside world. Yet in overcoming the dragon he learns that he must deal with the sources of evil within; eventually the quest in the outside world must turn inward.

Fairy Tales

Fairy tales and mythologies embody deep psychological realities and powerful instinctual drives. Symbols in fairy tales and myths are an attempt to set down eternal themes so that others can get in touch with such realities in their own lives. Childhood fables explain how those who deserve it will live happily ever after, how the weak and helpless are elevated, how evil is eventually punished, how the poor become rich and how the ugly duckling becomes beautiful. Fairy tales, told again and again, prepare the child to deal with the challenges of each developmental stage of life.

For example, in the tale of the Wizard of Oz, Dorothy and her companions head down the yellow brick road on a search for wholeness: the lion is seeking courage, the Tin Man will be happy if only he has a heart and the Straw Man is looking for a brain. Just like a child, all of them are plagued by inner questioning and people telling them, "Why aren't you smarter?" or "Why are you afraid?" Their adventure to find these virtues is much like the child's experience of growing up. When Dorothy and her friends finally encounter the Wizard, to their surprise they find they don't need him. In the struggle of their journey to Oz each of them had achieved what he or she wanted. Once the characters faced the mighty Wizard, they saw that in reality he was only a tiny man behind a big machine, a lesson not to be afraid of the roar of adults. From the Wizard Dorothy and her friends learned that the special powers had been potentials within each of them all along.

Fairy tales are symbolic of the passage from one developmental stage into another. On her thirteenth birthday Sleeping Beauty goes to visit her grandmother in a forbidden part of the castle. She pricks her finger and falls asleep. Soon the whole castle begins to slumber, only to be awakened by the prince who climbs through thorny rose bushes which have grown around the castle and kisses Sleeping Beauty.

Psychoanalyst Freida Fromm-Reichman's interpretation is that the blood symbolizes how Sleeping Beauty begins to menstruate at thirteen and her grandmother explains to her the facts of life:

> However, she remains an unawakened female until the male partner opens the hedge (the hymen) which has separated the young virgin from her self-realization as a woman.[11]

Little Red Riding Hood is dressed in red as a symbol of menstruation, Erich Fromm tells us. Mother warns Red Riding Hood not to run off the path, otherwise she might encounter wolves, just as parents warn their adolescent daughters to beware of men. Leaving the straight and narrow path represents a loss of virginity. In the fable the male is portrayed as a ruthless and cunning animal.[12]

In the 19th century Italian tale of Pinocchio, a wooden puppet carved from a block of wood is eventually transformed through suffering and love into a caring, responsible

After Pinocchio told the third lie in a row his nose grew so long he couldn't even turn around. Seeing his misery the Blue Fairy "clapped her hands together, and at this signal a thousand giant woodpeckers flew into the room through the window. They perched on Pinocchio's nose and pecked away at it so furiously that in a few minutes that extravagant monstrosity was back to its normal size."[13] *"Pinocchio and the Woodpeckers," a painting by Roberto Ciabani from "The Authentic Story of Pinocchio of Tuscany" by Crystal Publications.*

human being. The story is symbolic of the human struggle to balance the desire to be an unbridled free spirit with love for other people. Initially, Pinocchio is an impulsive, self-centered, free-spirited, irresponsible puppet, symbolically pulled in all directions by the strings of passion and fantasy. As Pinocchio continually indulges in immediate gratification, ignoring those who care for him while being distracted by those who only pretend to care, he finds himself twisting the truth, unable to keep his word. As much as he tries to hide from the truth, he can't fool himself or others because his nose begins to grow longer with every lie. Pinocchio repeatedly gets into mischief, continually diverted by promises of easy riches or an easy life in Funland where boys have fun everyday and never go to school, but eventually grow long ears and become donkeys. All the while his father, Geppetto, is sacrificing so Pinocchio can go to school. Later Geppetto almost dies as he desperately tries to find his lost son. Throughout the story Pinocchio says he wants to be good, like a real boy, and repeatedly promises himself and the Blue Fairy he will keep his promise. Eventually, after causing much suffering for himself and those who love him, just as all seems lost, his love for his family transforms him into a conscious, responsible human being who helps take care of those he loves, bringing happiness to himself and his family.

Now consider Beauty and the Beast, a story of a young woman awakening to adult life. In the story, Beauty, an unselfish and kind girl, asks her father for a white rose. Unfortunately the rose grows in an enchanted garden belonging to a beast. Her father is caught stealing the rose and required to return to the garden for his punishment, presumably death. Yet the Beast, who seems cruel and kind at the same time, gives the father a reprieve to go home. Beauty pleads to return to the garden to accept her father's punishment. At first she's afraid of the hairy beast who visits her regularly asking her to marry him. She learns through a magic mirror that her father is ill and begs to go home. The Beast says that if she stays away for more than a week he will die. At home, detained by her sisters, Beauty dreams of the Beast dying and returns to him. He tells her that he can't live without her and now that she is nursing him he will die content. Beauty forgets his ugliness, tells him that she loves him and says she will be his wife if he does not die. All of a sudden the castle is filled with music and brilliant light, representing Beauty's awakening into womanhood. The Beast turns into a prince who confesses he was under a magic spell from which he couldn't be released until a young girl fell in love with him for his goodness alone.

Joseph Henderson, a Jungian psychoanalyst, describes the symbolism of the tale. He says that Beauty represents an innocent young girl who must break the bond with her father in order to become a woman. She jeopardizes her father so that she can become free of him. He is a symbol of platonic, spiritual love which is blocking her from expressing her sexual love to the Beast. The Beast, in turn, represents the animus, expressing cruelty and kindness combined. Through the Beast, who she's initially afraid of, she faces the erotic and animal side of her nature and awakens as a woman, able to love the spirit and nature of the Beast.[14]

The Individuation Process

Let's look again at what this all means. Each of us has a very personal life path to follow which we may drift away from due to distractions in our life. Jung believed that it is by getting to know the number two personality that we can find that secret design once again.

To find one's inner purpose requires, to a certain extent, giving up the learned social self. It calls for ego submission. This means acknowledging something more important than one's own wishful desires and recognizing an authority higher than one's own ego and social power. *Individuation* is very different from "individualistic," in fact the person must give up personal aims. Self-fulfillment springs from selflessness.

The conscious attitude of individuation involves self-acceptance, being unwilling to subordinate any aspect of the Self. One of Jung's patients wrote him a letter to explain how much he gained when he let go of control:

> Out of evil, much good has come to me. By keeping quiet, repressing nothing, remaining attentive, and by accepting reality—taking things as they are, and not as

Carl Jung says that we are much wiser than we know. *Photo copyright by Aniela Jaffe.*

I wanted them to be—by doing all this, unusual knowledge has come to me, and unusual powers as well, such as I could never have imagined before. I always thought that when we accepted things they overpowered us . . . . This turns out not to be true at all. What a fool I was! How I tried to force everything, to go according to the way I thought it ought to![15]

This means discounting the Western notion that everything has to have utility and to realize that:

to fulfill one's destiny is the greatest human achievement and that our utilitarian notions have to give way in the face of the demands of our unconscious psyche . . . we should give in to this almost imperceptible yet powerfully dominating impulse—an impulse that comes from the urge toward unique, creative self-realization. And this is a process in which one must repeatedly seek out and find something that is not yet known to anyone. The guiding hints or impulses come not from the ego, but from the totality of the psyche; the Self.[16]

Jung says that we are much wiser than we know, if only we respect ourselves enough to try to understand the language of the unconscious through our dreams. There are a number of ways to increase the likelihood of remembering your dreams. First, set a pad and pencil by your bed and write down the dream immediately upon waking before other conscious thoughts enter your mind and the dream slips back into the unconscious. Then read back over the dream later in the day, trying to decipher what the symbols mean to you personally. Another method to increase your recall is to use the power of suggestion by reminding yourself just before you close your eyes that you will remember your dream in the morning.

An important step in the individuation process is to differentiate oneself from the archetypes that emerge in dreams. For the man this would start with the process of an inner image of a woman, his anima. The first part is to acknowledge and accept the anima, to listen to her messages as though she is a separate entity from the self, to get to know her and how she can make a valuable contribution to one's life. This understanding comes about from an internal psychological dialogue and studying one's dreams. So, for example, by listening to her dreams, at some point a woman dominated by her animus will begin to question the soundness of her own opinions, arriving at the position in which she can examine her opinions as separate from herself.

This is a very deliberate practice which involves separating one's anima and animus from real people in the outside world as well. So for example, when a husband becomes enraged with his wife, he tries to determine whether his anger is for her or because an emotional, controlling anima figure was touched off in him. When differentiated from the women he encounters in the world his anima attitudes can be considered objectively rather than breaking out in emotional arguments and moodiness. In this way he slowly stops projecting his archetypes on others and listens more attentively to the internal dialogue. The anima is then experienced more positively.

The process of individuation develops gradually during one's lifetime, particularly during the second half of life, usually beginning between the ages of 35 to 40. Jung was the first to study what is now called a midlife crisis, when all of a sudden the person's life lacks meaning. The individual may have achieved a social position that is well established, a family, a satisfying sexual relationship, a sense of power; but, as Jung says, "a social goal is attained only at the cost of diminution of personality."[17]

The hero myth is dead for them; they have conquered external forces to a certain extent, yet evil still exists in the world. They are not the triumphant heroes, their lives need something deeper. In a midlife crisis the person may no longer feel satisfied with a job, a mate or some other component of life. The individual may feel that life is empty.

The process of individuation typically begins when the person confronts a seemingly unsolvable crisis which demands a deeper understanding. This need for a wider perspective may bring about a series of painful realizations of what is wrong with the individual and one's conscious attitude. Even the crisis of boredom can give way to an openness to messages of one's inner purpose transmitted from the unconscious.

Getting to know the number two personality entails renewing many aspects of the Self which were plowed under and blocked off during socialization. First of all, Jung says the human personality is naturally spiritual.

In an interview with the British Broadcasting Company Jung was asked if he believed in God. He answered, "That's a hard question. I don't believe in God, I know him." He had come to know the image of God within himself.

The quest for wholeness is the same for all people; it is cross-cultural and transcends all periods of history.

Culture and art are reflections of the collective unconscious. The ability for classical art over the centuries to touch and move us emotionally illustrates the timelessness of expressions of the collective unconscious. Within each of us is this great wisdom to be creative. One human being may reflect the history of all life.

Using a Jungian approach can deeply enrich life— through spending time on oneself studying one's dreams, reading many authors, pursuing interests in other cultures, in art and mythology, delving into the spiritual side of our nature and through getting to know and understand the Self.

Forging a link between the unconscious and conscious aspects of the psyche means the person operates with both aspects of the Self in everyday life. Jung explains:

> Conscious should defend its reason and protect itself and the chaotic life of the unconscious should be given the chance of having its way too—as much of it as we can stand. This means open conflict and open collaboration at once. That evidently, is the way human life should be.[18]

Wholeness is resolving the deepest division of the human personality on a symbolic plane, transcending to a more spiritual notion of the Self and an integrated, fully developed personality in its own right.

Cultural Psychology:
Awareness and Self-Direction

Cultural Psychology: Awareness and Self-Direction

A. Cultural Awareness and Cultural Competency
B. Successful and Enjoyable Intercultural Relationships
C. What Is Culture?
D. Could You Be a Successful Aborigine in the Outback?
E. Environmental Opportunities and Development
F. Cross-Cultural Studies of Piaget's
   Theory of Cognitive Development
   1. Different Approaches To Problem Solving
   2. Can Children "Catch Up" With Those
      Who Have Had More Opportunities?
G. Values and Identity
H. Individualism and Collectivism
   1. Cultural Influences on Emotion
   2. A Collectivist Society: Italian Village Life
   3. An American Collectivist Society:
      Native Americans
I. Phenomenological Reality and
   Mutually Fulfilling Relationships
J. Cultural Psychology and Gender
   1. The Victorian Feminine Myth
   2. Cultural Standards of Feminine Beauty in
      19th Century China
   3. Twenty-first Century Standards of Beauty
   4. Role Conflicts in the 21st Century
K. Summary: Cultural Psychology and Self-Direction

Cultural Psychology: Awareness and Self-Direction

Are we the product of our culture? A group of Ethiopian women who were airlifted out of the bush into modern Israel were shown a photo of birds in flight. The newly arrived immigrants shook their heads as though they didn't understand. The Israeli teacher realized the women did not perceive the birds in the picture. The African women did not understand that the image on the glossy paper was an animal they had seen before.[1] What if we had grown up in a culture without photos? Would we recognize the birds in the picture?

In this chapter we are going to look at how our culture influences our perceptions and how understanding people from other cultures can increase our awareness and self-direction.

We live in a rapidly shrinking world where an estimated 4,000 cultures are coming into greater contact with each other. Global forces, including instantaneous world news coverage, worldwide Internet communication, jet travel and worldwide competition for jobs are breaking down the barriers of the past. No longer do we live in a time when villagers have the option of ignoring the people on the other side of the hill.

Cultural Awareness and Cultural Competency

Even societies such as the United States, which has been historically and economically dominant and relatively isolated, are now challenged. Those who have had little direct contact with other cultures now find that things are changing. Cultural psychologists such as Lonner and Malpass emphasize the importance of developing more understanding and respect for other cultures and ethnic groups in order to overcome cultural misunderstandings and competition for scarce resources worldwide.[2]

Social psychologists, such a Professor Troy Duster,[3] at UC Berkeley's Cultural Diversity Project, suggest that worldwide forces are redefining what it means to be an educated person and prepared to fully participate in the 21st century. It's no longer adequate to be just bilingual or even computer literate. Today, an increasingly valuable asset in business is to be able to function effectively in different cultural contexts from the culture one happened to be born into—to be *culturally competent*. This includes developing sensitivity and appreciation for various cultural and ethnic groups to function effectively in the emerging global economy.

Developing cultural competency today includes familiarizing oneself with psychology from around the world. Historically, psychology has had a relatively narrow perspective: most psychologists and psychological research originate from Western societies such as Canada, the United States and Western Europe. Today there is a growing interest in challenging and expanding psychology to make it more relevant to people of all cultures. Using the empirical, objective approach of scientific inquiry and culturally sensitive means, we can adapt the models of psychology to include culturally diverse communities of modern society.

This may contribute to a greater appreciation, understanding and cultural sensitivity in our local communities as well as in international affairs.

Culture is a silent and invisible determiner of our fundamental perception of ourselves and influences how we feel, think and act.[4] In fact cultural psychologists refer to *cultural lenses* that filter our perceptions in ways of which we are unaware, supporting the underlying assumptions we take for granted and determining how we interpret our own and others' behavior. Cultural Psychologist David Matsumoto recommends that the first step in gaining an understanding of such cultural influences on behavior is to recognize the effects of cultural filters on our own perceptions and thoughts and how they determine behavior. This means developing the skills to question our assumptions, what we take for granted.

Successful and Enjoyable Intercultural Relationships

Travel can help develop an awareness of our own cultural assumptions and new ways of thinking. Encounters with other cultures force us to question and become conscious of culturally determined assumptions because so many habitual ways of behaving simply don't work. Encountering people with different cultural values, thoughts, behaviors and ways of looking at the world requires a conscious effort to see ourselves and others in a new light. Outside the normal tourist routes there may be a sense of being different, of being an outsider, yet at the same time there is the excitement of learning about the worldviews and life experiences of people from other cultures while becoming more conscious of ourselves. We may develop some detachment from our culture, allowing for more self-direction to consciously choose values that are fundamental. Cultural competency includes this ability to "let go" of the persona, being sensitive to others and as Duster suggests, accepting being "different" or an "outsider" in some situations.

Sometimes travelers find that the locals actively seek them out, enjoying them, joining in a cross-cultural adventure of personal discovery. We can do this at home as well by seeking out travelers or by making friends from other cultures. This is much like traveling without the expense. Cross-cultural experiences provide people with the opportunity to discover more about themselves for personal development and fulfillment. One of the challenges in the modern world is for people of diverse ethnic backgrounds to develop a basis for mutually fulfilling relationships.

Being able to function effectively in cultural contexts different from the culture one was born into is increasingly valuable in today's world, seeing each other as resources and recognizing different competencies. Yet, it is not always easy. Duster suggests that there may first be a transition period of "self-segregation" that is sometimes difficult to penetrate. He says this may be a prerequisite to strengthening one's identity and sense of community, and then to bring that strength to the larger social arena. Some, especially the idealistic, may experience impatience, disillusionment and periods of conflict. This may be normal for such a process. Eventually, as people from different cultural experiences come together, new understandings and problem-solving strategies may result in a new level of enrichment for society and the individual.

What is Culture?

Just how much of our experience is determined by culture? Social scientists have discussed the importance of the individual's environment—whether it's supportive, warm, caring or authoritarian, whether the child's physical needs are taken care of and whether social factors exist that may interrupt or enhance the individual's development. Today there is a growing interest in the field of cultural psychology, studying human behavior with a global perspective; researching the subtle effects culture has on our ways of thinking, feeling, perceiving and understanding. Let's look at a few of the key ideas.

Culture refers to a way of life, the complex ways in which different groups of people live. It refers to the behavior patterns, beliefs, values, work patterns, music, dress, diet and ceremonies of people that are passed on from one generation to the next. It influences identity, what and how we learn, and social behavior. The shared rules of a culture let us know what kind of behavior is expected. These shared rules of a culture result from becoming socialized through learning rules, child-rearing practices and through the subtle, informal learning of enculturation.

North Americans have many ethnic identities. Our ancestors may have been Asian, Latino, Arab, English, African or come from many other origins. *Ethnic identity* is a sense of membership based on shared values, customs, and history of an ethnic group. Ethnic identity refers to characteristics of one's culture that the individual has incorporated internally, while *ethnicity* refers to external characteristics such as race, cultural heritage, nationality, religion or language. In contrast, a person may not identify with his ethnicity. For example, you may be Polish American (ethnicity) but may or may not identify with the culture (ethnic identity). It's important to note that people can be of the same race or nationality and not share the same values or behavior, that is, the same culture.[5] A *culturalist* may be of any particular race or nationality but acts in accordance with or identifies with the values or behaviors of a specific culture. In cultural psychology discussions, the term ethnicity (a socio-cultural term) is preferred to race (a biological, genetic term).

One must always allow for a vast array of individual differences that exist within each ethnic or cultural grouping. We want to be cautious of stereotyping. For example, not all Asians are excellent students; some even resent the pressure of such assumptions. Each person's behavior is determined by multiple causes. Diversity and individual differences exist in every group.

Cultural psychologists study how and why culture affects the individual's behavior. This includes ecological factors, cultural heritage, nationality, religion and language.

Ecological refers to the mutual relations between organisms and their environment.

Individualism refers to the degree a culture fosters individual needs, wishes and desires over group needs.

Collectivism refers to the degree which a culture emphasizes the sacrifice of individual wishes for the sake of the group.

Cross-cultural psychology compares ideas and principles across cultures to see which hold up universally and which are culturally specific.

Could You Be a Successful Aborigine In the Australian Outback?

Milpurra lives on the harsh dessert terrain in a remote area of Australia called the outback where his ancestors have lived for thousands of years. His lifestyle has not changed much from his distant ancestors, the Aborigines. Every day he ventures out across long expanses of arid land in search of enough water for the day. He and his family follow a nomadic lifestyle based on hunting and gathering, constantly moving over the vast landscape. Milpurra doesn't have many possessions; he has a spear, similar to his father's weapon. Women in his tribe carry digging sticks to dig for food. They are always traveling. He can move quickly with his tribe, sleeping in the open air, using vegetation to keep warm. Imagine what it would be like to be nomadic, without "things," living exposed to the raw elements of nature, on the edge of existence everyday, seeking out scarce new water supplies.

Milpurra's spiritual life is rich and active. He and his family create art incorporating many symbols; there are paintings that show various locations of the paths one must follow to find water. It is important to get around on the vast desert without getting lost. For Milpurra, survival depends on paying close attention to the artwork, to oral myths and stories that give meaning to each particular feature of the landscape and to routes traveled by ancestral spirits. The Aborigines believe every tree, rock and water hole contains the spirits of ancestors. Individuals not only learn their way around the desert, but they learn the legends of its spiritual inhabitants. In fact, they believe they are one with the spirits of their ancestors. Milpurra and his people share a very different relationship with the environment than those who live in post-modern industrial societies.

How do you think Milpurra might be different from you? Or how would you be different if you had been born an Aborigine? Would you be less materialistic? What cross-cultural psychology has shown us is how the human potential can be manifested in so many different ways.

Environmental Opportunities and Development

The Swiss Psychologist Jean Piaget and the Danish-born American Psychologist Erik Erikson say we develop from our experiences. It follows that if we have different experiences we will become different people. Erikson says that the problems we face at each life stage are a major factor in shaping our personalities, affecting our self-awareness, identity as well as cognitive and social development. These qualities do not emerge automatically, but rather must be cultivated and require environmental opportunities. Piaget, along with Erikson, says that our growth occurs in periods of crisis, struggle, tension and questioning. Piaget would say that children learn to think intelligently as a result of personally interacting with a lawful universe, through experiencing and discovering the laws of nature for themselves.

Piaget suggests that a child will naturally consider new variables unless inquiry is blocked. From our perspective of cross-cultural psychology we find a child's cognitive development can be blocked or encouraged by environmental and cultural limitations or opportunities.

John Berry developed a theory that says the individual's development is linked to the demands of the environment and culture. For example, people who live in an environmental setting where hunting is the basis for survival will reflect cognitive developmental skills adapted to the *ecological* demands of hunting. You'll recall that ecological refers to the relationship between the organism and the environment or in this sense the person's cultural adaptation to the environment. These cultural adaptations are transferred from one generation to the next through values, child rearing and socialization practices. They determine which human potentials will be developed.

Cross-Cultural Studies of Piaget's Theory of Cognitive Development

Cultural psychologists acknowledge the importance of Piaget's research on children's thinking processes. Piaget introduced the "clinical method" to study *cognitive development* (thinking processes) in which he would have an open, free-flowing dialogue with a child who was trying to solve a task. The result was a description showing the dynamics of how the child's thinking develops. He based his theory on questioning and carefully observing a few children at length. For example, his theory about motor development in infants was based on his own three children. While Piaget tested children's thinking processes in his homeland of Switzerland and generalized his results to include all children, cross-cultural psychologists decided to test whether his experiments would actually hold true in other cultures. The following experiments will also demonstrate how evidence can accumulate in psychology to support the universal applications of a theory.

Let's take a closer look at the thinking processes of the Aborigine children in Milpurra's tribe. One of Piaget's former students, Professor Pierre Dasen of the University of Geneva in Switzerland, decided to do just that when he visited the Australian Aborigines. Such landmark studies show how cultural psychology develops. He replicated Piaget's lemonade experiment on conservation in which children were asked whether the quantity of a liquid changed when it was poured from a short, wide glass into a tall slender glass and then back again. Piaget originally found that children, ages 5 to 7, realized that the amount of liquid remains the same, despite changes in appearance. However, Dasen found that while this type of reasoning took place in Australian Aborigine children, it was usually between 10 to

13 years of age and some never did achieve *conservation*, that is recognition that the quantity of liquid remained the same no matter what shape glasses were used.

In Piaget's lemonade study, the child replaces intuitive thought with concrete operational thinking. When the child realizes that the amount of lemonade doesn't change, *concrete operational thinking* has taken place. In other words, as long as the situation involves concrete examples the child is able to use reasoning. The child is not just responding to appearances but is beginning to have some understanding of the underlying reality. The seven-year-old realizes that the amount of lemonade is not solely determined by height but rather by height interacting with width.

What kinds of mental skills do you think children who were raised in the desert and hunt for water every day would develop? Since finding their way was very important, Dasen tested the Aborigines' spatial reasoning. First, they looked at a large picture of a landscape laid out on a table. They were told to point to a toy doll or sheep on the picture. In the second stage the sheep was removed and the picture was turned 180 degrees so it was upside down, and then the children were asked to point to where the sheep had been. The results showed that the Aboriginal children found the spatial tasks easier than the conservation of liquid while in contrast the Swiss children found the spatial tasks more difficult. Concrete operational reasoning in the spatial domain developed more rapidly than skills of quantification for the Aborigines.

Why would this be so? Which culture uses more quantifying, Western society or the Aborigines? Imagine for a moment what it would be like to be part of the non-materialistic Aboriginal culture. There is little need to quantify things since you don't store or sell things. You only use numbers up to five, anything more than five is "many." You search for water daily, although the exact amount of water is not an issue. You share the meat from the hunt; it is not sold or distributed by weight or quantity. Who receives a particular piece is determined by kinship. However, your ability to find your way around in order to find water, hunt, or find each other at the end of the day is essential to your survival. Spatial knowledge is therefore very important to your culture while quantification (counting or measuring) is not as important to your way of life.

So if spatial knowledge is necessary for survival in the outback, what kinds of *cultural aids* support its development? Oral traditions, mythologies, artwork and stories passed on from childhood are all cultural aids. Another cultural aid is artwork that uses symbols to show various locations and the paths between them. They give meaning to each particular feature of the landscape and focus attention to routes traveled by ancestral spirits to ensure the Aborigines' survival. If you were an Aborigine, you would need to pay attention to such details to survive and function successfully in your cultural context. There is not a lot of room for mistakes when you live in such a vulnerable state in nature.

In contrast, many of our cultural aids encourage quantification. Can you think of some? Even at a very young age our culture exposes children to counting and the accumulation of wealth through games such as Monopoly and comic book figures like Uncle Scrooge, who is always counting his money. So people raised in a materialistic, urban, industrialized society learn that their culture places a high value on quantification. Success, status, well being, acceptance, and even survival might well be based on the accumulation of material possessions, storing goods and measuring how much one owns or is "worth."

In short, the results of Dasen's study, which found differences between Aborigines' and Swiss children's skills in spatial reasoning, support Piaget's view that the child's development is shaped by experiences: different experiences result in different aspects of development. For example, getting around in the natural world would probably be a lower priority for urban children and adults who spend so much time contained in the space of predictable rooms. One shopping mall is much the same as another; one schoolroom is the same as another; one office cubical is the same as another. Even locating a drinking fountain is a far cry from the Aboriginal child's endeavor to find water in the desert. In industrialized societies the child pays more attention to bus route numbers while traveling from one place to another and may not even notice the lay of the land. Here again, the development of a child's skills at spatial tasks and quantification varies in different cultural settings depending on what contributes to survival. In turn, these skills are highly valued in the culture.

In follow up studies Dasen found similar results in his study of nomadic Eskimo children who were more developed at spatial tasks than were sedentary West African children from an agricultural culture who were more developed at quantification. Each group did best in areas supported and valued by their culture for survival. What is needed to survive is promoted in child-rearing practices and more easily expressed in the language.

In other words, culture acts as a lens, influencing our perceptions, assumptions, thinking and behavior. It focuses us on what is important in our society to ensure survival. Culture can be thought of as an accumulation of experience based on those who lived before us—a way of life.

By comparing the results of studies of multiple cultures, converging evidence may clarify and reveal phenomena that would have otherwise gone unnoticed. In contrast, traditional psychology with a narrow base of subjects, often college psychology students, may produce research findings that are questionable in terms of generalizing the assumptions to the larger population. To understand better how culture influences social and individual behavior and to overcome psychology's cultural bounds and ethnocentric tradition, we need to examine psychology from a multicultural perspective.

Different Approaches To Problem Solving. Could there be different mental approaches to solving problems in different environments? Psychologist Patricia Greenfield decided to test French West African children from both urban and bush environments. The bush children learned the oral traditions of their tribe but had no formal schooling.

Nearly all of the schooled children attained conservation by age 11 to 13 while only half of the unschooled children achieved conservation. Greenfield concluded the school children relied less on appearances and more on thinking while the unschooled bush children relied more on appearances.

However, when the bush children were allowed to pour the water for themselves into different shaped glasses, there was a dramatic increase in their understanding of conservation. Greenfield suggested that the bush children may have initially attributed the seeming change in the quantity of water to the "magical powers" of the adults in authority, but were less likely to believe in magic after pouring the water for themselves.

Surprisingly, Greenfield found that African children didn't distinguish between their own point of view and the object. For example, the children responded with silence when they were asked, "Why do you think one glass has more?" However, the children would answer the question when it was reworded as, "Why does the glass have more?" Researchers thought the children did not share Western self-consciousness and did not separate or distinguish between their own thoughts or statements and the thing or object itself, so the idea of explaining a statement was meaningless ("it is what it is"). They explain the external event without a reference to their thoughts. The idea that things may vary with a personal point of view may be less prevalent in non-Western culture.

Can Children "Catch Up" With Those Who Have Had More Opportunities?   Let's look more closely at a question that Greenfield's findings suggest: if children who have lacked certain experiences are given opportunities, is it possible to bridge the gap? Lemonade studies of Eskimo children and African children have shown they could indeed catch up if they were given the opportunity through a second chance or training. Dasen tested children from three different non-Western societies: Central Eskimo, Baoule of West Africa and Kikukiyu of Kenya, East Africa. He found that when they were trained to understand conservation in one medium, say liquid, they could generalize what they learned about conservation to other objects. Children realized the number of objects stayed the same no matter how they were grouped. This study demonstrates that a person may lack skills, not because he or she is incapable, but because of a lack of experience.

Of course, the idea of "catching up" should be understood in the context that all cultures are both advanced in some ways and not advanced in others according to Professor Lee Rode. If an African adolescent from the bush environment were to find herself alone in her environment, could she survive? Most assuredly. If a North American adolescent were to find herself alone in that same African environment, would she survive? The odds are not as good. But the North American adolescent might be fortunate enough to be taken in by an African bush population and given the training she needs to develop those survival skills. In other words, she lacks experience, but can advance. And in more collectivistic African societies, more help would likely be offered, while in individualistic North American society, people might be less likely to take a stranger in. It gives one pause as to how to define societies as "advanced".[6]

These landmark studies in cross-cultural psychology give support to the underlying premise of Piaget's conclusion that children's thinking develops from experiences. When children recognize inconsistencies and realize they have made a mistake, there is an opportunity for their thinking to become more complex and comprehensive to include underlying principles while freeing them from appearances. Studies also empirically support Piaget's assumptions that stages of cognitive development occur universally in sequence for people of all cultures, although the ages may vary. A review of studies on children from Great Britain, Australia, Greece and Pakistan confirms that children from very different cultures learn Piaget's stages of cognitive development in the same order. Some cultures tend to lag in specific areas of development while others are accelerated depending on how much opportunity they've had according to Matsumoto, a psychology professor at San Francisco State University and author of the review.

From such research we can better understand the differences among people of various cultures. Cognitive skills reflect the needs of a particular culture and whether they are required for survival. In some ways, tasks can be thought of as culture-bound, including those linked to the practices of formal schooling in Western society.[7] Rather than ranking people from one culture as smarter or better able to function at higher levels, these studies suggest that an individual's skills or strategies reflect the setting or cultural context in which he or she grows up.

Values and Identity

The Australian psychologist Norman Feather says values are more fundamental to the individual's self-concept than attitudes. They go beyond specific objects, events and situations. Feather used the Schwartz Value Survey, designed to access values in cross-cultural studies, to measure the values of 281 Australian college students in an introductory psychology classes. The results demonstrated that national identification with Australia was positively related to the importance of such values as hedonism, security and achievement for both sexes, while men identified with power and women identified with social values.

He concludes that the degree to which people identify with a specific culture is related to how well they perceive the culture supporting their values. People identify with their culture when their values are supported by the culture. Those who are in the minority, who do not feel that their values are supported by their society, may not identify with the society.

Individualism and Collectivism

In Thailand parents tell their children the following story about a father and his sons: the father gives each of his three sons a fish and asks them to make the fish last a year. The first son cut his fish into 10 parts and tried to eat them very slowly for lunch and dinner, but his fish was soon gone. The second son preserved his fish with salt and also ate it very slowly, but his fish was also soon gone. The third son made curry with his fish and gave jars of it away to all his neighbors. The next day one of his neighbors gave him a jar of curry, and the second day another neighbor gave him another jar and so on throughout the year. This story represents a cultural aid to teach Thai children the value of collectivism.

In the study of cultural psychology, we find cultures can be divided into those that value *collectivism*, working for the good of the group, or *individualism*, in which the focus is on the individual.

Individualism is a set of beliefs and practices that assumes the individual is separate from others and nature, identity is derived from one's inner world and the emphasis is on the individual. Collectivists believe that the individual is interdependent with society and nature, identity is derived more from the outer world of objective actions than inner experience and the group is more important than the individual. For the collectivists, the ultimate determinant of their personal identities is that their actions affect others.[8]

For example, in the study we discussed earlier about African bush children, cooperative social responsibility was most valued in the parents' belief system. Cognitive skills were only valued if used for the good of the group, not for individual gains. In other words, the focus was not on the individual excelling, but on how the individual, for example a child herding cattle in the Serengeti, contributed to the family and community.

In an attempt to develop a universal definition of individualism and collectivism free of any ethnocentric cultural bias, Hui and Triandis asked social scientists from around the world, including North America, Latin America, Europe and Australia, to judge how people in each of the two categories would respond differently to given situations. The test revealed clusters of beliefs and attitudes.

Collectivists characteristically would consider the implications of their ideas on other people. They have a higher degree of concern for how their decisions and attitudes affect their spouses, their mothers and their friends. They are also thought to be more likely to share their resources, their tools and appliances, while individualists would rather personally own things. Collectivists are more influenced by their social group, more apt to go along with the group for interpersonal harmony and acceptance and more vulnerable to feeling shame and loss of face if the group disapproves of them.

In contrast, individualists belong to many more groups and are less devastated if rejected by a particular one. Another survey suggests that individualism is a matter of being emotionally independent from the influence of groups.[9] Among employees in a large multinational firm, individualism was highest in the United States, Australia and Britain and lowest in Venezuela, Colombia and Pakistan. A study of Navy recruits found that Hispanics were among the highest in such collectivist values as those related to good interpersonal relationships, harmony, acceptance of authorities, loyalty, interdependence and reliability.[10]

Traditional American culture fosters individualistic values—the individual is encouraged to excel. People of

These children herding cattle on the Serengeti in Kenya, East Africa, illustrate the cooperative social values of collectivist cultures as they contribute to the family and the community.

some cultures value conformity more than Americans. In fact, many cultures foster more collective, group-oriented values: valuing conformity, compliance and obedience. In a review of the literature, Matsumoto found that the British endorse individualistic values such as independence and freedom more than Asian subjects who value conformity and obedience. Similarly, Indonesians[11] and Japanese[12] value conformity more than Americans.

A criticism of modern psychology is its ethnocentrism and conception of the self as individualistic. The ethnocentric history of American psychology has been reflected in certain concepts and models, sometimes resulting in a limited understanding, such as the emphasis on the self (self-fulfillment, self-actualization, etc.). Although individualists develop an awareness of self as being separate from the outside world, the concept of self is understood differently in collectivist cultures. For example, people in Asian culture see themselves as more connected and interdependent, largely defined by the group to which they belong.[13] Collectivist values include emphasis on humbleness, duty, obligation, inner harmony, forgiveness and perseverance. In the Euro-American cultural context the self is assumed to be more separate from others and nature.

Professor Bruce Lerro, cultural psychologist at Dominican College, says cross-cultural research finds the following differences between collectivism and individualism. For the individualist the self ends with the body while for the collectivist the self includes the in-group and nature. In the individualist society the individual has a "true self" separate from roles while in the collectivist society the individual's life cannot be separated from the life of the in-group. The values for the individualist include achievement and excitement.[14]

Lerro suggests that much of psychology and therapy is individualistic in its assumptions, such as social roles being separate from and a constraint on the true self.

"In contrast, in collectivist societies, your role *is* your identity," according to Lerro. "There is no imprisoned true self, trying to get out. To encourage this could invite anxiety."

Therapists who suggest that conflict in the family is the source of the client's problem will meet with tremendous resistance from collectivists. Whereas the individualist strives for self-expression and being true to the self, the collectivist will see preserving group harmony as the higher good.

Cultural Influences on Emotion.   Matsumoto stresses the importance of cultural influences on our emotions. He states that the distinction of individualism versus collectivism is such a meaningful measure of culture it should replace studying or classifying people in such categories as Caucasian, African American, Hispanic, and Asian or American, Irish, French, Japanese and British. He says that the way culture fosters putting the individual's needs and wishes first or the group's needs first is more useful in understanding differences in emotional expressions between cultures than one's race, ethnicity or country of citizenship. In other words, an individualistic or collectivist orientation may be more fundamental in determining emotional expression than race or ethnic group.

Understanding collectivism and individualism can contribute to more successful international business relations. Consider the following example of a cross-cultural misunderstanding between the director of an American business and the business representative in Germany. When he tells the American how to do something the American is offended. "American individualism comes into conflict with the German need for authority, directness and organization.

For the German, there is nothing inherently disrespectful, abrasive or incorrect about stating facts as givens: 'You will do it this way,' or 'you are wrong.' For Americans such statements might be true, but first they will react to the way the statement is made. If it sounds like a challenge to their authority as individuals to make their own decisions, they will take it as an affront." Americans may be more sensitive because of their emphasis on individualism to the blunt and direct German way of stating a fact. If the American business director had been aware of this classic cross-cultural interaction he found himself in, his buttons might not have been pressed so hard, says author Dean Allen Foster in *Bargaining Across Borders*.[15]

People fall somewhere on a continuum between collectivism and individualism, so there are many individual variations within a group. Studying collectivism and individualism sharpens our awareness of the impact of culture so that we may be in a better position to consciously choose how to balance these dimensions in our own lives. While modern American society encourages individualistic values, let's take a closer look at some cultures that have a greater emphasis on collectivism to clarify our own personal values and the options we have.

A Collectivist Society: Italian Village Life. To better understand collectivist society let's look at life in an Italian village at the foot of the Alps in Piedmont. It is common for multiple generations of families to live together in the same home. One household consists of an older woman living with her grandson and widowed son who fixes dinner for her everyday. They all eat together. Another older woman was widowed, so her brother moved in to help with the house and large garden. She has four grown daughters all of whom have their own children. One of her daughters and two grandchildren share her house. Two other daughters live a few houses away with their families. The fourth daughter's family lives less than a ten-minute walk away. Generations are in daily contact and help each other.

The cultural emphasis on family and personal life is supported by social-cultural structures. For example, Italian stores traditionally close from 1 to 4 p.m. so that shopkeepers have time during the day to spend with their families. This contrasts with some American businesses that are open 24 hours a day.

Many people tend their own home gardens and some produce surplus food for the village. Some neighbors specialize in raising chickens and rabbits. A landowner shares the harvests of his vineyards with his friends, who do much of the care and harvesting.

It is a strange experience for a person from another time and place, from a modern urban center, to sit and look out over a courtyard with open-ended barns and red tile roofs, realizing that this view has barely changed at all over the past four hundred years. Standing on the dirt floor of a 250-year-old cow barn gives a sense of going back in time.

One day the church bells start ringing loudly. From the church steeple two sets of large bells ring in a pattern for ten minutes alerting villagers who are tending fields on the outskirts of the village. The cadence of the bells announces the death of a villager, whether a man or woman, young or old. Later posters with the individual's photo and name appear around the village.

In such a collectivist, old world society, the deceased is kept at home for people to view, rather than at a funeral parlor. There is no embalming. Friends and neighbors come to the family home to pay their respects. One daughter says keeping her mother's body at home gives her time to get used to the idea that her mother is dead.

The day of the funeral, villagers stand in the aisles, overflowing the church and then go to the home of the deceased to carry the casket on foot in a procession to the cemetery. There an older son helps lay bricks in the family burial chamber even though a bricklayer is present. Generations of families are buried in family plots or small buildings. Some use a method of breaking and removing the coffin in an upper chamber when it is needed after a few years, allowing the remains to fall in a lower chamber with their ancestors' remains. In this small Italian village the whole community is aware of the family's loss and provides support. Contrast this to modern urban life in which people often seem to grieve the death of a loved one alone. Such a strong system of community support in this collectivist society may help the person deal with the sense of loneliness and loss.

An American Collectivist Society: Native Americans. Another collectivist culture closer to home is the traditional Native American culture in which the people also lived together in extended families. When the first settlers arrived, the Native American culture of North American included more than 600 languages and great variety from tribe to tribe. Yet there were certain common features among many of the Native Americans that conflicted with the early settlers way of doing things, in other words, they had cultural conflicts in values. The collectivist culture was in stark contrast to that of the newcomers, who pursued distinctly individualistic aims.

For example, the Native Americans couldn't understand why the settlers built fences, because for them land was held in common. The tribe shared the land, so when they sold it to the colonists, the Native Americans did not understand that they had given up the rights to fish and hunt. They were called "Indian givers" when they loaned something to a white man and then wanted it back. The white settlers believed the Indians had given these things as gifts for them to keep. For the Native Americans, possessions were to be shared and loaned, rather than owned. As a collectivist society they did not emphasize individual ownership and that resulted in misunderstandings.

These two collectivist cultures reflect certain characteristics: focusing on sharing and owning things in common and living in communities with extended families. Both cultures are close to the land, working the land in common. The emphasis is less on the individual excelling, but

Traditional Native American culture, a collectivist culture, emphasizes the individual's contribution to the group. *"Interior of a Mandan Earth Lodge" Watercolor and ink on paper. Courtesy of Joslyn Art Museum, Nebraska.*

rather on contributing to the good of the group. In the Native American culture and the traditional Italian village the individual's identity cannot be separated from the good of the group.

Phenomenological Reality and Mutually Fulfilling Relationships

Continuing our alternating multiple perspective approach, let us now turn to Psychologist Carl Rogers to further develop our cultural competencies and sensitivity to different cultures. Roger's approach is to take an internal frame of reference to better understand the life experience of others.

Rogers says people react to their "reality" as it is perceived from their own point of view so that two different people may experience the same thing but perceive and react to it very differently. Rogers calls this unique personal perspective one's *phenomenological reality*. It is not based solely on people and events as they are, but on likes and dislikes, values and what one reads into the world.

During the American hostage crisis in Iran in 1980, the U.N. Secretary General was sent to negotiate between the two countries. Secretary General of the U.N. Waldheim flew to Iran to seek the hostages' release. His efforts were set back when Iranian radio quoted him as saying that he had come as a mediator to work out a compromise. The Persian word compromise lacks a positive meaning; it means, "our integrity was compromised." In Persian the word "mediator" suggests meddler, someone who is uninvited. Within an hour after the radio broadcast the Secretary General's car was stoned.[16] From the perspective of the Persian people's phenomenological reality, the U.N. Secretary was perceived as a meddler while Americans saw him as a representative of their needs.

The concept of phenomenological reality can be useful for questioning our perceptions of others and developing cultural competency. Cultural misunderstandings can be minimized through sensitivity to other cultures using this theory. Roger's ideas on trust and communication have spread to the world of international relations.

Rogers says another important element of successful relationships is mutual *positive regard* that includes acceptance, liking, warmth, empathy and respect. It helps people to accept and to be themselves, reducing the need to be defensive and rigid in their perceptions, merely acting in social roles. In accepting and expressing themselves, people tend to develop feelings of positive regard for others without judgment, which facilitates communication and the development of healthy and mutually fulfilling relationships. This can take place in the context of cross-cultural experiences.

Cultural Psychology and Gender

How does one get inside the mode of thinking of another culture? Erik Erikson's ideas on *psychohistorical* studies are useful for developing skills to enter worldviews and modes of thinking of other cultures far different from our own. This involves looking at a particular historical moment and the opportunities and limitations that help shape the person's identity. Part of this approach is to take the person's internal frame of reference to understand why he or she would go along with certain cultural traditions. Such perspectives may help us see our own historical moment with greater objectivity.

Not all cultural values are positive: some actually work against the health and welfare of its members. Sometimes the values of a functioning society and the welfare of its members are in contradiction. Let's look at an example of how culture influences gender identity using two 19th century psychohistorical perspectives of female identity, one from China and the other from the United States.

Why would women participate in their own oppression? Why would a woman wear such tight fitting clothing that she couldn't breath properly and might faint at any moment? Or alternatively, why would women wrap their daughters' feet so they would barely be able to stand or walk? How does society get women to participate in behavior that works against their health in favor of certain cultural traditions?

The Victorian Feminine Myth. What if you were a young fashionable woman living in the Victorian era? You would have been required to wear a very peculiar undergarment which would have, in fact, changed your whole way of life, limiting your physical movement, your endurance, and even perhaps your self concept.

If you recall the tiny hourglass figure represented in pictures of women from the 1800's, you'll realize no one is born with such a tiny waist. It could only be achieved by cinching the waist with a corset. A highly fashionable woman would reduce her waistline by at least 4 inches for an hourglass figure, however the whalebone corset itself would expand the waist by 2 inches, so she had to make her waist 6 inches smaller. Well-to-do women strove for this ideal figure until the early 1900's. If you didn't wear the corset your clothes wouldn't fit, for fashions were designed for a tiny waist. You would be called "a loose woman." Not many women would take their corsets off during the day except those who worked in fields. The few women who wore pants to work in the fields were called radicals. Parenting books advised buying a girl's first corset at age nine, and

1889 picnic party near Pasadena, California on Thanksgiving Day. Can you imagine going to a picnic in such formal dress? Notice the facial expression on the fashionable woman with the hourglass figure. She is wearing a tight corset to make her waist smaller. Do you think she's relaxing at the picnic? *Courtesy of University Archives, Bancroft Library, University of California, Berkeley.*

although she would probably find it uncomfortable, make her sleep with it on until she got "used" to it.[17]

A fashionable woman's diary explains how much strain her body endured by narrowing her waist 6 inches by day. At night she could feel her organs shift around inside her body disturbing her sleep for hours. The fainting spells, the difficulty breathing and the strain on internal organs alerted some to the health consequences of wearing such undergarments. Rehabilitation centers opened to treat women who became ill as a result of corsets.

Health guides recommended that women should not wear more than 11 pounds of underwear! However, women were required by fashion to wear up to fifteen petticoats to achieve a full-skirted look that restrained their movement.

Garments restricted a woman's activity not only at home, but also at the beach. Accounts from Santa Cruz, California, describe how a young woman who went to the beach would wear a cloak covering her from head to foot. Under this was a woolen "swimsuit" covering the entire body. To preserve her modesty, if she wanted to go into the water she would take off her cloak inside a small house called a bathing machine. Then a gentleman would roll the bathing machine down to the surf where she could get in discreetly, holding on to metal cables so she wouldn't be washed away. She had to wear so much clothing that the weight of the wet material could wash her away if she didn't hold on.

How would this kind of attire, which placed tremendous physical restriction on you, make you see yourself? You would definitely be the weaker sex, expecting to faint at any moment, anticipating how someone would revive you with smelling salts. All this was considered very feminine. At night you would take off your corset and listen to your organs gurgle and feel them reposition themselves as you tried to sleep. You would have been indoctrinated as a child, before you had a chance to question this fashion. You would learn that you were not athletic, that you must wear a corset and expect difficulty breathing. You couldn't go swimming because women were required to wear so many pounds of heavy wool.

No wonder you would feel weak, like fainting and would probably believe that you needed someone to take care of you and would assume a role of being submissive.

This would compliment men's beliefs about the weaker sex. Men would see themselves as protectors. It all fits together. Everyone has experiences and assumptions that confirm this cultural myth. Contrast this with the Iroquois Native American culture in which women were not physically handicapped by their clothing and were treated as equals.

The Victorian era fashion gave substance to the feminine myth and today provides us with the opportunity to understand the dynamics of cultural influences. In the Victorian context it was assumed that women were weak and needed men to take care of them. As a result of social structures, women actually experienced themselves as weak, confirming the cultural myth. Even the furniture industry contributed to this myth by selling "fainting couches."

Let's take this myth apart in detail to understand its far-reaching effects on the individual. Breathing is a fundamental basic physiological need, tied to health, awareness and the ability to concentrate. A woman wears a corset that prevents her from breathing deeply so she becomes faint if she tries any strenuous activity. What are the ramifications of this? She doesn't see herself as a physically competent person. Through this socially fabricated experience she accepts an identity as the weaker sex. Although the problem was created by cultural values, its real source goes unrecognized.

The Victorian culture manipulated women to accept a myth and an identity that worked against their health. Women who didn't conform to the expectations of the time had to endure name-calling and labels such as "loose women," rather than "straight-laced women."

Their self-acceptance was undermined and taken away through social forces and institutions of their time, and then, in a sense, "sold" back to them in exchange for submission to cultural values that hurt them. We can see the power of such cultural influences when they result in people ignoring personal health and comfort in order to be accepted. These dynamics and mechanisms are not limited to Western culture.

Cultural Standards of Feminine Beauty in 19th Century China.   While Victorian women were called "loose" for not wearing a corset, Chinese women were told if they did not bind their daughters' feet, no one would want to marry them. In China up until about 1917, tiny feet were a sign of beauty and femininity. Just as their Western sisters were taught to believe they were the weaker sex, Chinese females were expected to be weak and physically vulnerable. In Pearl Buck's book, *The Good Earth,* she describes how the Chinese hero desires a woman named Lotus because she has such tiny hands and feet. He finds it very attractive and alluring how she teeters and almost falls as she tries to walk. Bound feet were considered erotic. Lotus is unable to walk any distance because of her small feet. The Chinese said a woman with bound feet walked "like a tender young willow shoot in a spring breeze."[18]

In her book, *Wild Swans*, Jung Chiang explains how her grandmother's feet were bound at two years old with 20 feet of cloth. The toes were bent inward under the sole and a large stone was placed on top to crush the arch. The girl screamed in pain so her mother stuffed her mouth with a rag. The bones were broken, but still bound day and night so the foot would not recover. The pain was terrible. When the child pleaded to have her feet untied, the mother said she was doing it for her child's future happiness.

What was a mother to do, to step outside the boundaries of her culture? If she did, her daughter might later blame her for being weak. Following the beliefs of her culture, a mother knowingly put her child in excruciating pain,

Notice the size of the Chinese princess' foot in the photo above.
Her feet rest on a cushion. As a woman of higher status her
feet were never to touch the ground, it was considered a sign
of impurity. *Courtesy of Stibbert Museum, Florence, Italy.*

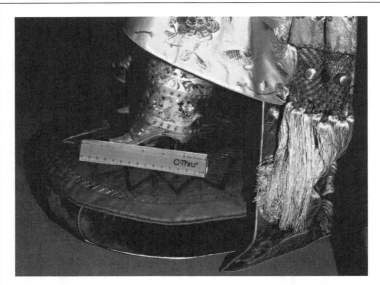

A closer look. These authentic shoes are on a life size model. As a standard for comparison the ruler is only 6 inches long. You can see then that her foot is about 4 inches long, the width of the line above the photo. Can you imagine trying to stand on such small feet? *Courtesy of Stibbert Museum, Florence, Italy.*

so that she would be more attractive to men and be chosen for marriage. The cultural values were in conflict with her motherly instincts. She knew that on her daughter's wedding day her future mother-in-law would lift the girl's skirt to look at her feet. If they were more than about 4 inches long the older woman would throw back down the skirt with a look of contempt on her face.

In China foot binding was a way to control females says Dr. Francesco Civita, curator of the Japanese Section at the Stibbert Museum in Florence, Italy. "Women of a higher social class were carried around on carriages, told not to walk. It was considered a sign of impurity to touch the ground. It was a way of controlling them in my opinion. Women were not physically controlled, but behaviorally controlled."[19]

Culture can be thought of as a built-in set of rewards and punishments for certain beliefs, values, standards of behavior or beauty. Because of the uniformities, the child learns to anticipate, remember and expect certain rewards and punishments, internalizing the culture's beliefs and values. Cultural-social sanctions used to enforce compliance include negative labeling that becomes part of the young child's thinking, forming his or her basic assumptions and conclusions regarding themselves and others.

Our culture shapes our experiences, thoughts and feelings. In the two cultural contexts we've studied, women experienced themselves as weak, confirming their cultural myths. Yet these were socially fabricated experiences. Women were taught they were objects of beauty to enhance the male status. These are some of the mechanisms society used to oppress women.

In short, Chinese girls learned from their mothers that they would not be desirable for marriage unless they submitted to torturous foot binding to keep their feet unnaturally small. They became acceptable, attractive to men, by having their feet crushed and bound while Victorian women wore corsets that reduced their oxygen supply, jeopardizing their health, in order to meet society's standards of beauty.

Twenty-first Century Standards of Beauty. What are some of the standards of beauty in modern society that influence and shape a woman's self-concept? Today, magazines and movies promote super thin models. In fact, female models weigh 20 per cent less than their counterparts in previous generations such as Marilyn Monroe who set the standard of beauty in the U.S. 40 years ago. The reader of a contemporary magazine may not realize that some of the images have been manipulated and computer enhanced; they are not of real women. In some cases two different bodies have been blended, a different face may be substituted and all blemishes are removed.

To what extent does the Victorian and 19th century Chinese cultural assumption, that women should be willing to distort their physical bodies in potentially harmful ways in order to be beautiful, still fit today? Is this different from magazines promoting thin models and an array of diets, so young women turn to anorexia to fit the culture's image of desirability? Despite the health risks of anorexia and silicon breast implants, women in American culture continue to feel they should try to achieve an idealized figure.

Consider the following poem reflecting a young woman's personal struggle against anorexia, to free herself from the culture's ideal of feminine beauty.

> *Starving for something else,*
> *Losing myself in the race of life,*
> *To become something I would never want to be,*
> *Becoming someone who is nothing like me.*
> *Looking in the mirror,*
> *Drained of all emotion.*
> *There was nothing left to help me show*
>   *who I am inside.*
> *I'm tired of hiding behind the absence*
>   *of my caloric intake,*
> *Thinking that no matter my personality,*
> *If body fits the ideal then I'll always be full,*
> *Fulfilling everyone else's desires but my own.*

> *August 15, 2002*

Social definitions of beauty bring up the question of how much are we willing to give up to 'fit in'? We have used these feminine myths to understand how culture shapes our expectations, experiences and thoughts. From this we can see how culture, a way of life, maintains the validity of people's perceptions of reality. Through understanding the mechanisms of how identity develops, we may be able to modify the culture's impact, avoiding those aspects that are unhealthy or destructive. Those traditions that are less fundamental to human nature or are detrimental to others could be the first to be modified.

Role Conflicts in the 21st Century. Let's look at role conflict in the psychohistorical context of the 21st century. Roles include social expectations and contribute to the maintenance and functioning of society. During a period of rapid transition and change, the economic and social forces within society may contribute to role conflict.

Today's woman continues to face culturally defined standards of beauty as well as new challenges to her role. To fit the media image she is supposed to be able to do it all: to be beautiful, to work, to have a family. While Victorian fashion harmed a woman's health, the modern woman's health can also suffer as she tries to balance different roles at home and at work, in some cases finding herself unable to feel success at any of them.

Men, as well as women, can be caught. There are economic pressures as well as social forces that often require both parents to work outside of the home to maintain the same quality of life their parents had in the 1950's when many mothers stayed at home. Two parents working outside the home is becoming the norm in many parts of the industrialized world.

Various forms of *work-family conflicts* can occur when the role demands of work and family are incompatible. In modern American society some jobs require aggressive, hard selling behavior, very different from the kind of approach used to function sensitively and effectively within the family scenario. *Conflict* occurs when the behavior used in the work domain is incompatible with the behavior required in the home domain or visa-versa. Work may require more aggressive behavior, while parenting requires empathy and understanding.

Parents can be caught between the needs of a sick child at home and a deadline at work, reducing the adult's ability to function in either domain. Sometimes there is the challenge not only to balance work and taking care of young children, but there may be aging parents as well who require assistance,[20] resulting in role overload.

From a psychohistorical perspective we can see that these role conflicts require consciousness and self-direction to keep one's balance while navigating through these competing and at times seemingly irreconcilable demands.

Summary:
Cultural Psychology and Self-Direction

This chapter illustrates several important reasons why studying cultural psychology is useful.

1. To develop our individual sensitivities and cultural competencies.

2. To relate successfully with people of other cultures for our own personal enrichment.

3. To contribute to greater understanding and success in international relations and the global economy.

4. To test the universality of psychological concepts through cross-cultural studies.

5. To reveal and gain perspectives and greater understanding of the cultural forces that determine our thoughts, emotions and identities so that we may further our capacity for conscious choices and self-direction in such areas as social roles and multi-cultural relations.

Culture influences how our thinking develops and is structured. We have used *cross-cultural psychology* to compare ideas and principles across cultures to see if they hold up universally. By comparing the results of studies of multiple cultures, phenomena are revealed that otherwise would have gone unnoticed. Studies show how specific cognitive development, whether spatial or quantitative, is a reflection of the requirements of a particular environment or culture. For example, the Aborigine is good at spatial skills while the American is good at quantitative skills.

The cultural response to the environment includes cultural aids such as mythology and art that shape our assumptions and help determine our perceptions. Culture shapes our values, the way we think, feel and how we perceive ourselves and the world; in other words it shapes our identity. We see the world through "cultural lenses" that filter our perceptions. This focuses us on what is important in our society for success or survival.

In cultural psychology we found that cultures can be divided into those that either value collectivism, in which the group's needs are put first, or individualism, in which the culture focuses on individual needs and desires over group needs. The way a culture fosters putting the group's needs or the individual's needs first may be more useful in understanding differences in emotional expressions between cultures than race, ethnicity or country of origin. Concepts like individualist or collectivist are composites of values, resulting in orientations, such as being independent and valuing personal success or valuing family and harmony. They define relationships between people. Consciously cultivating elements of both collectivism and individualism in one's life may be useful, depending on the issues at hand and the opportunities and limitations of a particular moment.

As we've seen in the context of cultural standards of beauty, social forces can sweep over the welfare of the individual. This demonstrates the importance of making constructive conscious choices and being self-directive. From the study of such cross-cultural/historical perspectives we may gain greater objectivity for understanding our own psychohistorical moment.

Cultures and identities are being challenged worldwide. There are many forces breaking the bonds of cultural traditions and the sense of continuity and belonging. The environments that allowed a person to be a successful Aborigine or a successful American are changing. As the values and orientation of the 4,000 cultures of the world impact each other through the media, politics, terrorism and economics, people may find their traditional ways of life and their identities challenged.

How can people of different cultures benefit from each other's point of view? The study of cultural psychology may offer a basis for people of different cultures to discover common aspirations and values as a foundation for greater world understanding. We have an opportunity in the 21st century to develop cultural competency and sensitivity to other cultures along with the openness to question our assumptions and develop an appreciation of characteristics of other cultures that may contribute to international understanding.

Studying people from many different cultures may result in a clearer view of the weaknesses as well as the strengths of our own cultural ways. Some cultures, such as East Indian, emphasize spiritual values. Other cultures, such as Native Americans and the Aborigines, have profound bonds with the earth and encourage living in harmony with nature. Some, such as Thai culture, de-emphasize the self and place more value on the family. Other cultures, such as Native American, de-emphasize material accumulation and place more value on leisure, while the United States emphasizes material productivity, high technology and science. So many cultures have rich, diverse traditions.

The goal of this chapter is to become more self-directive through developing an awareness of the impact of culture, to see its strengths and weaknesses through such perspectives as collectivist and individualist, in order to make conscious choices and to see ourselves on a continuum, better able to develop identity outside the restrictions of a single culture.

Conclusion

*T*here is no single theory of psychology which fully explains the individual and the uniqueness of human experience. Today accelerating global forces are further challenging our individual and group identities. Rather there are tentative, approximate and complementary explanations. We cannot just take ourselves and others for granted, we need continual attention to function fully as human beings. Developmental psychology points out that we are fluid, rather than static entities, which means there is continually a need to reassess changing motives, interest and direction. Freud has demonstrated that our past influences how we function today and designated the irrational, emotional self which can carry earlier limitations and frustrations into our present lives.

Not only personal vulnerabilities, but external forces influence how we think and act. In a demanding, distracting environment in which aspects of the personality are molded by social forces or distorted through conditioning, making it difficult to determine who we are, our highest potentials can be left undeveloped. In some cases social forces can even cause people to go against their own identities and morals. This is because the social definition of the self, which maintains the society, such as status or power, may not be fully consistent with the optimal well-being of the person. Discerning which attitudes are socially directed and monitoring how such behavior affects our well-being can increase the amount of control we exert over our lives for greater efficiency and health. Separating the personal definition of self from those social goals which are irrational and from the limitations of our past, we can concentrate on personal development.

This requires understanding and effort because physiological needs and the need for self-esteem shout at us, while the higher needs of self-realization merely whisper. Yet by listening we can come in contact with powerful resources within us for self-direction and self-development. There is the universal spiritual self, the collective unconscious, which can serve as an inner guide. There is the self-actualizing, creative self, which can emerge once the hierarchy of needs has been satisfied in a supportive environment of positive regard. A basic theme of these theories is that we have the opportunity to see what kind of organism we are psychologically, physiologically and socially, and to choose our attitudes and behavior to develop the self and our human potentials. As we acknowledge the inner self, apart from our past and our society, the direction for authentic self-fulfillment is clarified, and life becomes more personally satisfying.

Because we are tied to the biological, psychological and social world which is constantly changing, we must repeatedly monitor and balance our desires in these three realms. For example, the desire for self-esteem can prod the individual to forsake physiological well-being to over-achieve at work. Or social conformity can restrain the development of individuality, leading us away from the kind of experimentation which is necessary to evolve a sense of security based on inner resources and personal competence. There can be many misdirections: depending on others to satisfy conditions of worth, being a captive of the desire for a former dependent way of life, or being drawn to groups or cults which promise a sense of security at the cost of self-actualization.

Transformation

We've seen that being human is to experience continuous change in the process of transformation and growth. In a sense we are different people at each life stage as motivations, perceptions and intellectual understanding change. The process of growth includes making mistakes, incorporating a sense of inferiority or humility. If we can accept this inherent tension, the discomfort of trial and error, rather than being overwhelmed, it may help us grow, to become more personally fulfilled and socially productive.

Letting go of some aspects of the past also contributes to growth and transformation. Freud's theory is one of the most powerful for understanding our emotional fixations from negative childhood experiences and irrational aspects of socialization. As a result we no longer need respond to situations in an automatic, purely emotional and unconscious manner, which only compounds problems, but rather, have more energy and flexibility for rational behavior and growth. Developmental psychology also emphasizes the necessity of changing our former ways of being to become self-actualized. What was appropriate for an eighteen-year-old to be fulfilled may no longer work for a thirty-year-old with a family, who needs to live for "we" rather than solely for "I," cultivating another generation. Carl Jung speaks to us of giving up ego-oriented goals in midlife to experience the fulfillment of the spiritual and psychological side of the personality. He describes the death of the ego as a step in the individuation process. Similarly, the work on stress-related illness suggests that moderating desires for high-powered advancement on a material plane may be crucial to longevity and psychological well-being.

Opposites

As we begin to let go of former ways of being, on the threshold of new self-expression, there's often a sense of ambivalence between our dependency and our desire for independence, between a sense of confidence and a sense of inferiority. Part of healing the splits in our personality, knowing the whole self, entails incorporating these opposite feelings. Growth occurs through the struggle to integrate and balance opposing tendencies, consciously developing inferior functions to respond more completely to life.

Not acknowledging these ambivalences can prevent personality integration. A child is told to be perfect and to deny negative feelings such as jealousy for a sibling. A young man may be taught to respect women and repress his sexual fantasies and passion. A boy learns to be "macho" and unmoving, to suppress tenderness and sympathy. Although the person may hold such lopsided views consciously, the opposite feelings still exist, no matter how deeply they are buried. These unconscious characteristics may then be experienced as projections on others—our maleness or femaleness on the opposite sex, evilness on other people or even on other countries. Unrecognized, such feelings can break out without rational considerations, limiting intimacy and self-development. Ignored, the opposite feelings may in time overwhelm and dominate us, reducing our ability to perceive reality clearly and to consciously direct our own lives. Carl Jung speaks to us about getting in touch with our own shadow and with the male and female archetypes within us, to become more aware of who we really are as individuals, differentiated from others. To struggle with evilness outwardly can be a misdirected attempt which must eventually take place inwardly.

Recognizing these opposite characteristics can clarify more personally appropriate and fulfilling goals. As we know ourselves better there is a sense of singularity of movement, of less dissension within. A feeling of wholeness and purpose dominates as one's priorities become clear.

With a better sense of our ambivalences, our attitudes in the world may become more tentative and open. Alternating perspectives, cultivating the ability to imagine more than one way of resolving a situation, helps overcome the limitations of socialization and one-sided thinking. Being in touch with all of our resources we can respond more fully to our present circumstances. The theories we've studied can be used for such alternating views, as a lifetime reference as new challenges unfold.

This book is designed for easy review. For instance, in male-female relationships, reading the section on Freud's Oedipus complex can help clarify the split between passion and respect; or Jung's work on the anima and the animus may be useful in understanding how we project feelings. Humanistic psychology's focus on the importance of unconditional acceptance can help build a relationship based on trust and positive regard. If external powers seem overwhelming, it may be of benefit to review sections on behaviorism and social forces to see how we are socially influenced, to differentiate the self from situational forces. The study of cultural psychology reminds us of how our feelings, thoughts and even our identities can be shaped by our culture. Distinguishing ourselves from our environment, from our archetypes and from the past, we can be more objective in the present moment. The chapter on self-actualization and Jung's work on the individuation process are relevant for getting in touch with the sources of power and direction within.

Rather than trying to offer a single viewpoint, this book is designed to provide concepts which are useful for self-direction, for you to be an active participant in your own continuing personality integration and growth, to make better decisions in moments when there is a need to be more objective, to incorporate different perspectives or to call on your own higher resources.

ADDENDUM

Identity,
Terrorism and Globalization

Identity, Terrorism and Globalization

Identity,
Terrorism and Globalization

At 8:46 on the morning of September 11, 2001, the United States became a nation transformed. An airliner traveling at hundreds of miles per hour and carrying some 10,000 gallons of jet fuel plowed into the North Tower of the World Trade Center in Lower Manhattan. At 9:03, a second airliner hit the South Tower. Fire and smoke billowed upward. Steel, glass, ash, and bodies fell below. The Twin Towers . . . both collapsed less than 90 minutes later.[1]

The 9/11 Commission Report

September 11th was burned into the American psyche forever as people around the world watched in horror and disbelief as commercial jet liners became missiles of destruction and people jumped out of exploding skyscrapers. The most powerful nation in the world suffered the most destructive terrorist attack in history while millions of people watched. Each individual was left to struggle with his or her sense of security and identity. So many questions followed. What is it to be an American? Who am I? What motivated the terrorists? How did it affect the way we look at ourselves? Can the study of psychology help us to understand these issues?

"The baseline of anxiety in our culture has risen," according to San Francisco Psychologist Mark Levy. "We are now all primed. It takes less for our fear signals to go off."[2]

The Method and Purpose

The following is meant as a starting point, to stimulate our thinking in our search for understanding, illustrating how the scientific approach of psychology can contribute to developing greater objectivity to grapple with today's pressing issues, such as terrorism, globalization and identity. In the beginning of this text we discussed how different models of thinking could be useful, even if not necessarily true, because they may have a *heuristic value,* which means they encourage further independent investigation and questioning. The following ideas are not presented as complete or final answers or even necessarily true, but rather as different perspectives to increase our awareness so we may develop innovative critical thinking skills outside the limitations of our cultural assumptions.

This chapter illustrates how the *alternating multiple perspectives approach* can be applied to specific issues. So far, we've studied individual theories—now we are going apply them to larger, more complex issues by using multiple theories for alternating perspectives. We will use two significant yet very different real-life examples, the identity of Americans following 9/11 and the psychology of terrorists, as illustrations of this approach. Webster defines *terrorism* as the systematic use of terror, especially as a means of coercion.

The Identity Dilemma After 9/11

College students are supposed to be finding their place in the world, not just a profession but also an intellectual framework for learning and understanding their lives. After the terrorist attacks, that goal seems more urgent and yet more elusive than ever.[3] This statement frames the identity dilemma following 9/11.

Terrorism not only threatens our lives, but can also be seen as an attack on both one's world and one's cultural worldview, which includes shared beliefs about the nature of reality and gives one's life meaning and purpose. Identity is more elusive after the terrorist attack. Today, global conflicts may be more an issue of identity and challenged worldviews than an issue of territory according to Professor Christine S. Dunkel, psychology professor at UCLA.[4]

Identity formation can be seen as a process of exploring worldviews, adapting a worldview and then finding one's place within that worldview. The formation of a worldview may seem even more important and pressing but also more difficult.[5]

Erikson's Theory of Identity

Identity has long been a central concept in psychology—how we think of ourselves and how our feelings are shaped. Noted psychologist Erik Erikson says identity is a major psychological crisis in the modern world, reflecting the conflicts of our time. These conflicts include the effects of accelerating global forces as 4,000 cultures, or ways of life, come together as well as dealing with the aftermath of September 11, which can result in questioning personal assumptions and perceptions. We live in a time of transition in which boundaries and borders are becoming less defined.

More than 30 years ago Erikson discussed how accelerating global forces were experienced as a threat to the traditional American identity that included a sense of unlimited space and inexhaustible reserves. "The difficulties met in the attempt to integrate this old image of insulated spaciousness with the new image of explosive global closeness are deeply disquieting."[6]

Erikson defined identity crisis after working at San Francisco's Mt. Zion Veteran's Rehabilitation Clinic with former soldiers who had been on the battlefield. He described the toll of battle on their personalities; lost was the ego's shock absorbing capacity, the continuity of personal character and the confidence in knowing who they were—they were in the midst of an identity crisis. There was a distinct loss of ego identity; their belief in their social roles was gone. In other words, these young men were no longer relating to other people in ways in which they had become used to seeing themselves; instead they had been forced by the cruelties of war to kill, and as a result they saw themselves in totally different ways. They had lost the sense of security and control they had known through previously defined roles and expectations. They no longer knew who they were, nor did they feel safe. They were left with a sense of emptiness and a lack of meaning, in short, they were experiencing an existential crisis.[7]

According to Erikson's psychohistorical approach, the development of a sense of identity has both psychological and social aspects. He says the individual's identity reflects the crises, opportunities, conflicts and inconsistencies of one's time. Erikson studied creative people who had some success at wrestling with a sense of identity in order to overcome the limitations of their culture.

The issue of identity includes the continuity of shared worldviews, that is, shared beliefs about the nature of reality. Our worldviews have been challenged by terrorism, and with it the sense of sameness and continuity in our lives.

A marketing consultant, Bethany Hornthal, noted that Silicon Valley had always been a multicultural place where young people felt they could go anywhere in the world and fit in. They were global kids.

"Suddenly after 9/11, that changed," she said. "Suddenly they were Americans and there was a certain danger in that identity. [As a result] the world has become more defined and restricted for them. Now you ask, where is it safe to go as an American?"[8]

Erikson explains the quest for identity.

> Like a trapeze artist, the young person in the middle of vigorous motion must let go of his safe hold on childhood and reach out for a firm grasp on adulthood, depending for a breathless interval on a relatedness between the past and the future and on the reliability of those he must let go of and those who will "receive" him. Whatever combination of drives and defenses, of sublimations and capacities has emerged from the young individual's childhood must now make sense in view of his concrete opportunities in work and love...(and) he must detect some meaningful resemblance between what he has come to see in himself and what his sharpened awareness tells him others judge and expect him to be. [9]

> Erik Erikson, *Insight and Responsibility*

In a sense, as a result of September 11th, for some the trapeze apparatus may have broken, undermining the former safe secure position Americans once felt. The individual reaches for the broken trapeze and symbolically falls into the unknown. As a result, problems of identity may be more widespread than before. The struggle for identity can continue on into mid-life crises.

Globalization:
Identities and Cultures in Transition

Identity crises are not only taking place in America; they are worldwide.[10] It is not only Americans who no longer see the world as the same safe place they did before 9/11. Europeans, particularly frightened by the terrorist bombing of commuter trains at Madrid train stations in 2004 that resulted in almost 200 deaths, are afraid they will be next.

Exposures to other cultures can also threaten former ways of being. For example, some less technological societies may feel their way of life is being threatened by American culture and globalization. Our culture, with its fast pace and immediate gratification, has had an impact on the beliefs of other more tradition-based cultures. In India, as a result of outsourcing, young women, employed by American companies, are earning ten times more than they used to. Wealthy by Indian standards, they refuse to follow their parents' restrictions on dating and choose to live in apartments on their own, breaking the bonds of tradition and challenging the age-old views of their culture and their identities.

What happens to a young Indian woman's family? From a collectivist frame of reference the Indian family feels their daughter is being pulled away from them, as though they are losing their daughter. The Indian father's role as parent, as an elder, is significantly weakened; in short, his identity is being challenged. From a collectivist view Western individualist values are challenging their culture, the structure of their families and their identities.

The spreading influence of Western culture challenges people's worldviews and identities, particularly in response to the influence of the media and multinational corporations.

According to deMause, Director of the Institute for Psychohistories, "Many agree that American television programs are part of an extensive plot to wipe out religious and sacred values. Taliban leaders were shocked by the affluence and personal liberty of the average citizen in the west and by the promiscuity, alcohol and drug use of western youth. Only an absolute and unconditional return to conservative Islamism could protect the Muslim world. . . ."[11]

The forces of globalization such as television and outsourcing of jobs are permeating our lives on a daily basis. Globalization is about shifting forms of human contact, a transformation of present conditions that are still fluid and unfolding. The persistent experiences of global interdependence gradually change people's individual and collective identities and thus dramatically impact the way they act in the world according to Professor Manfred Steiger of the Globalization Research Center in Hawaii.[12] He suggests that terrorism is one manifestation of the forces of globalization as they impact various cultures. There are many contradictions in globalization. High tech equipment, the Internet, satellites to transport news, have allowed bin Laden to communicate although he admonishes modernity from a mountain cave.

The Image of America at Home and Abroad

As I watched a four-year-old boy in a tiny Northern Italy village playing with blocks, I heard him say the blocks represented the Twin Towers in New York, and then he knocked them down. Because of the powerful impact of the mass media, even he knew the World Trade Center had blown up. On a daily basis the mass media exposes us to people from other cultures, with different beliefs and values from our own, which can lead to questioning our own culture and values.

When television showed some Middle Eastern children celebrating the Twin Towers explosion Americans were shocked. We had always thought of ourselves as a big brother, as well liked. Why was this happening?

If we frame this dissonance in terms of Erikson's identity theory, Americans' identities had been challenged. Since the end of World War II, Americans have been generally well liked abroad, commended by Europeans for sending soldiers to free them from the Third Reich and later supplying funds to help rebuild war-torn countries. Now the image of America abroad is changing.

Our image of ourselves has also changed. Unseen, uncontrolled threats undermine our security, affecting the way we see ourselves as well as the image we portray to the outside world, no longer the cool, confident protectorates of the world. The very symbols society prides itself on, the World Trade Center and the Space Shuttle, have exploded. Feeling more vulnerable now, some Americans turn to bigger cars such as SUVs, perhaps to feel protected and safe.

Cultural Conflicts

Cultural clashes reverberate throughout societies as exposures to other cultures challenge former ways of thinking and being. Individuals, as well, can personally experience cultural inconsistencies and clashes in their own lives. An Iranian-American college student describes his experience when a coworker told him she hoped there were no Middle Easterners on a flight she had arranged. He felt anger and confusion, caught between American and Iranian cultures.

He observes that the contact between these two cultures is often shallow or limited: Middle Easterners associate Americans with pop culture while Americans associate Middle Easterners with Islamic extremists and terrorists. Yet he is proud to be from both cultures, citing that they both offer so much richness.

Identity is tied to former ways of thinking and being, a sense of continuity and predictability of experience within one's culture. We feel similar to the way we felt yesterday; we know when we wake up we will find the orange juice in the same place in the refrigerator, we'll drive the same route to work, find the same job waiting there and talk to the same people. This continuity of experience contributes to our identity: we see ourselves in terms of how we relate to these objects and people.

What happens to this predictability of experience when formerly isolated cultures come in contact with each other? It can challenge the sense of continuity, particularly when one culture is pushed upon another. Consider the effects on traditional societies that have evolved slowly over thousands of years when they are thrust into the modern world. The Australian aborigines, who have lived a semi-nomadic existence on the desert and suddenly find themselves in a big city, have difficulty coping with the lack of continuity of their former existence. They find their culture and sense of identity threatened and may feel they have "lost their soul." Similarly, displaced Native Americans have suffered disproportionably from such problems. Sometimes such experiences can result in symptoms such as alcoholism. In conservative Muslim countries in the Middle East, Western billboards of scantily dressed females sit next to ancient spiritual shrines where women still cover their bodies from head to foot.

Such challenges to traditional ways of being can threaten an individual's sense of security and self-concept. The in-group can become increasingly important in providing a sense of security. A greater sense of tension may develop towards an out-group when it is perceived as a threat to the in-group's way of life, undermining what the group values.

The Psychology of Terrorists

How do you explain people getting caught up with bin Laden and the Al Qaeda? Why would nineteen men get on airplanes in the U.S., coerce the passengers and pilot into submission and then use the planes as missiles and kill themselves in the process? Why do people turn to terrorist groups? There are multiple causes contributing to terrorism. The list could include poverty, unemployment, cultural clashes, dwindling natural resources and competition for limited fossil fuels. While economics, power, limited resources, world politics, globalization and religious ideologies may all impact the development of terrorism we are going to focus on what psychology has to offer.

Let's look at what we know about the most sought after terrorist, Osama bin Laden. Bin Laden was the seventeenth son of 51 children, born in 1957 in Saudi Arabia.[13] His mother was one of his father's many wives. He amassed a fortune with a construction company and Saudi government contracts and was not known to have been very involved with the children. His father died in a plane crash in the United States when Osama was thirteen-years-old. Later Osama may have looked for a strong father figure in the religion of Islam. As he grew up and entered college, bin Laden began going to nightclubs, drinking and dating many women. DeMause, Director of the Institute of

Psychohistory, says that bin Laden soon felt extremely guilty for his "sins" and began preaching about the need to kill Westerners for their sinful enticement of Muslims.[14] These "temptations" were clashing with the values of his culture.

From a Jungian perspective, bin Laden's desire to participate in Western temptations may have been relegated to his shadow, that which he couldn't accept in himself, allowing him to deny and project the evil feelings he found unacceptable. Rather than admit to the dark side of his personality, Jung says there is a tendency to project these qualities on others. The more restrictive the culture or subculture is, the greater the shadow. Seeing another as absolute evil may give one an unreal sense of self-righteousness, missing any chance to deal rationally with the other group. Such projections remain unconscious and outside of rational considerations and limitations. They distract the person from dealing with undesirable urges at their original source and create distance and problems with the people or countries on which the feelings are projected.

Eric Fromm's Theory: Giving Up The Self to Escape the Anxiety of Aloneness

After viewing the atrocities of Nazi concentration camps, social psychologist Eric Fromm said in order to understand human behavior we must also look at the society in which people live. By studying the developmental life histories of terrorists, we may be able to reduce future terrorism says deMause. He says many terrorists grew up without economic opportunities in a repressive society in war-torn centers: growing up amid ongoing war, they lacked the base to make the normal plans of young adulthood for a job, a house, a family. Although some terrorists are educated,

according to the U.S. government's 9/11 Commission
Report, most of the 9/11 terrorists were not well educated.
It takes tremendous resources to fully cultivate a human being. If people don't see a future, they may feel they have
nothing to lose.

Their motives can be seen as personal, religious, as
well as political. Islamic teachings include values of submission to and sacrifice for God. While many of the terrorists had limited opportunities, they were told to expect joy
in the afterlife, similar to the teachings of the Middle Ages
in Western Europe. Their daily training included discussions of suicide and homicide as a guaranteed admission to
heaven. Terrorists are willing to commit acts of violence
against innocent civilians in order to achieve political goals
according to Dean Michael Gohlman, UC Berkeley School
of Public Policy.

According to the U.S. government 9/11 report:

> The history, culture, and body of beliefs from which
> bin Ladin shapes and spreads his message, are largely
> unknown to many Americans. Seizing on symbols of
> Islam's past greatness, he promises to restore pride to
> people who consider themselves the victims of suc-
> cessive foreign masters. He appeals to people disori-
> ented by cyclonic change as they confront modernity
> and globalization."[15]

9/11 Commission Report

In an attempt to escape the sense of emptiness and
powerlessness that some people feel as they move into the
modern world they may give up the self. According to
Fromm's theory, individuals join terrorist groups to provide
a sense of belonging, identity and power. Terrorists share

many of the same motives as gang members and cult members, including submission to a leader who provides a strong sense of belonging and identity. Looking back on our study of the Jonestown cult may help clarify the inner workings of bin Laden's terrorist group. Both the cult and terrorist groups provide a sense of identity, belonging and meaningfulness for their followers, offer the promise of paradise, while cutting members off from the outside world, not allowing them to leave and making decisions for them, relieving them of the "burden of freedom."

But how can freedom become a burden? Fromm says when the traditional bonds that provided security are broken without the opportunities to develop the self, people experience the world as overwhelming. They achieve "freedom from" based on awareness of being separate, but not "freedom to" achieve something, lacking the necessary competencies. They are left with an overwhelming sense of alienation and vulnerability. Fromm says there is then an impulse to escape these feelings by giving up or losing the self through submission to a leader or a group to feel one again with the world.

Let's apply this model. Terrorists are exposed to the ways of the Western world that are in conflict with their culture. Exposure to this larger world may raise questions about who they really are. As they become aware of being separate from their traditional bonds the initial impulse is to give up this newfound freedom of choice. By surrendering to a social movement, the individual escapes the negative feelings. As traditional bonds are undermined a vacuum is created which terrorist leaders may fill. Pursuing a "holy war" gives life significance. The terrorists surrendered their freedom and individuality to bin Laden in exchange for a sense of meaning, belonging and pride.

Defense Mechanisms

Authoritarianism. Authoritarianism, with its blind obedience to authority, further helps clarify bin Laden's motivations and influence on his followers. Fromm says authoritarianism is a tendency to fuse with something on the outside to gain the inner strength one is lacking. The most important feature is the person's attitude towards power. The powerful are shown submission and the weak are dominated, attacked, humiliated or made to suffer. The aim of the person is to escape unbearable feelings of insignificance through dominating a group to enlarge the self or by being swallowed up in a group. This results in losing the integrity of the self.

Conformity. Another of Fromm's defense mechanisms is conformity. A person may conform to escape the feelings of loneliness associated with freedom when opportunities to develop the self are not present. As a result of submission to convention, cultural beliefs, duty or the simple pressure of situational forces, people may mistakenly conclude that they are consciously making their own decisions when in fact they are trapped in the assumptions of the group. In order to belong to the group, members give up their own thoughts and independence to conform to their leader's beliefs.

Destructiveness. The living of life is inversely related to destructiveness. Destruction is the last desperate attempt to save the self from being crushed by comparisons. Fromm says it is an attempt to escape from the unbearable sense of individual powerlessness and isolation by removal of all objects to which the individual has to compare the self. Through violence and terrorism, an individual obliterates ideals, institutions and other people that might cause an unfavorable basis for comparison. Destruction of the Twin Towers, symbols of Western influence and power, can be seen as an attempt to deal with feelings of powerlessness through destruction.

The Power of Situational Forces: Abu Ghraib

With many people still on full alert from threats of terrorism, Americans and the world were shocked when photographs of prisoners at Abu Ghraib prison in Baghdad, Iraq showed U.S. military personnel torturing and humiliating naked Iraqi detainees. According to Senate hearings some prisoners died as a result of being repeatedly hit.

Was this just another horrible, unexplainable event?

The classic study by Zimbardo, the Stanford Prison experiment, conducted more than 30 years ago on college students, is one of the main models cited to explain the soldiers' behavior, revealing many of the underlying dynamics that led up to the Abu Ghraib scandal. Zimbardo found that situational circumstances could contribute to destructive behavior.

He says, "The social psychological factors at play in the Stanford Prison Experiment correspond almost exactly with those at play in the Iraqi prison: extreme power differentials, the diffusion of responsibility for immoral deeds and the sense of anonymity that freed the guards from any awareness of personal responsibility for their actions, the individual guards who model abusive behavior for peers . . . and the dehumanization. . . ."[16]

Guards and prisoners in the Stanford experiment were healthy, intelligent, middle-class male college students. Yet within 36 hours, the first prisoner showed acute emotional disturbance, with uncontrolled crying, disorganized thinking and rage.

Zimbardo ended the study early because "guards were escalating their abuse of prisoners in the middle of the night when they thought no researchers were watching."

Prisoners in Abu Ghraib, as well as the Stanford experiment, wore bags over their heads. Zimbardo's study suggests that up to a third of normal, intelligent males will engage in sadistic behavior when put in total control of others. The study also suggests that those who do not engage in this behavior will not interfere with those who are abusing power, just as at Abu Ghraib where pictures show bystanders who are not taking part in the abuse.

The study shows the power of conformity to social roles such as prison guard or prisoner. "It was remarkable how we all slipped into our roles, temporarily gave up our identities. It almost becomes like walls, it isn't me at all. I do have my own will, I'm not the kind of person who enjoys this kind of thing," said one of Zimbardo's subjects.

Reports from Abu Ghraib soldiers' friends and family in the U.S. maintain that these young soldiers were normal and not capable of performing such atrocities on their own. "Everybody knows that boy, and if he did it, he was ordered to do it," says a typical resident in the hometown of a soldier who was later sent to prison. Could the men and women at Abu Ghraib have been in an identity crisis, feeling threatened, living in a foreign culture, forced by the atrocities of war to perform acts outside of their identity?

Understanding how good people can become perpetrators is an area Zimbardo is investigating. Zimbardo, president of the American Psychological Association, grew up in poverty in a New York City ghetto.

"I am primarily concerned with understanding the psychological and social dynamics involved when an ordinary 'good' person begins to act in anti-social ways, and in the extreme, behaves destructively towards the property or person of other people. I have seen first hand my childhood friends go through such transformations and always wondered how and why they did and whether I could also change like that," reflects Zimbardo.[7]

Another study that is often cited to explain the abuse of Iraqi prisoners is the classic research on obedience by Stanley Milgram at Yale (previously discussed in Chapter 5). He found that some subjects continued to obey instructions to shock "learners" at dangerously high levels even while believing the "learners'" lives were at risk. They did so over the screams and protests of their subjects. Milgram found that the structure of the situation could lead people to do unexpected things, to become "caught up in the moment." *Situational forces* can develop their own momentum in which the dominating force is not within the person, but within the environment. Once the person pressed shock button #3, there was a tendency to press #4 and so on. Milgram concludes that if the request comes from a seemingly legitimate authority (even if it's irrational), many people will do what they are told regardless of the consequences. It follows, he says, that government with its prestige and power can exercise a great deal of authority over its citizens.

These studies can help explain why the soldiers participated at Abu Ghraib in acts they knew were wrong. This research demonstrates how situational forces contribute to destructive behavior. The environment, including situational forces and conformity to roles, can overwhelm the person's sense of identity. These experiments demonstrate the power of conformity to situational forces and how seemingly otherwise normal people may follow an irrational authority if it seems legitimate, even to the point of threatening the lives of others.

Can these studies also add to our understanding of the power terrorist leaders exercise over their followers? Situational forces and the defense mechanisms of conformity, authoritarianism and destructiveness, which involve submission to irrational authority, can help to explain how terrorist leaders get their followers to carry out acts of atrocities.

The Effects of Stress Overload

The individual's ability to make decisions can break down under stress. In Ivan Pavlov's conditioning experiment (in Chapter 4), dogs that had previously learned to distinguish between a circle and ellipse were unable to make the same distinctions after the shapes had been manipulated so as to be indistinguishable and then returned to the original shapes. The dogs became agitated, barked and tore at the apparatus. Stimuli that become indistinguishable can result in inescapable conflict and produce what is called *experimental neurosis,* a condition in which the animal loses its ability to discriminate. Such studies can help us understand neurosis in humans. Similarly, cultural conflicts, like the threats of terrorism and war, coupled with the conflicts of modern life, may result in people being overwhelmed, finding it more difficult to function at high levels. When the individual is pushed beyond his or her capacity, their ability to differentiate may totally break down leaving them functioning at a lower level than initially and unable to even make what were formerly easy choices.

In such stressful situations, decision-making is not the only ability to suffer. Under stress the quality of life may diminish as the person's attention and motives shift from higher, self-actualizing creative expressions to more basic drives of security and safety according to Maslow. Immediately following 9/11 many Americans, seeking security, stayed home more, watching movies and eating dinner rather than going out or traveling. Safety and security are deficit motivations. In other words, the individual may end up just coping with life rather than pursuing the higher levels of growth and creativity because he or she no longer feels safe.

Another result of stress can be a sense of overwhelming emotion, which according to Freud, can result in regression and activate old unresolved conflicts, leaving less energy available to rationally deal with the present adult issues. In fact, if the ego's integrity is threatened or overwhelmed, it may abandon truth and compulsively reframe its perceptions of reality in an attempt to avoid the overwhelming anxiety.

Given the serious effects of stress overload, it is important to take stress seriously and know how to manage it: take breaks, try to resolve stressful situation and learn how to relax. Stress management can contribute to functioning at our best.

A Summary of Psychological Perspectives on Identity, Terrorism and Globalization

The purpose of this chapter was two fold: to see in what ways various psychological perspectives might illuminate two of the crises of our time, identity and terrorism, and to demonstrate the use of the method of alternating multiple perspectives. We have used several different psychological theories to demonstrate the usefulness of this approach in dealing with modern problems including: Erikson's identity theory and psychohistorical approach, Fromm's social psychological theory, Maslow's hierarchy of needs, Pavlov's experimental neurosis, Jung's theory of the shadow, Freud's defense mechanisms and cultural psychology. Alternating multiple perspectives, cultivating the ability to use the concepts of several theories simultaneously, may result in a more complex and complete understanding that can help to overcome cultural limitations.

These ideas were not presented as complete or final answers or even necessarily true, but rather as different perspectives to increase our awareness. Although there are many factors contributing to terrorism such as economics, religion and world politics, this chapter focused on what psychology may have to offer.

Identity is a central concept in psychology. It includes who we think we are and how our feelings and perceptions are influenced by culture and social institutions. Developmental psychologist Erik Erikson views identity as a major crisis in the modern world. We see ourselves differently as a nation following the attack of 9/11. Identity is a central issue in global conflicts and many cultural clashes. Some cultural psychologists suggest that today's global conflicts may be more an issue of identity and challenged worldviews than an issue of territory. People from more tradition-based cultures also feel their identities are threatened by the modern world. Many find their beliefs challenged and their way of life undermined and as a result feel vulnerable. Terrorism, globalization and 4,000 cultures coming together all influence the struggle for identity. Terrorism and identity crises can be seen within the broader historical context of globalization.

Erikson discusses how accelerating global forces are experienced as a threat to traditional identities. As these global forces sweep across the world, they increasingly impact our personal lives, challenging our ways of life, occupations, family relationships, security and even how we see ourselves. There is a growing awareness of the connection between the local and the distant as a result of globalization with its worldwide interdependence and interactions of people.

To better understand the psychology of terrorism, we used Jung's and Fromm's theories to analyze the motivations of terrorist leaders and their recruits. From a psychological perspective the terrorist leader bin Laden may have felt guilty for his indulgences in Western society. Repressing the desires he considered to be evil, he then projected the evil onto America, which became part of his shadow. Since the projection was unconscious, the evil was perceived as absolute, resulting in behavior beyond rational limits according to Jung.

As a result of globalization, poverty and growing up in worn-torn centers, bin Laden's followers found their more traditional ways of life being undermined. When young adults are unable to make plans for adulthood, such as having jobs and families, they may be easier to recruit. Fromm says in a society that does not support the development of personal competencies, freedom can be a burden. People may turn to terrorist groups or cults to try to escape feelings of meaninglessness, vulnerability and alienation according to Fromm. Defense mechanisms such as conformity, authoritarianism and destructiveness are used in order to fuse with something larger or to destroy the ideals, institutions and people that might result in an unfavorable basis for comparison.

Pavlov's work on experimental neurosis can also be applied to the crisis facing the modern world with the threat of terrorism. It demonstrates how important it is to moderate stress because it can reduce our level of functioning. The stress of the threat of terrorism and war can undermine not only the ability to function at the highest rational level and to reach the most effective solutions but also our quality of experience. As Maslow points out, when the individual doesn't feel safe, the basic needs of safety and security will override the higher needs for self-development, growth and creativity.

If identity lies at the root of many modern crises, it becomes increasingly important to differentiate what is fundamental to all human beings in a search for common ground. We've seen how environmental situational forces can override rational constructive elements of human behavior. An awareness of the powerful forces that shape our values and identities contributes to our ability to be more self-directive.

Rather than just accepting cultural views as truths, we can continue to search for understanding using the empirical, objective approach of scientific inquiry. This takes place with an awareness of the psychohistorical moment in which we live and the influence of social and situational forces. As global forces accelerate, these issues are not going to recede; no country is immune from their impact. As cultures of the world increasingly come in contact, the challenge is to work together for greater understanding based on mutual respect.

Acknowledgements

Aldus Books, London, of J. G. Ferguson Publishing Company:
Man and His Symbols, by Carl G. Jung, et al. Copyright 1964.

Collodi, Carlo. *The Authentic Story of Pinocchio of Tuscany* (M. L. Rosenthal, Trans.). Berkeley, California: Crystal Publications, 2002.

Clark University Archives. Photo of Sigmund Freud, G. Stanley Hall, et al.

Ciabani, Roberto. Acrylic painting for the Centennial of Pinocchio, Florence, Italy, for the Carlo Collodi Foundation.

Holt, Rinehart and Winston, CBS College Publishing, reprinted by permission of. "Inverted U Function" from *Textbook of Psychology* by D. O. Hebb. Copyright 1972 by W. B. Saunders Company.

Houghton Mifflin: *Client-Centered Therapy* by Carl Rogers. Copyright 1965.

Houghton Mifflin: *On Becoming a Person* by Carl Rogers. Copyright 1961.

Real People Press: *Person to Person: The Problem of Being Human* by Carl Rogers and Barry Stevens. Copyright 1967.

Viking Penguin Inc.: *C. G. Jung* by A. Storr. Copyright 1973.

W. W. Norton and Company, Inc.: *Insight and Responsibility* by Erik Erikson. Copyright 1964.

Zimbardo, Philip et al. The Psychology of Imprisonment: Privation, Power and Pathology. 1973.

Photo Credits
Unless otherwise acknowledged,
photos are the property of Crystal Publications.

INTRODUCTION
8 Vase/Face Illusion, Archives of the History of American Psychology, University of Akron.

CHAPTER SIX
243   Martin Luther King, Library of Congress.
251   Shadow, Estate of C.G. Jung.
260   Mato-Tape, Joslyn Art Museum, Omaha, Nebraska. Gift of the Enron Art Foundation.
261   Hawaiin Feathers, Bishop Museum Archives, Hawaii.
262   Mandala, photo copyright by Estate of C.G. Jung.
267   "Pinocchio and the Woodpeckers," Acrylic painting on canvas by Roberto Ciabani, Florence, Italy, from *The Authentic Story of Pinocchio of Tusccany,* Crystal Publications.
270   Carl Jung, photo copyright by Aniela Jaffe.

CHAPTER SEVEN
301   Native American Earth Lodge, Joslyn Art Museum, Omaha, Nebraska.
305   1889 Picnic Party, University Archives, Bancroft Library, University of California, Berkeley.
309   Chinese Princess, Stibbert Museum, Florence, Italy.
310   Chinese Princess, Stibbert Museum, Florence, Italy.

Notes

INTRODUCTION

1. Kruger, Justin and Dunning, David. "Unskilled and Unaware of It: How Difficulties in Recognizing One's Own Incompetence Lead to Inflated Self-Assessments," *Journal of Personality and Social Psychology,* 1999, Vol. 77, No. 6, 1121–1134.

2. Elliot, Jane, ABC News "The Eye of the Storm," 1970.

CHAPTER ONE

1. Cowan, P.A. *Piaget With Feeling.* New York: Holt, Rinehart and Winston, 1978.

2. Stevens, B. and Rogers, C. *Person to Person: The Problem of Being Human.* Walnut Creek, Calif.: Real People Press, 1967, pp. 9–11.

3. Goleman, D. "Erikson, in His Own Old Age, Expands His View of Life," *New York Times,* June 14, 1988. pp. C1, C4.

4. Erikson, E. *Childhood and Society.* New York: W.W. Norton, 1963.

CHAPTER TWO

1. Gray, P. "The Assault on Freud," *Time*, November 19, 1993.

2. Ibid.

3. Stone, A. A. "Where Will Psychoanalysis Survive," *Harvard Magazine,* Cambridge, Mass. January-February, 1997, pp. 35–39.

4. Solms, Mark. "Freud Returns." *Scientific American,* Vol. 290, No. 5, May 2004 p. 85.

5. Anderson, Michael et al. "Neural Systems Underlying the Suppression of Unwanted Memories," *Science*, Vol. 303, January 9, 2004, p. 23.

6. Heim, Christine and Newport, D. Jeffery et al. "Pituitary-Adrenal and Autonomic Responses to Stress in Women After Sexual and Physical Abuse in Childhood," *Journal of the American Medical Association,* August 2, 2000, Vol. 284, 592–597.

7. *New York Times,* "Physical, Sexual Abuse in Girls Tied to Abnormal Stress in Women," *San Francisco Chronicle,* August 2, 2000.

8. Solms, Mark. *Scientific American,* p. 88.

9. Ibid. p. 88.

10. Hobson, J. Allan. "Freud Returns? Like a Bad Dream," *Scientific American,* May 2004, Vol. 290, No. 5, p. 89.

11. Levine, M. "On the Myth That Freud's Ideas Defy Scientific Validation," *New York Times,* February 10, 1984.

12. Gray, 1993.

13. Cohen, J. *Personality Dynamics,* Chicago: Rand McNally, 1969, p. 17.

CHAPTER THREE

1. Rogers, Carl. *Client-Centered Therapy.* Boston: Houghton Mifflin, 1965, pp. 484–85.

2. Ibid, p. 486.

3. Ibid, p. 499.

4. Ibid, p. 501.

5. Ibid, p. 502.

6. Ibid, p. 503.

7. Ibid, p. 490.

8. Rogers, Carl. *On Becoming a Person.* Boston: Houghton Mifflin, 1961, p. 170.

9. Maslow, Abraham, *Toward a Psychology of Being.* New York: Van Nostrand, 1968, p. 214.

10. Ibid, p. 58.

CHAPTER FOUR

1. Knowles, John. U.S. Department of Health, Education and Welfare, *Forward Plan for Health,* 1975.

2. Thoresen, Carl; Friedman, Meyer; Gill, James and Ulmer, Diane. "The Recurrent Cornary Prevention Project," *Acta Medica Scandinavica* (Suppl.) 660: 1982, pp. 172–192.

3. Harlow, H.F. "Sexual Behavior in the Rhesus Monkey," In, F. Beach (ed.) *Sex and Behavior.* New York: Wiley, 1965.

4. Epel, Elissa and Blackburn, Elizabeth. "Accelerated Telomere Shortening in Response to Life Stress." *Proceedings of the National Academy of Sciences,* December 7, 2004, Vol. 101, No. 49, 17312–16.

5. Thoresen, Carl, et al. "The Recurrent Coronary Prevention Project: Initial Findings." In M. Horvath and E. Frantik, (ed.), *Psychophysiological Risk Factors of Cardiovascular Diseases (Psychosocial Stress, Personality and Occupational Specificity),* Supplement 3, Prada, Prague, Czechoslovakia: Avicenum-Czechoflovack Medical Press, 1982, pp. 518–524.

6. Stout, C. et al. "Unusually Low Incidence of Death from Myocardial Infarction," *Journal American Medical Association,* 188, 1964, p. 845.

7. Ornish, D.; Brown, S.E.; Scherwitz, L.W.; Billings, J. H. et al. "Can lifestyle changes reverse coronary heart disease? The lifestyle heart trial." In: *Psychosocial processes and health: A reader;* A. Steptoe, J. Wardle, ed., Cambridge England: Cambridge University Press, 1994. p. 507–521.

8. Chamberlain, K. and Zika, S. "The minor events approach to stress: Support for the use of daily hassles." *British Journal of Psychology* (1990), 81, 469–481.

9. Brown, J.D. "Staying fit and staying well: physical fitness as a moderator of life stress." *Journal of Personality and Social Psychology,* 1991, 60, 555–561.

10. Thayer, R.E. , Newmann, J.R. & McClain, T.M. "Self-regulation of mood: strategies for changing a bad mood, raising energy and reducing tension." *Journal of Personality and Social Psychology,* 1994, Vo. 67, No. 5, 910–925.

11. Williams, R.; Powell, L. et al. "Behavior change and compliance: keys to improving cardiovascular health." *Circulation,* 1993, Sept. 88 (3): 1406–7.

12. Ellis, Albert. *Growth Through Reason: Techniques for Disputing Irrational Beliefs (DIB's),* New York: Institute for Rational Living, 1974.

13. Kobasa, S.C., Maddi, S.R., Puccetti, M.C. "Personality and Social Resources in Stress Resistance," *Journal of Personality and Social Psychology,* 1983, 45, 839–850.

14. Goss, J. D. "Hardiness and Mood Disturbances in Swimmers While Overtraining," *Journal of Sport and Exercise Psychology,* 1994, 16, 135–149.

15. Stout, C. et al. Unusually low incidence of death from myocardial infarction. *Journal American Medical Association,* 1964, *188,* p. 845.

16. Buckley, K.W. "The Selling of a Psychologist: John Broadus Watson and the Application of Behavioral Techniques to Advertising." *Journal of the History of Behavioral Sciences,* 1982, 18, 207–221.

CHAPTER FIVE

1. Zimbardo, Philip. "The Psychology of Imprisonment," 1973, p. 9

2. Ibid., p. 18.

3. Ibid, p. 12.

4. Ibid.

5. Brewer, Judith, *Families in Focus,* U. S. Population Council, 1995.

6. Zimbardo, P. *Shyness: What it is and what to do about it.* Reading, Massachusets.: Addison-Wesley.

CHAPTER SIX

1. British Broadcasting Company. "The Story of Carl Jung. Part I: In Search of Soul," 1973.

2. Jung, Carl. G. et al. *Man and and His Symbols.* London: Aldus Books, 1964, p. 102.

3. Ibid. p. 50.

4. von Franz, M.L. The Process of Individuation. In C. G. Jung, ed., *Man and His Symbols.* 1964, p. 162.

5. Jung, Carl G., et al. *Man and His Symbols.* p. 94.

6. Ibid., p. 49.

7. Ibid., p. 61.

8. Salinger, Piere, ed., *A Tribute to Robert F. Kennedy.* New York: Doubleday, 1968, p.3.

9. Jung, Carl. *Analytical Psychology: Its Theory and Practice. The Tavistock Lectures.* 1935. New York: Pantheon Books, pp. 11–12.

10. Fordham, F. *An Introduction to Jung's Psychology.* Harmondsworth, Middlesex, Great Britain: Penguin Books, 1966, p. 26.

11. Fromm-Reichman, F. *Principles of Intensive Psychotherapy.* Chicago: University of Chicago Press,1950.

12. Fromm, E. *The Forgotten Language, An Introduction to the Understanding of Dreams, Fairy Tales and Myths.* New York: Grove Press, 1951, p. 240.

13. Collodi, Carlo. *The Authentic Story of Pinocchio of Tuscany.* (M.L. Rosenthal, Trans.). Berkeley, CA: Crystal Publications, 2002, p. 59.

14. Henderson, J.L. Ancient Myths and Modern Man. In C. G. Jung ed., *Man and His Symbols.* p. 139.

15. Storr, A. *C. G. Jung,* New York: Viking Press, 1973, p. 82.

16. von Franz, M.L. *The Process of Individuation,* 1964, p. 163.

17. Campbell, J., *The Portable Jung,* New York: Viking Press, 1972.

18. Fordham, F., *An Introduction to Jung's Psychology,* p. 77.

CHAPTER SEVEN

1. Professor Susan Goldstein, Lecture, Diablo Valley College, Pleasant Hill, CA. 12 April 1995.

2. Lonner , W.J. & Malpass, R., ed., *Psychology and Culture.* Boston: Allyn and Bacon, 1994.

3. Duster, T. et al., Diversity Project. Berkeley: Institute For the Study of Social Change, University of California, Berkeley, 1991.

4. Matsumoto, D., *People-Psychology from a Cultural Perspective.* Pacific Grove: Brooks Cole, 1994.

5. Matsumoto, D., Ibid.

6. Professor Lee Rode, Personal Interview, 22 October 2004.

7. Packer, Martin. "The Problem of Transfer and the Sociocultural Critique of Schooling." *The Journal of the Learning Sciences,* 2001, *10*(4)493–514.

8. Lerro, Bruce, *Power of Eden,* Victoria, British Columbia: Trafford Books, 2005, 328–342.

9. Hofstede in Hui, C.H. and Triandis, H.C., "Individualism-Collectives: A study of cross-cultural research," *Journal of Cross-Cultural Psychology,* 1986, 17, 222–248.

10. Triandis, H.C. in Ibid.

11. Hadiyono, J. E. P. and Hahn, M .W., "Personality Differences and Sex Similarities in American and Indonesian College Students," *Journal of Social Psychology,* 1985, 125, pp. 703–708.

12. Buck, E.B., Newton, B.J. and Muramatsu, Y. "Independence and Obedience in the U.S. and Japan," *International Journal of Intercultural Relations,* 1984, 8, pp. 279–300.

13. Markus, H. and Kitayana, S. "Culture and the Self: Implications for Cognition, Emotion and Motivation," *Psychological Review,* 1991, 98, pp. 224–253.

14. Lerro, Bruce. *Power of Eden,* Ibid.

15. Foster, Dean Allen, *Bargaining Across Borders: How to Negotiate Business Successfully Anywhere in the World.* New York: McGraw-Hill, Inc., 1992, p. 173.

16. Fisher, R., et al. *Getting to Yes: Negotiating Agreement Without Giving In.* New York: Penguin Books, 1991. p. 34.

17. Southworth, Jan, Naturalist Lecture at Ardenwood Historical Farm, 20 October 1996.

18. Chiang, Jung, *Wild Swans,* New York: Doubleday, 1991, p. 24–25.

19. Dr. Francesco Civita, personal interview, Stibbert Museum, Florence, Italy. 26 March 2003.

20. Frone, M. R., Russell, M., & Cooper, M. L. (1992). "Antecedents and Outcomes of Work-family Conflict: Testing a Model of the Work-family Interface." *Journal of Applied Psychology,* 77 , 65–78.

ADDENDUM

1. United States Government 9/11 Commission, *Final Report of the National Commission on Terrorist Attacks Upon the United States,* Official Government Edition. (Washington D.C. July 2004) p.1.

2. Fernandez, Elizabeth, "Americans Turn Inward," *San Francisco Chronicle,* October 2, 2001: A9.

3. Kantrowitz, B. and Maughton, K., "Generation 9/11," *Newsweek.* November 12, 2001.

4. Dunkel, C.S., "Terror Management Theory and Identity: The Effect of the 9/11 Terrorist Attacks on Anxiety and Identity Change," *Identity: An International Journal of Theory and Research,* 2002, Vol. 2, No. 2, 377–389.

5. Dunkel, C.S., Ibid.

6. Erikson, Erik, *Identity, Youth and Crisis.* New York: Norton, 1968. p. 69.

7. Ibid, p.67.

8. Friedman, Thomas, "Wired and Worried," *San Francisco Chronicle,* May 28, 2002.

9. Erikson, E., *Insight and Responsibility.* New York: Norton, 1964. p. 90.

10. Dunkel, C.S., Ibid.

11. deMause, L., "The Childhood Origins of Terrorism." *The Journal of Psychohistory,* 2002, 29, No. 4.

12. Stegar, Manfred, *Globalization, A Very Short Introduction.* England: Oxford University Press, 2003. p.2.

13. Alexander, Y. and Swetnam, M. S., *Osama bin Laden's Al Qaida: Profile of a Terrorist Network.* Ardsley, New York: Transnational Publishers, 2001.

14. deMause, L., "The Childhood Origins of Terrorism." *The Journal of Psychohistory,* 2002, 29, No. 4.

15. United States Government 9/11 Commission. Ibid. p. 11.

16. Zimbardo, Phillip, "The Virtue of Action," *San Francisco Chronicle,* May 17, 2004. B7.

Bibliography

Adler, A. (1964). *Social interest: A challenge to mankind.* New York: Capricorn Books.

Alexander, Y., & Swetnam, M.S. (2001). *Osama bin Laden's Al Qaida: Profile of a terrorist network.* Ardsley, New York: Transnational Publishers.

Anderson, M., et al. (2004, January 9). Neural systems underlying the suppression of unwanted memories, Science, 303, 23.

Atkinson D.R., Morten G. & Sue D. W. (1989). *Counseling American minorities: A cross cultural perspective,* Dubuque, IA: Wm. C. Brown.

Baumeister, R.E. & Muraven, M. (1996). Identity as adaptation to social, cultural, and historical context. *Journal of Adolescence.* 19, 405–416.

Bennet, Sandra K. (1994). The American Indian: A psychological overview. In Walter J. L. and Malpass, R. (Eds.), *Psychology and Culture,* Boston: Allyn and Bacon.

Bennett, P. & Carroll, D. (1994). Cognitive-behavioral interventions in cardiac rehabilitation. *Journal of Psychosomatic Research. 38,* 169–182.

Berkowitz, L. & Devine, P.G. (1995). Has social psychology always been cognitive? What is "cognitive"anyhow? *Personality and Social Psychology Bulletin, 21* (7), 696–703.

Berry, J. & Dasen, P.R. (1982). Cross-cultural aspects of Piaget's theory: The competence/performance model. In L. L. Adler (Ed.), *Cross-Cultural Research At Issue* (pp. 163–170). New York: Academic Press.

Blum G. S. & Miller, D. R. (1952). Exploring the psychoanalytic theory of the "oral character." *Journal of Personality,* 20, 287–304.

Blum G. S. (1954). An experimental reunion of psychoanalytic theory with perceptual vigilance and defense. *Journal of Abnormal and Social Psychology,* 49, 94–98.

Bhushan, R. (1993). A study of family functioning variables as predictors of identity achievement. *Indian Psychological Review (Monthly Journal of India), 40*(1–2), 29–34.

Boxberger, D.L. (1991). Individualism or tribalism? The dialectic of Indian policy. *American Indian Quarterly,* 15, 29–31.

Brant, W. D. (1980). The effects of race and social distance on obedience. *Journal of Social Psychology, 112,* 229–235.

Breakwell, G.M. & Millword, L.Y. (1997). Sexual self-concept and sexual risk taking. *Journal of Adolescence, 20.* 29–41.

Brazil, E. & Ness, C. (1997, March 2). Experts describe culture and cults: An interview with Margaret Singer. *San Francisco Examiner,* p. A20.

British Broadcasting Company. (1973). *The story of C. G. Jung. Part I: In search of soul. (videotape)*

Brock, T. C. & Buss, A. H. (1962). Dissonance, aggression and an evaluation of pain. *Journal of Abnormal Social Psychology, 65,* 197–202.

Brown, J.D. (1991). Staying fit and staying well: physical fitness as a moderator of life stress. *Journal of Personality and Social Psychology, 60,* 555–561.

Buck, E.B., Newton, B.J. & Muramatsu, Y. (1984). Independence and obedience in the U.S. and Japan. *International Journal of Intercultural Relations, 8,* 279–300.

Buckley, K.W. (1982). The selling of a psychologist: John Broadus Watson and the application of behavioral techniques to advertising. *Journal of the History of Behavioral Sciences, 18,* 207–221.

Buehler, R. & Griffin, D. (1994). Change-of-meaning effects in conformity and dissent: Observing construal processes over time. *Journal of Personality and Social Psychology, 67*(6), 984–996.

Buss, A. H. & Brock, T. C. (1963). Repression and guilt in relation to aggression. *Journal of Abnormal Social Psychology, 66,* 345–350.

Byler, W. (1977). The destruction of American Indian families. In Unger, S. (Ed.), *The destruction of American Indian families.* New York: Association on American Indian Affairs.

Campbell, J. *The portable Jung.* New York: Viking Press, 1972.

Chamberlain, K. & Zika, S. (1990). The minor events approach to stress: Support for the use of daily hassles. *British Journal of Psychology, 81,* 469–481.

Chiang, Jung. (1991). *Wild swans.* New York: Doubleday.

Civita, Francesco. (2003, March 26). Personal interview at Stibbert Museum, Florence, Italy.

Cohen, J. (1969). *Personality dynamics.* Chicago: Rand McNally,

Cohen, R. J. (1994). *Psychology and adjustment: Values, culture, and change.* Boston: Allyn and Bacon.

Collodi, Carlo. (2002). *The authentic story of Pinocchio of Tuscany.* (M. L. Rosenthal, Trans.) Berkeley, California: Crystal Publications.

Cooper, J. B. & McBaugh, J.L. (1963). *Integrating principles of social psychology.* Massachusetts: Schenkman Publishing.

Cote, J.E. (1996). Sociological perspectives on identity formation: the culture-identity link and identity capital. *Journal of Adolescence, 19,* 417–428.

Cowan, P.A. (1978). *Piaget with feeling.* New York: Holt, Rinehart and Winston.

Cowley, G. (2003, February 24). Fear and the brain (Our Bodies, Our Fears) Boulder, Colorado: *Newsweek,* 42–46.

Cross, S.E. (1995). Self-construal, coping, and stress in cross-cultural adaptation. *Journal of Cross-Cultural Psychology, 26,* 673–697.

Dasen, P. R. (1982). Cross-cultural aspects of Piaget's Theory: The competence/performance model. In L. L. Adler (Ed.), *Cross-Cultural Research At Issue* (pp. 163–170). New York: Academic Press.

Dasen, P.R. (1994). Culture and cognitive development from a Piagetian perspective. In Lonner, W.J. & Malpass, R. (Eds.), *Psychology and culture.* Boston: Allyn and Bacon.

De Lisi, L.E., Maurizo, A. et al. (2003). A survey of New Yorkers after the Sept. 11, 2001 terrorist attacks. *The American Journal of Psychiatry, 160,* 780–783.

de Mause, L. (2002).The childhood origins of terrorism. *The Journal of Psychohistory, 29*(4).

Domino, G. (1992). Cooperation and competition in Chinese and American children. *Journal of Cross-Cultural Psychology, 23,* 456–467.

Dunkel, C.S. (2002). Terror management theory and identity: The effect of the 9/11 terrorist attacks on anxiety and identity change. *Identity: An International Journal of Theory and Research, 2*(4), 287–301.

Durodie, B., & Wessely, S. (2002). Resilience or panic? The public and terrorist attack. *The Lancet, 360,* Issue 9349, 1901–1902.

Duster, T. et al. (1991). *Diversity project.* Berkeley: Institute For the Study of Social Change, University of California.

Elkind, D. (1974). *Children and adolescents: Interpretive essays on Jean Piaget.* London: Oxford University Press.

Elliot, J. (1970). In ABC News, "The Eye of the Storm."

Ellis, A. (1962). *Reason and emotion in psychotherapy.* New York: Lyle Stuart.

Ellis, A. (1974). *Growth through reason: Techniques for disputing irrational beliefs. (DIB's).* New York: Institute for Rational Living.

Emmons, R.A., & McCullough, M.E. (2002). Counting blessings versus burdens: An experimental investigation of gratitude and subjective well-being in daily life. *Journal of Personality and Social Psychology, 84*(2), 377–389.

Epel, E. & Blackburn, E. (2004, December 7). Accelerated telomere shortening in response to life stress. *Proceedings of the National Academy of Sciences, 101,* issue 49, 17312-16.

Eriksen, C.W. (1952). Individual differences in defensive forgetting. *Journal of Experimental Psychology, 44,* 442–446.

Eriksen, C.W. (1963). Perception and personality. In Wepman, J.M, & Heine, R.W. (Eds.), *Concepts of Personality* (pp. 31–62). Chicago, Illinois: Aldine Publishing Company.

Eriksen, C.W. (1958). Unconscious processes. In M. R. Jones (Ed.), *Nebraska symposium on motivation* (pp.169–227). Lincoln, NE: University Press.

Erikson, E. (1963). *Childhood and society.* New York: W.W. Norton.

Erikson, E. (1964). *Insight and responsibility.* New York: Norton.

Erikson, E. (1968). *Identity, youth and crisis.* New York: W.W. Norton.

Evans, R. I. (1964). *Conversation with Carl Jung.* New Jersey: D. Van Nostrand.

Fagan, K. (2002, May 26). Psych Sleuth. An interview with Margaret Singer. *San Francisco Chronicle Magazine,* pp. 8–13, 25.

Fancher, R. (1973). *Psychoanalytic psychology, The development of Freud's thought.* New York: W.W. Norton.

Feather, N.T. (1994, April). Values and national identification: Australian evidence. *Australian Journal of Psychology, 46* (1), 35–40.

Fernandez, E. (2001, October 2). Americans turn inward. *San Francisco Chronicle,* A9.

Fisher, R., Ury,W. & Patton, B. (1991). *Getting to yes: Negotiating agreement without giving in.* New York: Penguin Books.

Fordham, F. (1966). *An introduction to Jung's psychology.* Harmondsworth, Middlesex, Great Britain: Penguin Books.

Foster, D. A. (1992). *Bargaining across borders: How to negotiate business successfully anywhere in the world.* New York: McGraw-Hill, Inc.

Fredrickson, B.L., Tugade, M. M. et al. (2003). What good are positive emotions in crises? A prospective study of resilience and emotions following the terrorist attacks on the United States on September 11th, 2001. *Journal of Personality and Social Psychology, 84,* 365–376.

Freud, S. (1920). *A general introduction to Psychoanalysis.* New York: Washington Square Press.

Freud, S. (1949). *An outline of Psychoanalysis.* New York: W.W. Norton & Co.

Freud, S. (1952). *An autobiographical study.* New York: W.W. Norton & Co.

Freud, S. (1952). *On dreams.* New York: W.W. Norton & Co.

Freud, S. (1953). *The future of an illusion.* Garden City, New York: Doubleday Anchor Books.

Freud, S. (1959). *Beyond the pleasure principle.* New York: Bantam Books.

Freud, S. (1961). *Civilization and its discontents.* New York: W.W. Norton & Co.

Friedman, M., & Rosenman, R.H. (1974). *Type A behavior and your heart.* New York: Alfred A. Knopf.

Friedman, M., & Thoresen, C. E. et al. (1986). Alteration of Type A behavior and its effects on cardiac recurrences in post myocardial infaction patients: Summary results of the recurrent coronary prevention project. *American Heart Journal, 112*(4) 653–665.

Friedman, T. (2002, May 28). Wired and worried. *San Francisco Chronicle.*

Fromm, E. (1951). *The forgotten language.* New York: Grove Press.

Fromm, E. (1968). *The revolution of hope.* New York: Bantam Books.

Fromm, E. (1963). *The art of loving.* New York: Bantam Books.

Fromm, E. (1963). *Escape from freedom.* New York: Holt, Rinehart & Winston.

Fromm, E. (1973). *The anatomy of human destructiveness.* New York: Holt, Rinehart & Winston.

Fromm-Reichman, F. (1950). *Principles of intensive psychotherapy.* Chicago: University of Chicago Press.

Frone, M. R., Russell, M. & Cooper, M. L. (1992). Antecedents and outcomes of work-family conflict: Testing a model of the work-family interface. *Journal of Applied Psychology, 77,* 65–78.

Frost, S.E. Jr. (1959). *Ideas of the great philosophers.* New York: Barnes & Noble.

Geller, D. M. (1978). Involvement in role-playing simulations: A demonstration withstudies on obedience. *Journal of Personality and Social Psychology, 36,* 219–235.

Gidron, Y. (2002). Posttraumatic stress disorder after terrorist attacks: A review. *The Journal of Nervous and Mental Disease, 190*(2), 118–121.

Gilbert, S. J. (1981, December.) Another look at the Milgram Obedience Studies: The role of the graduated series of shocks. *Personality and Social Psychology Bulletin, 7*(4), 690–695.

Goleman, D. (1988, June 14). Erikson, in his own old age, expands his view of life. *The New York Times,* C1, C4.

Goldstein, S. (2004, October 3). Personal interview at Diablo Valley College, Pleasant Hill, CA.

Goss, J. D. (1994). Hardiness and mood disturbances in swimmers while overtraining. *Journal of Sport and Exercise Psychology, 16,* 135–149.

Gray, P. (1993, November 19). The assault on Freud. *Time,* New York.

Greenberg, J. S. (1983). *Comprehensive stress management.* Dubuque, Iowa: Wm. C. Brown Co.

Greenfield, P. M. (1966). On culture and conservation. In J.S. Bruner, J.S., Olver, R.P. & Greenfield, P.M. (Eds.), *Studies in cognitive growth.* New York: Wiley.

Grossmann, L. (2003, January, 20). Freud's complex: Can the talking cure make a comeback? *Time,* New York. 161(3), 76–81.

Gutherie, R. (1976). *Even the rat was white.* New York: Harper & Row.

Hall, C.S. & Lindzey, G. (1962). *Theories of personality,* New York: John Wiley & Sons.

Haney, C., Banks, C. & Zimbardo, P. (1973). Criminology: Interpersonal dynamics in a simulated prison. *International Journal of Criminology and Penology,* 1, 69–97.

Harlow, H.F. (1965). Sexual behavior in the Rhesus Monkey. In F. Beach (Ed.), *Sex and Behavior.* New York: John Wiley and Sons.

Hadiyono, J. E. P. & Hahn, M .W. (1985). Personality differences and sex similarities in American and Indonesian college students. *Journal of Social Psychology,* 125, 703–708.

Han, G. & Park, B. (1995, May). Children's choice in conflict: Application of the theory of individualism-collectivism. *Journal of Cross-Cultural Psychology,* 26 (3), 298–313.

Heim, C., Newport, D. J. et al. (2000, August 2). Pituitary-adrenal and autonomic responses to stress in women after sexual and physical abuse in childhood. *Journal of the American Medical Association,* 284, 592–597.

Henderson, J. L. (1964). Ancient myths and modern man. In C. Jung *Man and his symbols.* London: Aldus Books.

Hoffman, E. (1992, January, February). The last interview of Abraham Maslow. *Psychology Today,* 89, pp. 68–73.

Hobson, J. A. (2004, May). Freud returns? Like a bad dream. *Scientific American,* 290 (5), 89.

Horney, K. (1942). *Self analysis.* New York: W. W. Norton & Co. Inc.

Horney, K. (1945). *Our inner conflicts.* New York: W. W. Norton & Co. Inc.

Hui, C.H. & Triandis, H.C. (1996). Individualism-collectives: A study of cross-cultural researchers, *Journal of Cross-Cultural Psychology,* 17, 222–248.

"Intellect and Illness." (1980, June 21–22). University of California, Santa Cruz Seminar, Palo Alto.

Jaffe, A. (Ed.), (1979). *C. G. Jung, word and image.* Princeton, New Jersey: Princeton University Press.

Jahoda, G. (1992). Cultural psychology: Essays on comparative human development. *Journal of Cross-Cultural Psychology,* 23, 538–540.

James, W. (1892). *Psychology*. New York: Henry Holt and Company, pp. 189–226.

Jones, W.H., Hobb S.A. & Hockenbury, D. (1982). Loneliness and social skills deficits. *Journal of Personality and Social Psychology, 42,* 682–684.

Jing, Q. (1994). Development of psychology in China. *International Journal of Psychology, 29*(6), 667–675.

Jung, C. G. (1935). The Tavistock lectures, Analytical psychology: Its theory and practice. In H Read, M. Fordham & G. Adler (Eds.), *The collected works of C.G. Jung* (Vol. 18, pp. 3–182). Princeton, NJ: Princeton University.

Jung, C. G. et al. (1964). *Man and his symbols.* London: Aldus Books.

Kaczynski,T. (1996). Text of the Unabomber's manifesto, *Oakland Tribune.*

Klineberg, O. (1960). *Social psychology.* New York: Henry Holt & Company,

Knight, G.P., Bernal, M. E., Garza, C.A., Cota, M.K. & Ocampo, K. A. (1993). Family socialization and the ethnic identity of Mexican-American children. *Journal of Cross-Cultural Psychology, 24,* 99–114.

Kobasa, S.C. (1979). Stressful life events, personality and health: An inquiry into hardiness. *Journal of Personality and Social Psychology, 37,* 1–11.

Kobasa, S.C., Maddi, S.R. & Kahn, S. (1982). Hardiness and health: A prospective study. *Journal of Personality and Social Psychology, 42,* 168–177.

Kobasa, S.C., Maddi, S.R. & Zola, M.A. (1983). Type A and hardiness. *Journal of Personality and Social Psychology, 6,* 41–51.

Kobasa, S.C., Maddi, S.R., Puccetti, M.C. & Zola, M.A. (1985). Effectiveness of hardiness, exercise, and social support as resources against illness. *Journal of Psychosomatic Research, 24,* 525–533.

Kramer, S.N. (Ed.), (1961). *Mythologies of the ancient world.* New York: Doubleday.

Knowles, J. (1975). *U. S. Department of Health, Education and Welfare, Forward plan for health.* Washington, DC: U. S. Government Printing Office.

Kruger, J. & Dunning, D. (1999). Unskilled and unaware of it: How difficulties in recognizing one's own incompetence lead to inflated self-assessments. *Journal of Personality and Social Psychology, 77*(6), 1121–1134.

Lachkar, J. (2002). The psychological make-up of a suicide bomber. *The Journal of Psychohistory, 29*(4), 349–367.

Lerro, B. (2005). *Power of Eden.* Victoria, British Columbia: Trafford Books.

Levine, M. (1984, February 10). On the myth that Freud's ideas defy scientific validation. *The New York Times.*

Levy, J. & Munroe, R. (1959). *The happy family.* New York: Alfred A. Knopf.

Long, R. E. (Ed.), (1994). *Religious cults in America.* New York: H.W. Wilson.

Lowenfeld, J. (1961). Negative affect as a casual factor in the occurrence of repression, subception and perceptual defense. *Journal of Personality, 29,* 54–63.

Lewin, Tamar. (1995, May 31). Families in trouble all over: Economic pressures alter parental roles. *The New York Times,* p. C1.

Lonner, W. J. & Malpass, R. (Eds.), (1994). *Psychology and culture.* Boston: Allyn & Bacon.

Macrae, C. N., Bodenhausen, G.U., Milne, B. & Jetten, J. (1994). Out of mind but back in sight: Stereotypes on the rebound. *Journal of Personality and Social Psychology, 67* (5), 808–817.

Madden, E. (1960). *The structure of scientific thought.* Boston: Houghton Mifflin Co.

Madden, E. (1962). *Philosophical problems of psychology.* New York: Odyssey Press.

Malik, A. & Katyal, S. (1993, January). A comparative study of frustration in daughters of working and non-working mothers. *Indian Psychological Review, 40,* 9–13.

Mantell, D. & Panzarella, R. (1976). Obedience and responsibility. *British Journal of Social and Clinical Psychology, 15*(3), 239–245.

Markus, H. & Kitayana, S. (1991). Culture and the self: Implications for cognition, emotion and motivation. *Psychological Review, 98,* 224–253.

Mascetti, M.D. (1990). *The song of Eve: Mythology and symbols of the goddess.* New York: Simon and Schuster.

Maslow, A. (1968). *Toward a psychology of being.* New York: Van Nostrand.

Maslow, A. (1971). *The farther reaches of human nature.* New York: The Viking Press.

Matsumoto, D. (1994). *People-psychology from a cultural perspective.* Pacific Grove, CA.: Brooks/Cole.

May, R. (1961). *Existential psychology.* New York: Random House.

McGinnies, E.C. & Sherman. H. (1952). Generalization of perceptual defense. *Journal of Abnormal and Social Psychology, 47,* 81–87.

McLeod, R. (1995, April 24). "Why more families are without a father. *San Francisco Chronicle,* p. A2.

McLynn, F. (1996). *Carl Gustav Jung.* New York: Bantum Press.

Meyer, P. (1970, February). If Hitler asked you to electrocute a stranger would you? *Esquire.*

Milgram, S. (1963). Behavioral study of obedience. *Journal of Abnormal and Social Psychology. 67,* 371–378.

Milgram, S. (1965). Some conditions of obedience and disobedience to authority. *Human Relations, 18,* 57–75.

Miller, W. A. (1981). *Make friends with your shadow.* Minneapolis: Augsburg Publishing House.

Monfries, M.M. & Kafer, N.F. (1994, July). Private self-consciousness and fear of negative evaluation. *Journal of Psychology, 128*(4), 447–454.

Montessori, M. (1964). *The Montessori method.* (Anne George Trans.). NewYork: Schocken Books.

Morton, F. (1979). *A nervous splendor: Vienna 1888,1889.* Boston:
Little Brown.

Munroe, R. (1955). *Schools of psychoanalytic thought.* New York:
The Dryden Press.

Nye, R. (1992). *The legacy of B.F. Skinner.* Pacific Grove, CA:
Brooks/Cole Pub. Co.

Olson, R. (1962). *An introduction to existentialism.* New York: Dover
Publications.

Olsson, P. A. (2002). A malignant Pied Piper: Osama bin Laden.
Journal of Applied Psychoanalytic Studies, 4(4), 465–468.

Organista, K. (1995, October). Lectures on ethnic identity. University
of California, Berkeley.

Organista, K. (1995). Cognitive behavioral treatment of depression
and panic disorder in a Latina client: Culturally sensitive case
formation. *In Session: Psychotherapy in Practice.* New York:
John Wiley and Sons, Inc., *1*(2), pp. 53–64.

Orgler, H. (1963). *Alfred Adler: The man and his work.* New York:
Capricorn Books.

Ornish, D., Brown, S.E., Scherwitz, et al. (1994). Can lifestyle
changes reverse coronary heart disease? The lifestyle heart trial.
In Psychosocial processes and health: A reader, Steptoe, A. &
Wardle, J. (Eds.), Cambridge England: Cambridge University
Press, pp. 507–521.

Payot, J. (1893). *The education of the will: The theory and practice of
self-culture.* New York: Funk & Wagnalls Co.

Phillips, J.L., Jr. (1969). *The origins of intellect: Piaget's theory.* San
Francisco: W.H. Freedman.

Piaget, J. (1952). *The construction of reality in the child.* (M. Cook,
Trans.). New York: International Universities Press.

Piaget, J. (1952). *The origins of intelligence in children.* (M. Cook.
Trans.). New York: International Universities Press.

Piaget, J. (1962). *Play, dreams and imitation in childhood.* New York:
W.W. Norton & Co.

Popplestone, J.A. & McPherson, M.W. (1994). *An illustrated history of American psychology.* Dubuque, IA.: William C. Brown Communications, Inc.

Powell, L. & Mendes, C. et al. (1991). Change in coronary-prone behaviors in the recurrent coronary prevention project. *Psychosomatic Medicine, 53,* 407–419.

Powell, L. (1992). The cognitive underpinnings of coronary-prone behaviors. *Cognitive Therapy and Research, 16*(2), 123–142.

Puner, H. (1978). *Freud: His life and his mind.* New York: Charter Books.

Punetha, D., Giles, H. & Young, L. (1987). Ethnicity and immigrant values: Religion and language choice. *Journal of Language and Social Psychology, 6,* 229–241.

Putney, S. & Putney, G.J. (1964). *Normal neurosis: The adjusted American.* New York: Harper & Row.

Putney, S. (1972). *The conquest of society.* Belmont, CA.: Wadsworth Publishing Co.

Red Horse, J., Lewis, R., Feit M. & Decker, J., (1978, February). Family behavior of urban American Indians, *Social Casework,* 67–72.

Rickman, J. M.D. (Ed.), (1957). *A general selection from the works of Sigmund Freud.* Garden City, N.Y.: Doubleday & Co., Inc.

Roberts, R. (1983). *Tales for Jung folk.* San Anselmo, CA.: Vernal Equinox Press.

Rode, L. (2004, October 22). Personal interview at Diablo Valley College, Pleasant Hill, CA.

Rogers, C. (1942). *Counseling and psychotherapy.* Boston: Houghton Mifflin.

Rogers, C. (1951). *Client-centered therapy.* Boston: Houghton Mifflin.

Rogers, C. (1961). *On becoming a person.* Boston: Houghton Mifflin.

Rogers, C. (1970). *Carl Rogers on encounter groups.* New York: Harper & Row Publishers.

Rogers, R. & Prentice-Dunn, S. (1981). Deindividuation and anger-mediated interracial aggression: Unmasking regressive racism. *Journal of Personality and Social Psychology, 41,* 63–73.

Sackhoff, J. & Weinstein, L. (1988, July). The effects of potential self-inflicted harm on obedience to an authority figure. *Bulletin of the Psychonomic Society, 26*(4O), 347–348.

Salinger, P. (Ed.), (1968). *A tribute to Robert F. Kennedy.* New York: Doubleday.

Saltz, E., & Loreto, A.D. (1965). "Defense" against traumatic concepts. *Journal of Abnormal Psychology, 70,* 281–284.

Shaw, L.L., Batson, C. D. & Todd, A. M. (1994, November). Empathy avoidance: Forestalling feeling for another in order to escape the motivating consequences. *Journal of Personality and Social Psychology, 67*(5), 879–887.

Sheehy, G. (1977). *Passages: Predictable crises of adult life.* New York: Bantam Books.

Shute, N. (2002, September). Madam Montessori, *Smithsonian, 33*(2), pp. 70–74.

Singer, Margaret. (1997, June). Personal interview at Berkeley, CA.

Sinha, D. (1994). Origins and development of psychology in India: Outgrowing the alien framework. *International Journal of Psychology, 29* (6), 695–705.

Skinner, B. F. (1954). Critique of Psychoanalytic concepts and theories. *Scientific Monograph, 79,* 300–305.

Smith, R. (1995). *Challenging your preconceptions.* Pacific Grove, CA: Brooks/ Cole Publishing Co.

Solms, M. (2004, May). Freud returns. *Scientific American,* 290 (5), 85–88.

Southworth, J. (1996, October 20). Naturalist lecture at Ardenwood Historical Farm, Newark, CA.

Spence, K.W. (1964). *Behavior theory and conditioning.* New Haven: Yale University Press.

Stafford-Clark, D. (1965). *What Freud really said.* New York: Schocken Books.

Steele, J. (1965, March). Lectures on the oral-passive marriage, the anal fixation marriage, the Oedipal-Electra marriage. San Jose State University, San Jose, CA.

Stegar, M. (2003). *Globalization, a very short introduction.* England: Oxford University Press.

Steinburg, L.D. (1986). Latchkey children and susceptibility to peer pressure: An ecological analysis. *Developmental Psychology, 22,* 433–439.

Stevens, B., & Rogers, C. (1967). *Person to person: The problem of being human.* Walnut Creek, CA.: Real People Press.

Stone, A. A. (1997, January-February). Where will psychoanalysis survive. *Harvard Magazine,* Cambridge, Mass. pp. 35–39.

Storr, A. (1973). *C. G. Jung.* New York: Viking Press.

Stout, C. et al., (1964). Unusually low incidence of death from myocardial infarction. *Journal American Medical Association, 188,* p. 845.

Sue, D.W. & Sue, D. (1990). *Counseling the culturally different: Theory and practice* (2nd ed.). New York: John Wiley & Sons.

Thayer, R.E., Newman, J.R. & McClain, T.M. (1994). Self-regulation of mood: Strategies for changing a bad mood, raising energy and reducing tension. *Journal of Personality and Social Psychology, 67*(5), 910–925.

Thorensen, C. et al. (1982). The recurrent coronary prevention project: Initial findings. In M. Horvath and E. Franktik (Eds.), *Psychophysiological Risk Factors of cardiovascular diseases (Psychosocial stress, personality and occupational specificity).* Supplement 3, (Praka), Prague, Czechoslovakia: Avicenum-Czechoslovak Medical Press, pp. 518–524.

Thoresen, C., Friedman, M., Gill, J. & Ulmer, D. (1982). The recurrent coronary prevention project. *Acta Medic Scandinavica (Supp.)* 660, 172–192.

Thoresen, C. (1983, February). Personal interview.

U. S. Department of Health, Education and Welfare. (1975). *Forward plan for health.* Washington DC: U.S. Government Printing Office.

United States Government 9/11 Commission. (2004, July). *Final report of the national commission on terrorist attacks upon the United States, official government edition.* Washington DC: U. S. Government Printing Office.

Verkuyten, M. & Masson, K. (1996). Culture and gender differences in the perception of friendship in adolescent. *International Journal of Psychology, 31*(5), 207–217.

von Franz, M.L. (1964). The process of individuation. In C.G. Jung (Ed.), *Man and His Symbols.* London: Aldus Books.

Watson, D., & Tharp, R. (1993). *Self-directed behavior.* Pacific Grove, California: Brooks/Cole Publishing Company.

Weinstein, R. S. (1994). Pushing the frontiers of multicultural training in community psychology. *American Journal of Community Psychology, 22*(6), 811–820.

Wiebe, D.J. (1991). Hardiness and stress moderation: A test of proposed mechanisms. *Journal of Personality and Social Psychology, 60*(1), 89–99.

Williams, R., Powell, L. et al. (1993, September). Behavior change and compliance: Keys to improving cardiovascular health. *Circulation, 88*(3),1406–7.

Wollheim, R. (1971). *Sigmund Freud.* New York: The Viking Press.

Zimbardo, P. G. (1969). *The cognitive control of motivation.* Glenview, Illinois: Scott, Foresman & Co.

Zimbardo, P. G. (1972, April). Pathology of Imprisonment, *Society.*

Zimbardo, P. G., Haney, C., Banks, W.C. & Jaffe, D. (1973, April 8). The mind is a formidable jailer: A Pirendellian prison. *The New York Times,* pp.38–60.

Zimbardo, P.G., Haney, C., Banks, W.C. & Jaffe, D. (1973). *The psychology of imprisonment: The Stanford prison experiment,* (paper presented with slides). Palo Alto: Stanford University.

Zimbardo, P. G. (2004). A Situationist perspective on the psychology of evil: Understanding how good people are transformed into perpetrators. In A. Miller (Ed.), *The social psychology of good and evil: Understanding our capacity for kindness and cruelty.* New York: Guilford.

Index